Francis Buckley ... is the closest thing America has
to a Jonathan Swift.
SPENGLER (David Goldman)

F. H. Buckley is a national treasure.
STEPHEN B. PRESSER

His prose explodes with energy.
JAMES CEASAR

Praise for this book

F. H. Buckley shows us how a seeming contradiction can lead to
the healing of a fractured country.
ROGER L. SIMON, award-winning novelist
and editor, *Epoch Times*

Praise for THE REPUBLIC OF VIRTUE

This is Buckley at his colorful, muckraking best – an intelligent,
powerful, but depressing argument laced with humor.
GORDON S. WOOD, Pulitzer Prize winner

Praise for CURIOSITY

You are our Montaigne!
CHRISTOPHER DeMUTH

Praise for THE WAY BACK

Frank Buckley marshals tremendous data and insight
in a compelling study.
FRANCIS FUKUYAMA

Praise for THE ONCE AND FUTURE KING

Penetrating ... iconoclastic. No US political scientist has achieved
what F. H. Buckley does in this ambitious book.
TIMES LITERARY SUPPLEMENT

PROGRESSIVE CONSERVATISM

HOW REPUBLICANS WILL BECOME

AMERICA'S NATURAL GOVERNING PARTY

F. H. BUCKLEY

BOOKS

NEW YORK · LONDON

First American edition published in 2022 by Encounter Books, an activity of Encounter for Culture and Education, Inc., a nonprofit, tax-exempt corporation. Encounter Books website address: www.encounterbooks.com

Manufactured in the United States and printed on acid-free paper. The paper used in this publication meets the minimum requirements of ANSI/NISO Z39.48-1992 (R 1997) (*Permanence of Paper*).

FIRST AMERICAN EDITION

LIBRARY OF CONGRESS
CATALOGING-IN-PUBLICATION DATA

Names: Buckley, F. H. (Francis H.), 1948– author.
Title: Progressive Conservatism: How Republicans Will Become America's Natural Governing Party / F. H. Buckley.
Description: First American edition. | New York: Encounter Books, 2022. | Includes bibliographical references and index. |
Identifiers: LCCN 2022000676 (print) | LCCN 2022000677 (ebook) | ISBN 9781641772532 (hardcover) | ISBN 9781641772549 (ebook)
Subjects: LCSH: Republican Party (U.S.: 1854–) | Conservatism—United States.
Classification: LCC JK2356 .B89 2022 (print) | LCC JK2356 (ebook) | DDC 324.2734—dc23/eng/20220210
LC record available at https://lccn.loc.gov/2022000676
LC ebook record available at https://lccn.loc.gov/2022000677

1 2 3 4 5 6 7 8 9   20 22

FOR ESTHER

CONTENTS

CHAPTER ONE

The Dream of Republican Virtue

As we age, we slip softly from one country to another, and what began in innocence led down a path littered with betrayals and smelly compromises. Charles Péguy understood how it happens. After defending Alfred Dreyfus, he found himself allied to unscrupulous and opportunistic politicians. "Everything begins in mystique and ends in politics," he wrote.[1] But the dreams of our youth never quite die, and without quite knowing it we continue to yearn for something we had lost along the way. And that is purity.

For Americans, purity is a dream of republican virtue, a shining city on a hill free from baseness and corruption and peopled by secret romantics who are hard on the outside and soft on the inside. Our heroes aren't kings or princes but common folk, the knights-errant of the dusty trail and mean streets in search of their private grail. When surrounded by cynics, they keep their integrity, like John Wayne in *Stagecoach* and Humphrey Bogart in *Casablanca*.

Like them, our country was touched by grace. We knew there was something special about America, that this was the country of the Declaration of Independence, of equality and liberty, where lingering injustices are in time corrected. We were the country of the American Dream, the idea that, whoever you were, wherever you came from, you can flourish and know that your children will have it better than you did. In any struggle, we'd always be on the right and winning side.

That was how we used to see America. In the 1930s, the US Communist Party spied on us for Russia, but party leader Earl Browder was constrained to say that "communism is 20th century Americanism." Protestors took to the streets but told us that that was how we began as a country and assured us that dissent was true patriotism. After struggling to rid ourselves of the legacy of racism, we came at last to understand that republican virtue calls for love of country and that love of country requires that our government advance the common good without discrimination.

More recently, however, the Left has made love of country seem indecent and republican virtue a fraud. Every patriotic instinct was scorned and every sacred institution mocked. Our pathways crumbled beneath our feet, and we peered dizzily down unfathomable depths – the *ivresse des grandes profondeurs*. Everything, everything you loved, is dirty, said the Left. On the Right, the madness was paid back with interest by the millions of Americans who even now think that Trump won the 2020 election and by reactionaries who blame the country's ills on the founders' liberalism. In a national apostasy, extremists on both Left and Right abandoned our liberal heritage.

We have come to a dead end, and we'll not see a way back except through a recovery of the mystique of American purity in the republican virtue of the founders and the GOP's great leaders – Abraham Lincoln, Theodore Roosevelt, and Dwight Eisenhower – and the content they gave to our idea of the common good. That is the party's task, and in embracing it the Republicans will restore the American Dream and become the country's natural governing party.

The Enormous Tragedy of the Dream

The Left has asked us to remember everything terrible about our country and ignore anything good, for example how in 1619 the New World's first democratic assembly convened in Jamestown, Virginia. That's been forgotten, and what's remembered is how, a few miles away, 1619 was the year when the first African slaves were brought to America. That was the springboard for the *New York Times*'s 1619 Project, which asks readers to rethink all our history from the perspective of slavery. "Out of slavery grew nearly everything that has truly made America exceptional: its economic might, its industrial power, its electoral system."

To be sure, our pride in the American Revolution tends to

obscure the compromises on the Patriot side,[2] but the 1619 Project is so extreme that even the *Times* had to walk back some of it. Nevertheless, the Project appeals to people who despise America. Nikole Hannah-Jones, who wrote the Pulitzer-winning essay kicking it off, took pride in how she might have encouraged the 2020 riots. She approvingly retweeted a *New York Post* op-ed entitled "Call them the 1619 Riots." I'd be honored if that's what they're called, she said.[3] But if that's her idea of America, one might wonder why she would choose to live in so infamous a country.

It comes down to hate, and there's not much you can do to change a hater's mind. You say that the American Revolution was fought to preserve slavery, and I say no. That's really a factual dispute, where it becomes important to understand whether the Patriots thought that slavery was threatened. If we could clear that up, we might agree with each other. When the 1619 Project appeared, therefore, several eminent historians weighed in to pick holes in it. But it really wasn't a dispute about the facts. It's more like the breakup of a marriage, where the same behavior might inspire either the deepest love or the most corrosive hatred. So, too, for those who love or hate America. The hater isn't going to be brought around by contrary evidence any more than a broken marriage can be cured by a calm weighing of the facts. As Dido learned, there's no end to the things of the heart.[4]

Still, one might have expected the 1619 Project to collapse of its own weight, by the tendency of hatreds to dissipate over time. The Project asks people to stay angry, and as Philippa Foot noted, people consumed by *ressentiment* live wretched lives.[5] But the anger didn't go away. Instead, it was the impetus for the abandonment of America's traditional liberalism.

In the past the Left adhered to free speech principles. That worked in leftists' favor when they were the dissenters but not after they ascended to power. Then the conservatives were the dissenters, and the Left became the censors. They call themselves liberals. But labels can lie.

Conservatives found themselves spurned in higher ed and bounced from social media. An army of online Robespierres and LGBT bullies searched them out to get them canceled. Fox News was a special bête noire. It's the top-ranked cable network, but compared to the rest of the media it is right of center and therefore should be blacklisted. A *New York Times* columnist wants cable companies to drop Fox News from basic cable TV packages,[6] and the *Washington Post*'s media columnist (!) asks us to blacklist its advertisers.[7] That's not enough for another *Post* columnist, who thinks Fox should be required to give airtime to left-wingers.[8] In the past this might have been checked by an appeal to the free speech beliefs of the founders. But such impediments were removed when the founders were revealed to be evil racists, and in place of liberalism the Left embraced an explicitly anti-liberal ideology called Critical Race Theory (CRT).

There is no single definition of CRT, but what unites its adherents is a single-minded focus on race and the totalitarian's rejection of liberal principles of fairness and liberty. CRT denigrates Western civilization, its great works of art and literature, Judeo-Christian ethics, the Enlightenment, free markets, and America's founders. It is the creed of primitive vandals who are abetted by the nihilism and cynicism of a *nekulturny* Left. Who knew that fifty years after the Kenneth Clark miniseries *civilization* would become a dirty word?

For CRT, everything came down to a smash-and-grab struggle for power from which civility and gentleness were banished, and ideas we had thought well-established were turned upside down. Immanuel Kant said that rules aren't moral unless they can be applied universally, and Jeremy Bentham thought that everyone should count as one and no one as more than one. This comes down to saying that all lives matter, but now that's become toxic and taken as an assertion that black lives don't matter. Unsurprisingly, this annoys Republicans who think that, with their education, immigration, economic, and criminal justice policies, it's really the Democrats who harm blacks. In addition, religious conservatives don't think that blacks are helped by permissive abortion laws. Black lives do matter – from conception to death, in both this world and the next.

It's gone beyond the humdrum politics of past years. The Left no longer seems to like America. First, it refought the Civil War and took down the Confederate statues. Fair enough, but then it refought the American Revolution. It relabeled schools named after Thomas Jefferson and George Mason, and it questioned George Washington's place in the American pantheon.[9] As a nation we might not exist but for Washington, but the *Washington Post* took to labeling him an "enslaver." We'll wait to see what will happen to that monument to racial oppression, Mount Vernon.

The Left told us this was normal or that if it wasn't, we deserved it. We deserved to have our faces rubbed in the mire; we deserved it because we were hateful. It wasn't about redemption because we were irredeemable, and it wasn't about forgiveness because our sins were unforgiveable. It wasn't about repairing the world because reparations could never make things whole again. And yet reparations were asked for and confessions of guilt demanded.

The Left no longer had stopping points. Homosexuality was decriminalized, and that was all well and good. Then the Supreme Court held that there was a right to same sex marriage, and conservatives remained silent. Next the Left turned on a dime to take up the cause of transgendered bathrooms, and conservatives sucked it up. Finally came the drag queen story hours in elementary schools. The changes happened so quickly that it didn't seem to be about homosexuality at all. Instead, the point was to stick it to religious conservatives and make them kowtow if they wanted to keep their jobs.

We all know what has happened, and yet no one is permitted to say it. We know that democracy isn't threatened when we adopt the same election rules as every other country. We know that open border immigration policies aren't good for the country. We know that nothing frightens elite socialists more than workers of the world who peacefully unite. We know that when an Arab terrorist takes hostages in a synagogue, the real victims aren't Moslems. We know that anything we say may be used against us and that in many workplaces there'll be informers who'd happily turn us in. We've even stopped telling jokes. They used to do so in the former East Germany, but in our intolerant society joke-telling marks one as an anti-party element.

A newly dominant culture, sure of itself and contemptuous of dissenters, flexes its muscles and asserts its power. And power doesn't count unless it cuts across the grain. It doesn't show itself by affirming that water is wet and that puppies are cute. Instead, it imposes a belief in things that are false, degenerate, or impossible, the idea that we're racists at heart, that there are sixty-two genders or that 2 plus 2 is 5. It tells us to silence the still, small voice of our conscience and praise the degraded, perverse, and unnatural.

Our culture became transgressive and even anti-American. Conservatives found themselves living in a country where the *Band of Brothers* miniseries could no longer be made. Those soldiers were just a bunch of racists, says the *Washington Post*.[10] Father Bing Crosby would be revealed to be a child molester in *Going My Way II*, while June would divorce Ward in a new *Leave it to Beaver*. As for the Beaver, he'd get a sex change operation. The dream had become a nightmare, and we waited for someone to rouse us from it.

The Hegelian Hero

The sense that we had lost our way led to the rise of Donald Trump and his defense of America's essential goodness. He came out of a celebrity culture without any ties to or affinity with the Republican establishment, and he created a new Republican Party, one that rejected the right-wing orthodoxy of the conservative think tanks. The Republican Right didn't care for him, and he had no use for them. They called themselves "Never Trumpers" and asked how a man so personally impure could be expected to convey a message about purity and republican virtue.

I see your point, said the Trump supporter, but who else is there in a time of crisis? You had your chance with a gentlemanly Mitt Romney, and where did that get us? If we saw Trump's rough edges, we took them as a sign that he wouldn't succumb to the Republicans' fatal wish to please. If he was sometimes rude, at least he wasn't going to apologize to people who wanted to cancel us and who lacked the most basic sense of fairness. We had elected Republicans to hold fast to conservative principles but remembered how George W. Bush collaborated with Ted Kennedy on the federal takeover of K–12 education and how his father broke his "no new taxes" pledge. That wasn't going to happen with Trump. Fortitude is also a virtue.

Besides, we had tired of the Never Trumpers' right-wing policies. Libertarian principles had left millions of people behind, and Trump was a different kind of Republican, one who thought that whoever you are and wherever you live, you should be able to get ahead and know that your children will have it better than you did. That is the American Dream, and he said that the government has a duty to make it happen. Second, he promised a return to republican virtue by draining the swamp and ending rule by interest groups and the elites who line their own pockets while ignoring the common good. Third, he told us of his unapologetic pride in America, his belief that our country is a beacon to the world that has always surmounted its difficulties and would continue to do so. That is what "Make America Great Again" meant, a return to the country we had loved and that the Left had asked us to hate.

Those were the same principles of an earlier Republican Party, that of Lincoln, Theodore Roosevelt, and Eisenhower, and which sadly had been abandoned. In voicing them Trump became a world-historical figure. He was a Hegelian great man who incarnated the spirit and needs of his time, the need to break with the stale policies of a Goldwaterite Republican Party and a divisive race-and-gender Democratic Party. Even if he couldn't fully articulate the ideas he was unfolding, it was enough that he sensed what was ripe for development. He was the clear-sighted one, and the more he was reviled, the more he became the champion for the forgotten American, for whom he was what Napoleon was to G. W. F. Hegel (1770–1831), the world soul on horseback, the hero evoked by history.

Like Trump, the Hegelian hero is not so nice as the rest of us. He breaks things, and that didn't trouble Hegel. The German philosopher thought that the hero's misdeeds might be justified by the logic of history, which excused Caesar and Napoleon for their wars.[11] But we're now in an After-Trump era, and it's time to move on. Trump has self-destructed, just as Hegel would have predicted. His world-historical figure is a troubled hero whose life is one of conflict, and when history is done with him, he falls away "like empty hulls from the kernel."[12]

The Never Trumpers told us that if we nominated Trump, it wouldn't end well. But it's so much better than anything you have, we answered.

It turns out that we were both right.

But while Trump was defeated and left in disgrace, the mystique of the dream lives on. More than seventy-four million people voted for him, and they're not going away. Many weren't traditional Republicans, and the party will never elect another president if it leaves them behind. And yet that obviously won't suffice. The Republican Party is going to need both the Trump supporters and those who can't stand him, and this book explains how it can do so, both now and into the future.

I · PROGRESSIVE AND CONSERVATIVE

The Republican Party must be known as a progressive
organization or it is sunk.

Dwight Eisenhower

CHAPTER TWO

After Trump

A NEW REPUBLICAN PARTY, shorn of Trump but faithful to the policies he brought to the party, will emerge to unite the country. What this won't be is a snapback to the way conservatism was defined for the last fifty years. The Goldwater movement, whose touchstone was economic liberty but which opposed civil rights reforms and national welfare policies, ran its course and was repudiated by Trump's victory in the 2016 Republican primaries. In doing so, Trump added a new meaning to conservatism, one that represents a rejection of the self-styled keepers of the flame and a return to an earlier kind of Republicanism, one that sought the common good for all Americans. If this was defeated in 2020, that was because it was 2020 and a year not to be repeated.

In office Trump began to deliver on his promises. What followed the 2016 election was a reversal of decades of policies that had enriched an elite but abandoned those beneath them. The civilian unemployment rate fell from 5.0 percent to 3.5 percent, the lowest rate in fifty years.[1] Trump's trade protectionism cost him the support of libertarians but appealed to communities that had seen 3.4 million US jobs exported to China between 2001 and 2017.[2] Real gross domestic product grew at an annual rate of 2.5 percent. Remarkably, this was an egalitarian recovery, where the wealth gains accrued to lower- and middle-class Americans and the richest families saw a decline in their income.[3] By 2020 most of us reported that we were better off than we had been four years earlier.[4]

This was especially true for black Americans. The black unemployment rate fell from 16.8 percent in 2010 to 5.8 percent in 2020 before the pandemic shutdown. That was an all-time low, and while the white rate was always lower, the gap between them narrowed as the economy picked up. Other indices of black well-being, such as household income, life expectancy, and number of people sentenced, also showed substantial progress. Whatever the reasons for the George Floyd protests, you'll not find them in the Bureau of Labor Standards statistics, and the Trump administration can be proud of its record on minority job creation and its First Step Act that helped bring former inmates back into the labor force.

Trump made our NATO allies pony up their military spending and was the first president since Eisenhower not to get us into any new wars. There were no Russian invasions, as there had been under Obama and would be under Biden. Trump eliminated energy imports and kept inflation well in check. Though Congress blocked his plans to build a border wall, Trump almost ended illegal immigration. How quickly it all changed when he left office!

The major media outlets refused to give Trump any credit, however. Instead, they defined themselves through their opposition to him. If he said that new federal buildings should be in a classical style, they would discover that brutalism was cool again.[5] If he wanted to make America great again, they answered that it was never great. The peace treaties he brokered between Israel and its neighbors were ignored. Instead, the Left falsely accused Trump of collusion with Russia, blocking a reset of relations with that country, a missed opportunity whose loss is so painfully obvious today.

There was no basis for believing that the piddling amounts the Russians had spent on social media made any appreciable difference in 2016, and when it looked for collusion, the two-year Mueller investigation came up blank. Nevertheless, the Left's media outlets continued to spread the charge, and Democratic voters continued to believe it.[6] In fact, whatever collusion there was came from the Democrats, who had paid for the fabricated and Russian-tainted opposition research in the Steele Dossier and who peddled the lies to produce the Mueller investigation and the lingering left-wing paranoia.[7] The intelligence agencies, staffed by Trump-haters, forgot about the Taliban and spied on his administration and did not let their failure to find anything stop them. And with all their fact-checkers, the media collaborated on a Big Lie.

A Democratic House impeached Trump for opening up an investigation of Joe Biden, when it was Biden who had shut down an investigation of his very corrupt son, Hunter Biden.[8] For all of this, not a peep from the left-wing media. In October 2020, Facebook and Twitter censored stories about Biden family corruption, which if generally known might have changed the election's outcome. National Public Radio, which is supposed to be nonpartisan, dismissed the evidence of the family's malfeasance with a sneer. "We don't want to waste our time on stories that are not really stories, and we don't want to waste the listeners' and readers' time on stories that are just pure distractions."[9] But the Left did make time for gag-making stories about how wonderful Hunter was and how close he was to his father. "Joe Biden loves his son," said the *Washington Post*. "We should all be so lucky."[10] The son was discharged from the Navy for his cocaine use and fathered a child with a stripper while dating his brother's widow, but the *New York Times* thought the real story was Hunter Biden's new career as an amateur painter. "There's a New Artist in Town. The Name Is Biden."[11] If you want some doors opened for you, perhaps you might want to buy one of his paintings. They're going for $500,000.

The major media outlets had always tilted left. They swooned over Obama and made Mitt Romney's claim that he had "binders of women" for possible appointments seem anti-women. But now all restraints, any sense of fairness or decency, were cast off, and for partisanship and sycophancy the media rivaled the Soviet press during the communist era. Trump wasn't a normal candidate, wrote a *Washington Post* contributor, and journalists would have to do things they'd never done before.

> They may even have to shock us.... They may have to call Trump out with a forcefulness unseen before.... Hardest of all, they will have to explain to the public that Trump is a special case, and the normal rules do not apply.[12]

The *Post* quickly took the hint. It adopted "Democracy Dies in Darkness" as its page one motto, which implied that Trump's America was a fascist state and that it took courage to mimic what every thought leader in the country was saying. It was all meant to elect a Democrat, and for promoting the hysteria over Russia, the *Post* and the *New York Times* were shamefully awarded a Pulitzer Prize.

Like the print media, the TV news media enjoyed a profitable "Trump bounce," in which its core left-wing listeners tuned in to feed their desire for hatred. The CBS president took notice of this, commenting that while he thought the Trump movement wasn't good for America, "it's damn good for CBS." And if the audience wanted animus, why that's what it would be given. At a Trump COVID-19 press conference, the CNN chyron at the bottom of the screen read "Angry Trump Turns Briefing Into Propaganda Session." CNN's Jim Acosta said of another Trump press conference, "he was ranting and raving for the better part of the last hour." It had become a bad joke, and most Americans stopped trusting the mass media to report the news.

What was especially galling was the way the media covered up Biden's failing mental capacities. During the 2020 campaign, the babbling and botoxed-to-the-gills candidate struggled to find the right word, experienced mood swings, and had difficulty following a storyline, all symptoms of early dementia. Incontinent in both body and word, he was hidden from the public with the connivance of the press. Day after day he called a lid on events or appeared before no more than ten or twenty of his supporters. Later, when the wheels came off with the fall of Kabul, we learned how the media had betrayed us. Democracy Dies in Darkness.

The Year of Living Dangerously

In spite of the media, Gallup pollsters told us in early 2020 that Trump was America's most admired man, and it looked as if he would be reelected. But then came the COVID-19 pandemic, which has killed nearly a million Americans. It was a Black Swan calamity that could not have been anticipated, but voters blamed it on Trump, and Jane Fonda called it God's gift to the Left. The media persuaded them that he had failed to protect us even though this was hindsight bias at work and there was no evidence that the Democrats would have done any better.

In 2020 the *New York Times*'s star reporters told us that Trump's decision to let the states take the lead in fighting the pandemic was a "catastrophic policy blunder" and "perhaps one of the greatest failures of presidential leadership in generations."[13] But there was not a hint of blame when 2021 COVID-19 deaths exceeded those in 2020, and Biden told reporters, "there is no federal solution. This gets solved at a state level."[14] He had repeated what the *Times* reporters had labeled a catastrophic blunder and then left for the beach, but not a word of apology from them. Their failure to condemn Biden proved that the point was simply to smear Trump.

We were told to believe the science, but that was a matter of guesswork, and the story kept changing. The Centers for Disease Control couldn't make up its mind about airborne transmission of the virus and the need for masks. In March 2020 Dr. Anthony Fauci encouraged healthy Americans to sign up for ocean cruises, but by October he was asking everyone to stay home for Thanksgiving. It was always a matter of trading off the costs of the pandemic (which the scientists knew something about) versus the costs of shutting down the economy (which they didn't), without knowing what was up the road.

When we saw the first signs of the virus, the Democrats were obsessed with Trump's impeachment and told us that his 2020 travel bans were racist (presumably unlike Biden's 2021 travel bans). New York's Democratic Governor Andrew Cuomo forced nursing homes to admit COVID-19 patients, where they infected and killed thousands of elderly residents, but he was rewarded by an Emmy for his "masterful" COVID-19 briefings. Trump had launched Operation Warp Speed, which expedited the development and delivery of lifesaving vaccines, but before the election Kamala Harris cast doubt on them.[15] Then, when they were ready, Big Pharma held back the announcement until after the election in order to deprive him of the credit.

The pandemic made the 2020 election a one-off and not to be repeated. But if that weren't enough, what followed was the Black

Lives Matter protests and the Left's calls to defund the police. What had begun as a simple demand for justice soon metastasized and became a permission slip for looting and violence. At the same time, Antifa rioters took to the streets to attack random businesses. The local police were ordered to stand down, and if anyone was arrested, Kamala Harris asked her supporters to pony up the bail money. As it happened, that wasn't going to be necessary since in nearly all cases left-wing prosecutors dropped the charges.[16] Throughout, the media treated the rioters with kid gloves. "Quick to vilify antifa, but slow to explain it," tut-tutted the *Washington Post*'s media columnist.[17]

The machinery of criminal deterrence quickly broke down. After George Floyd's death in Minneapolis, the city reduced the police budget, and there was a surge in officer retirements. The cops who stayed on the beat remained in their police cars or hid out at the station. Why be proactive if that's going to get you in trouble? Predictably, shootings doubled and murder rates were up 50 percent from the year before. Nationwide, there were 4,901 more murders in 2020 than in 2019, the biggest jump since national records started in 1960.[18]

In a nice example of the totalitarian mind at work, real violence was excused, and "white silence" was labeled violence. We go to restaurants for the food and also for a respite from real-world concerns. But that's just what annoyed some BLM activists, who roamed the streets to harass random patrons at outdoor restaurants. They chanted "silence is violence" and demanded that diners raise their hands in solidarity. When one couple refused to do so, they were swarmed by the activists, who leaned over them to scream obscenities.[19]

Soon even passionate leftists became aware of the costs of ignoring crime. They might rail against the Second Amendment, but they'll still go out and buy handguns for themselves. It's different when it hits home. The mayor of Seattle yielded control of a Capitol Hill area of Seattle to a mob – until they spray-painted her house. A Portland, Oregon, city commissioner who demanded $18 million in police budget cuts called the cops on her Lyft driver in an argument about open windows and then patted herself on the back for opposing white racism.[20] In 2020 the Portland mayor condemned the police when they pepper sprayed Antifa rioters, but by 2021 he felt differently about criminal deterrence. He had been confronted by a middle-aged man who objected to the maskless mayor and tried to take a video of him. The mayor pepper sprayed him. "I became imminently concerned for my personal safety," he explained.[21]

We wanted it all to stop, and we weren't reassured when the left-wing media called the George Floyd riots "mostly peaceful." They were anything but peaceful. Six days after Floyd was killed, eighteen people were murdered in mainly black Chicago neighborhoods.[22] Compared to that, the January 2021 riot at the Capitol was a walk in the park. Which is to say that "mostly peaceful" doesn't cut it. When we go to baseball games or symphony concerts, we'll want an *entirely* peaceful experience. Nevertheless, we elected Biden in the hope that this would quiet everything down. There was little enough enthusiasm for the doddering Democratic nominee, but given the media's wall-to-wall hatred, ridicule, and contempt for Trump, they were gambling they could run anyone as their nominee. The clincher was the implicit promise that it would all stop if Biden were elected.

The Left had discovered the political uses of revolutionary violence and in doing so copied from a playbook written by Georges Sorel (1847–1922). In his *Reflections on Violence*, Sorel described how French trade unions had used the threat of violence to wrest the changes they wanted. So, too, the looting and riots became political leverage for an opportunistic Democratic Party.

Before revolutionary violence succeeds in its political goals, three things are required. First, the violence must be seen to serve the goal of resisting an illegitimate state, and that is just what the Democrats told us America had become under Trump. He had not been legitimately elected, they said, because his opponent had received more votes. Under our Constitution that can happen and did happen four times before 2016. It also happens in our sister parliamentary countries, as it did in the 2019 and 2021 Canadian elections, when the Tories won the popular vote but the Liberals won more seats and formed the next government. That didn't raise a fuss in Canada, but then the American Left is less likely to play by the rules of the game.

Second, frightened conservatives must show themselves to be unwilling or unable to suppress the violence. "The most decisive factor in social politics is the cowardice of the government," wrote Sorel.[23] And for all its bluster, the Trump administration did little to quell the riots. It might have declared a state of insurrection, and in a *New York Times* op-ed Sen. Tom Cotton (R-AR) urged the president to do just that. But nothing was done apart from federalizing local cops and sending in federal marshals to protect federal property. All that Cotton's op-ed did was get a *Times* editor shown the door.

Lastly, a party allied to the rioters must be able to promise credibly that, if given its way, it can cabin the violence and prevent things from descending to mere anarchy. In that case, said Sorel, "a parliamentary group *sells peace of mind to the conservatives*, who do not dare use the force they command."[24] And that is what the Democrats ran on. Elect Trump and all hell will break loose, they implied. Elect us and it will go away. It looked like extortion, but for many voters it worked and plausibly tipped the scales in 2020. Biden represented a return to normalcy, voters thought. We had seen four years of unhinged craziness from the Left, and the country had had enough.

That wasn't an unqualified endorsement of the Democrats, however, for if American voters had spoken with a single voice, they wanted Trumpism without Trump. We might have been dismayed by Trump, but we didn't care for Adam Schiff's bug-eyed paranoia and the Squad's socialism. We saw how the Democrats had become the party of Michael Avenatti and Stormy Daniels, of Defund the Police and Critical Race Theory, and they lost twelve seats in the House and nearly saw the GOP take it back. The Republicans might have retained control of the Senate had Trump conceded the election, but he didn't, and this likely tipped the two Georgia Senate seats to the Democrats. At the state level, Republicans held sixty-one of the ninety-nine legislative chambers, six more than they had before the election. Biden won but without coattails, and voters turned away from the radicalism they saw in prominent members of his party.

Though they've made a sweep of the White House and both houses of Congress, the Democrats are poised for a fall. They can't trot out the Sorel playbook again, not after 2020's violence was repeated in 2021 and 2022. Encouraged by the Left's zero-bail policies and lax Democratic prosecutors, we've seen looters empty out stores in big cities and murder rates return to levels not seen in thirty years. Nor can the Democrats blame Trump for the 2021 US COVID-19 deaths, which were nearly 70 percent higher than in the year before. Their nominal head, the president, is seventy-nine, and the signs of his mental decline are painfully evident. In office, he reads inflammatory speeches written by twenty-somethings without showing much understanding of the words coming out of his mouth. The fall of Kabul revealed a callous man wholly out of his depth, pulled by invisible strings held by shadowy people. When he effectively invited a Russian invasion of Ukraine in a press conference, we learned why his minders don't want to let him out of the basement. In spite of an obsequious media that gushed over his choice of ice cream flavors, his approval ratings declined more quickly than any president's in memory. But for the fact that, were he removed, he'd be replaced by the obscenely cackling and deeply unpopular Kamala Harris, the Democrats would likely have ditched him.

He has presided over a train wreck of an administration. Prices at the pump and in the grocery store have skyrocketed. The left-wing media thinks it can make Americans forget the fall of Kabul, but our adversaries remember it and provoke us in ways they would never have dared when Trump was president. The Chinese launch hypersonic missiles, and we throw at them a transgender four-star admiral.

Biden has surrounded himself with one of the weakest cabinets in memory, a defense secretary who obsessed over critical race theory as Kabul fell, a transportation secretary who took a two-month maternity leave with his husband during a transportation crisis, an attorney general who sent in SWAT teams to spy on parents at PTA meetings, an energy secretary who shut down pipelines, and a treasury secretary who thinks we'll whip inflation if the federal government spends more money.

The Democrats have become the party of open borders, big city crime, inflation, and military humiliation. Self-righteous and contemptuous of half of America, their only answer to critics is to call them racists or link them to Jefferson Davis and Bull Connor as Biden has done. They tell us democracy is at risk if they lose elections when it's talk like that threatens democracy. And while Biden promised to unify the country, that's not at all how he has governed or spoken, and in any event it wouldn't go over with those who are mired in what the *New York Times's* Charles Blow praised as the Left's "insatiable rage."[25] Things are broken, and in alarming numbers we support secession.

What the Democrats chiefly have going for them is Trump, which is why they can't let go of him. He's the boogeyman who hid under their beds when they were children, and while he's left for Mar-a-Lago, they're still trying to run against him. The Alexandrine poet C. P. Cavafy wrote about the quandary one finds oneself in when threats just go away. People had been terrified by the thought of a barbarian invasion. Except one day everyone realized that the barbarians wouldn't show up. "Now what's going to happen to us without barbarians? Those people were a kind of solution."

The Need to Move On

If the Democrats so desperately need Trump, that should tell Republicans that they're better off without him. He received eleven million more votes in 2020 than he did in 2016 and increased his support among white women, Hispanics, and blacks. But the Democratic nominee received fifteen million more votes than Hillary Clinton had in 2016, and it wasn't because of Joe Biden's sparkling personality. It had more to do with the personality of the Republican candidate. The faltering Democratic nominee was merely Chance the Gardener, the un-Trump.

In future elections, smart Republicans will keep Trump at arm's length, as Virginia's Glenn Youngkin did in 2021. While supporting the policies the man brought to the party, it's necessary to recognize Trump's failures. Elected to drain the swamp, he became its prisoner, the subject of endless investigations by the spy agencies and plagued by daily leaks from disloyal subordinates. He permitted apocalyptic figures to pose as his spokesmen and never learned how to staff his administration with competent allies. Many of his senior appointees, the Betsy DeVoses and Alex Acostas, were wholly out of their depth. He brought in a few respected figures – the Jim Mattises and Rex Tillersons – but he couldn't get them to agree with him, and they seldom lasted very long. Such friends as he had, crude fixers like Michael Cohen and pushy sycophants like Anthony Scaramucci, made our flesh creep, and we were happy to see the last of them. The man became the kind of person he used to mock: a loser.

Trumpism, the speeches he gave, and the policies he favored spoke to the needs of an ailing America and the hypocrisy of our left-wing elites. But Trump the man was prickly and surly. He lacked Dwight Eisenhower's reassuring manner and George W. Bush's self-deprecating sense of humor. He picked a stupid fight with John McCain that might have cost him Arizona's electoral votes in 2020, and his graceless show of contempt for Jeff Sessions revealed a person without a spark of gratitude for or understanding of an old-fashioned Southern gentleman. After he lost, his inability to move beyond himself and make a proper case for Republican candidates in the January 5, 2021, Georgia run-off elections cost the party control of the Senate, with the result that every law the Democrats enact is on him.

Then came the January 6, 2021, riot at the Capitol. It was a chaotic free-for-all and not an insurrection. Unarmed loonies in raccoon skins and horns don't overthrow a government. Of those who entered the Capitol, about a hundred fought with the police, but the videos reveal that hundreds more were ordinary-looking people who waltzed through the open doors.[26] Six Capitol police officers were brought up on charges, apparently for saying, "Right this way, folks."[27] Only one person was killed, and she was a Trump supporter who was shot by the police.

For passive-aggressive Democrats, however, the riot became a gold mine. The event lasted only a few hours, but for Democrats it's a permanent insurrection and an everlasting threat to democracy.[28] They're using it as an excuse to say that the expected Republican victory in 2024 would amount to a coup,[29] which might justify who knows what extreme response. We got a hint of what might lie ahead when Democrats in the summer of 2020 thought Trump might win the election and senior members of the party game-planned what to do next. California might threaten to secede, they suggested, and the military might have to decide the issue.[30]

With their self-righteousness and sense of entitlement, the Democrats are quick to project onto Republicans their own willingness to depart from constitutional norms. Nevertheless, what happened on January 6 was an outrage, and Trump fanned the fires by claiming that the election had been stolen and asking his supporters to show up in Washington on the day Congress was to vote on electing a new president.

There had been fraud at the polls, to be sure. There always is, but it wasn't enough to change the result, as Attorney General Bill Barr concluded. Still, Trump persisted and at the Ellipse told the crowd that "we're going to walk down to the Capitol ... You have to show strength, and you have to be strong." He said, "if you don't fight like hell you're not going to have a country anymore."

It's true that whatever he said in his January 6 speech didn't incite the rioters. They were a mile and a half away when he spoke and couldn't have heard him. He might have recited the Pledge of Allegiance, and the attack would still have happened. Nevertheless, he had asked the protesters to come to Washington, and when they did he ignored the danger to members of Congress, even to those in his own party. He told his supporters that Vice President Pence had the authority to refuse to certify the election, and that sent the rioters looking for him. As they did, Trump tweeted, "Mike Pence didn't have the courage to do what should have been done to protect our Country and our Constitution." But it was Pence and people like him who followed the law. Not Trump. If you liked him, was the riot your idea of American Greatness?

We had put up with a great deal, but for many Trump supporters this was the breaking point. He wanted to overturn an election and was a self-absorbed egotist. In case there was any doubt, he announced that no one should vote Republican in 2022 or 2024 unless the fraud in the 2020 election is "solved."

That makes him an extreme narcissist, but it doesn't make him a fascist. He disputed the election results, but that's what Hillary Clinton did in 2016, and Biden has said that the predicted Republican victory in the 2022 Congressional elections will be illegitimate. Trump was censored by social media, and that doesn't happen to real authoritarians. Instead, they do the censoring. They also don't face a hostile press or lose elections. He adopted immigration policies to protect Americans, but when he was blocked by the courts, he meekly revised his policies or dropped them. He asked his top lawyers to overturn the election but backed down when they rebelled. He made clear what he thought of journalists, but unlike Obama he didn't prosecute or wiretap them.[31] Nor did he ask the intelligence community to spy on the Democrats, as Obama had done to him while knowing that this was grounded on baseless Democratic opposition research.[32]

What especially annoyed Republicans was how Democrats tried to pass themselves off as the party of law and order. They told us there was nothing to see when cities burned and stores were looted, and when Antifa injured 140 federal officers in Portland, they blamed the cops. Speaker Nancy Pelosi compared them to Nazi stormtroopers, and Sen. Mazie Hirono (D-HI) said that it was Antifa that needed protection from the police. "The hearing we should be having is one called the right of the people to peaceably assemble without being beaten up by unidentifiable federal agents." For Democrats, the police were the villains and the thugs were social justice heroes, which explains the degradation and crime we're now seeing in Democrat-run cities, the homeless encampments and the looting, dangerous driving, and carjackings. Still, Speaker Pelosi can take some pleasure in the thought that, because of cop-killers, there are fewer of those stormtroopers around today.

Occupying Pelosi's office was terribly wrong in 2021, but apparently not in 2018 when a different set of protesters piled into the office of Senate Judiciary Chairman Chuck Grassley (R-IA) during the Kavanaugh hearings. The Left also excused and celebrated the protesters who occupied the Wisconsin statehouse in 2011.[33] The Republicans knew hypocrisy when they saw it and (like Billy Joel) said that we didn't start the fires.

That didn't justify the riots at the Capitol, but it did tell Republicans to scorn the Left's attempt to use this as an excuse to turn American into a one-party state. Even before the riot, Clinton's

Labor Secretary Robert Reich tweeted that we'll need a Truth and Reconciliation Commission "to name every official, politician, executive, and media mogul whose greed and cowardice enabled this catastrophe." Speaker Nancy Pelosi called Trump supporters "enemies of the state,"[34] and Anne Applebaum compared them to Nazi collaborators.[35] The *Washington Post*'s Jennifer Rubin thought it wasn't enough that Trump lost. "We have to collectively burn down the Republican Party. We have to level them. Because if there are survivors ... they will do it again."

Conservatives have known for years that they were despised by the Left, but the January 6 riots paired back the last shreds of civility. It wasn't just the rioters, said the *Washington Post*. What about your neighbors? The people at the Capitol on January 6 had been regular people, park workers, hairdressers, and piano teachers, seemingly just like the rest of us except that they were conservative. Now we need to dig down and scrutinize the people who say hi when we meet them on the street. Just what is behind their smiles? "Back in the quiet, well-to-do neighborhoods of America, the constitution of the mob raised unnerving questions. *Do I know any of these people?*"[36] As for Nikole Hannah-Jones, she wants the seventy-four million Americans who voted for Trump to be deprogrammed.[37]

The Left concluded that Hillary Clinton was right after all. The Trump supporters are deplorables, and any grievances they voice should be ignored. But what if those grievances are legitimate? What if the Left had excused violence when it suited them and became the party of law and order only when this was politically advantageous? What if they had portrayed Republicans as racists when it is they who embrace racism through their racial preferences? What if the party that said it championed equality and mobility had really made us unequal and immobile and abandoned the common good to become the party of, by, and for its elites? What if turning America into a one-party state won't promote democracy? In that case, the honest voter who desires a better country won't turn to the Democrats.

Which raises the question of where we'll be now that Trump is in the rearview mirror. If you loved him, you might ask yourself whether you're better off without him. And if you hated him, why he's left for Mar-a-Lago. And while he might think he's coming back, it's not going to happen. At most, he'll hover over his enemies in the Republican Party like an exterminating angel. But while he's gone, what remains is what he brought to the Republican Party, a defense of the American Dream, a rejection of corruption, and the nationalist's pride in America.

These are not new principles. They defined the Republican Party for most of its history, and I call them progressive conservatism and say it is an authentically American tradition and the party's hidden yet ever-recurring driver. Republicanism was born in the West, the home of progressivism, and its greatest leaders – Abraham Lincoln, Theodore Roosevelt, and Dwight Eisenhower – may fairly be called progressives. They were also conservatives even if they didn't reduce every issue down to economics.

Progressive conservatism is what Americans yearn for. It's not a thin ideology that ignores our need to bond with others, our family, neighbors, and nation. When told that an act was freely chosen, the progressive conservative will ask whether it was well chosen. He knows that we are all a little self-deceived and, like Aleksandr Solzhenitsyn, thinks that the line between good and evil runs through each of our hearts. He prefers culture to anarchy and thinks there are some paintings and sculptures that are objectively beautiful, some music that is deservedly loved, some novels that everyone should read, some traditions that should be followed, and some ideas that should be preserved.

In all those ways, progressive conservatives are conservative. But they're also progressives who think that we've seen enough craziness from the Left and that we don't need more of the same from the Right. Left-wing hysteria doesn't justify right-wing end-of-the-world chiliasm. If the Left has given up on America, we don't need reactionaries telling us that the American experiment was a big mistake. Free market principles have brought prosperity to billions of people, and we can do without the perfect conservative idiot who complains about neoliberalism. If the right-wing weirdo is a monarchist, we're still republicans. If he thinks that Hungary is the future, we'll stick with America.

We are poised for a revival that affirms America's essential goodness and the republican virtue of the founders. After the rise of a woke Democratic Party, only Republicans can provide this, and only they can govern without discrimination for the common good, which is as close to the ideal of purity in government as you'll find. Republicans will not ask voters to ally themselves with shabby teachers' unions or grievance monsters, with corporate welfare bums or dogmatic libertarians, or with anything that degrades a person. And thus, as progressive conservatives, Republicans will become America's natural governing party.

CHAPTER THREE

What Is Progressive Conservatism?

BUT WHAT DOES progressive conservatism mean? Labels can confuse more than they clarify, and sometimes they lie. People asked how Obamacare could raise healthcare costs. It was labeled the "Affordable Care Act." And how could the mobs in Portland be dangerous? They call themselves anti-fascists.

Similarly, the progressive label is often dishonest. Is it progressive to sneer at working class people and call them deplorable? And if the self-styled progressive is intolerant, what's progressive about that? He's given up on the liberal's free speech rights and searches out thought crimes with the goal of canceling people and getting them fired. There's even something a little passé about the label. Not so long ago, it meant Enlightenment principles and left-wing economic policies such as Medicare for all, but today's progressive has reverted to the premodern identity politics of tribe against tribe, race against race, that is destructive of democratic dialogue. When liberals and conservatives debate one another, some positive new ideas might emerge. If it all comes down to race or sex, however, there's nothing left to say except to clamor that the least racist and the least sexist society that has ever existed is a Mount Everest of racism and sexism.

Old-fashioned Democrats would have been horrified at this. They were patriots who supported free markets and fought to expel communists from their party. With progressive Republicans they helped heal their country's racism and sexism. Unlike todays leftists, they defended Western civilization and weren't cultural barbarians. They stood up for what was right and did great things, and their errors (the Great Society) were mistakes of the mind and not the heart.

Their passing has left a hole in American politics. But if today's Democratic Party has given up on those older values, so much the worse for them. If they turn every question into one of race, let the Republicans be the party of all lives matter and the common good. If the Left has bought into cancel culture, let the GOP defend free speech and the free exercise of religion together with old-fashioned Democrats who have been abandoned by their party.

Conservative Progressives

Right-wingers detest the progressive label without knowing a great deal about it. They trace the modern regulatory state all the way back to Theodore Roosevelt's embrace of administrative agencies and think that that's when it all went to hell. But then a lot of things needed regulating 120 years ago. The municipal corruption and slum conditions described by muckraking journalists such as Lincoln Steffens, Ida Tarbell, and Roosevelt's friend Jacob Riis would disturb everyone today.[1] No one would want to go back to the unregulated meatpacking industry portrayed in Upton Sinclair's *The Jungle.*

Right-wingers are Manicheans who see things in terms of black or white, but the attempt to read everything malign into progressivism distorts it "as if through a fun-house mirror," in the words of Ken Kersch.[2] In truth, there was no one progressive movement but a variety of them. Some were recognizably left of center, such as that of Herbert Croly (1869–1930) with his mistrust of "extreme individualism" and faith in centralized government and scientific planning by a body of experts.[3] Others, especially the western agrarians, were conservative and individualistic and more Jeffersonian than the Hamiltonian Croly. What they wanted, and what every conservative wants today, was a mobile society where everyone who puts in the effort can get ahead.

The conservative strain in progressivism arose in the west, the land of free soil and free labor where the Republican Party was born, and found its champion in the first great progressive historian, Frederick Jackson Turner (1861–1932).[4] What made Turner both a conservative and a progressive was his celebration of democracy and freedom, which he said were the gifts of the frontier. Our history was forged not in Jamestown or Boston but in Stephen Vincent Benét's Tucson and Deadwood and Lost Mule Flat and the way in which America had constantly reinvented itself in its restless movement westward, even as the dude became Mark Hanna's "damn cowboy" when Theodore Roosevelt bought a ranch in the North Dakota badlands.

Eastern states were corrupt, undemocratic, and immobile, said Turner, while western states were the repository of republican virtue, democratic, and mobile. They had to be to attract the settlers they needed, and so they competed for people by offering them fresh starts, free land, and egalitarianism. They gave women the franchise, enacted initiative and referendum laws, and supported the popular election of senators under the Seventeenth Amendment.[5] They liked competition and didn't think there was enough of it back east. All this came to define the American Dream, the idea that there were boundless possibilities of self-improvement in this country. In time, the eastern states that were losing people to the west began to compete for people by liberalizing themselves. It all came from the west. "The reign of aristocracy is passing," said Turner. "That of humanity begins."[6] He was a conservative progressive.

If progressivism lacks a clear meaning, conservatism isn't better defined. You might think that, if nothing else, conservatives would all oppose radical change, but progressive conservatives sound like revolutionaries when they talk about taking back the culture. The Left's long march through our institutions has silenced and excluded conservatives, and progressive conservatives say we should break up the monasteries. That's progressive, but it's not how conservatives used to think. Evidently, progressive conservatism represents a blending of former labels.

Progressive conservatives support our country's free-market economic institutions. But if conservatism means a bias against change and innovation, the label doesn't fit free market progressive conservatives. Nothing is more radical than the way in which free competition churns our economic institutions, burying one corporate behemoth after another in what Joseph Schumpeter called the "creative destruction" of capitalism.[7] Take a look at a magazine from sixty years back and see who advertised in it. They're mostly gone now, and only Exxon cracks the top-ten list in both 1960 and 2020. Many of today's biggest firms – the Apples, Amazons, and Walmarts – weren't even around sixty years ago. Trump was a progressive conservative when he objected to trade treaties that subject American firms to unfair foreign competition, but he didn't attack free market capitalism. That job he left for the Democrats.

Progressive Conservatives

If the meanings of progressivism and conservatism are both contested, is the ambiguity compounded when they're combined in the term "progressive conservative"? But then progressive conservatism is a well-understood term in our sister democracies. There it means a conservatism that is alive to changed circumstances that call for reform and that is unwilling to let the party of the Left become the sole agent of progress.

Edmund Burke was the founder of modern conservatism, but that didn't make him a reactionary. Like his fellow Whigs, he supported the post-1689 British constitution, urged conciliation when American Patriots were on the verge of revolt, and backed Catholic emancipation in Ireland. It's not enough to look backward, he thought, and society must incorporate a principle of progress. "A state without the means of some change is without the means of its conservation." And like all progressives, Burke loathed corruption in government and prosecuted Warren Hastings, the governor of Bengal, for exploiting his office. But if he wasn't a reactionary, neither was he a modern progressive who scorns the past. Wise policy, he said, always looks back to our heritage in charting a course for the future. "People will not look forward to posterity, who never look backward to their ancestors."[8]

That was a progressive conservative.

Burke's appeal to the age of chivalry and his contempt for the radical band of "sophisters, economists and calculators" defined another element in what became modern conservatism, the romantic rebellion against arid eighteenth-century rationalism. One saw the same yearning for premodern virtue and community in Oliver Goldsmith's protest against the enclosure movement and in William Blake's horror of dark, satanic mills. It could also be found in Thomas Gray's *Elegy*, which on the eve of battle James Wolfe said he would rather have written than take Quebec. In France, romanticism meant the rediscovery of Christianity for the youthful François-René de Chateaubriand and Alphonse de Lamartine. In America, too, you'll find a romantic conservatism in the preference for localism and agrarianism and especially in the desire for a virtuous republic by both our founders and today's progressive conservatives.

You'll not find abstract theories of government in Burke. He didn't think they existed and mocked anyone who thought they did. Instead, he said, a statesman should be guided by his sense of his country's identity and the circumstances before him, the people to be persuaded, and the obstacles to be overcome. He thought Britain should make peace with the American colonists not because he agreed with their principles but because he thought it imprudent to make war upon them. Questions of sovereignty and inalienable rights were quite beside the point. Like Gerd Gigerenzer and Friedrich Hayek, Burke thought we're often better off relying on our instincts than on the rationalist's theories.[9]

The progressive conservative is curious about people and how they fare, not theories. Like William Butler Yeats's *Seven Sages*, he'll learn from those who have walked the roads and mimicked what they heard. In 1822 this was William Cobbett, a progressive Tory who wanted to travel from Kensington to Uphusband to report on the lives of ordinary Englishmen. By coach he could have done so in eight hours, but he decided against this. "My object was, not to see inns and turnpike-roads, but to see the *country*, to see the farmers at *home*, and to see the laborers in the *fields*; and to do this you must go either on foot or on horse-back."[10] The result was *Rural Rides*, an account of the agricultural distress and ministerial corruption that he learned about from his rambles.

Then, in the nineteenth century, a distinct school of progressive conservatism arose led by Benjamin Disraeli, prime minister of Great

Britain in 1868 and from 1874–80. In the 1840s, he created the modern progressive conservative Tory party by opposing the free trade policies of the Sir Robert Peel's Conservative Party. Like Trump, Disraeli thought free market orthodoxies had ignored the plight of forgotten classes of his fellow citizens, and these included not only Britain's farmers but also the industrial worker in the new factory towns. In *Sybil*, Disraeli said England was divided into two nations:

> Between whom there is no intercourse and no sympathy; who are as ignorant of each other's habits, thoughts, and feelings, as if they were dwellers in different zones, or inhabitants of different planets.... *The Rich and the Poor.*[11]

Right-left distinctions often make little sense when imposed on the past, but to the extent they do, Disraeli was on the left of Peel's Conservative Party. His fellow conservatives wanted nothing to do with English radicals, but Disraeli signaled his sympathy with them. "Although we do not approve of the remedy suggested by the Chartists, it does not follow that we should not attempt to cure the disease complained of."[12] And a year before Friedrich Engels shocked readers with his description of the wretchedness of East End London in *The Condition of the Working Class in England* (1845), Disraeli had written no less passionately about economic inequality.[13]

Then, like Trump, Disraeli campaigned on issues that his opponents thought they had owned. As prime minister, he extended the franchise to all adult male heads of households in the 1867 Reform Bill. If Peel thought the Tory party should make its peace with the middle class, Disraeli proposed a different national party based on an alliance between the country's farmers and the then-disenfranchised poor. Since electoral reform was going to happen anyway, some thought this cynical. Yet it was simply an application of the ideas he had put forward years before, in *Coningsby* (1844) and *Sybil* (1845), and in stealing the issue from Gladstone's Liberals he had "dished the Whigs," as Trump was to do in 2016.

Like Trump, Disraeli was also a nationalist who understood that this imposed a duty to promote the common good and the well-being of all fellow citizens and not simply a favored few.

I have always considered that the Tory party was the national party of England. It is not formed of a combination of oligarchs and philosophers who practice on the sectarian prejudices of a portion of the people. It is formed of all classes, from the highest to the most homely, and it upholds a series of institutions that are in theory, and ought to be in practice, an embodiment of the national requirements and the security of the national rights.[14]

What Disraeli had created was a socially conservative and economically centrist Tory party, the ancestor of Trump's Republican Party. He had taken the Whig's issues away from them, just as Trump had done in dishing the Democrats in 2016.

The Tory party's progressive conservative tradition continued with people such as Lord Randolph Churchill (Winston's father) and his idea of a left-of-center "Tory Democracy."[15] It was also taken up by Tory writers such as John Ruskin (1819–1900), who began his autobiography by proclaiming, "I am, and my father was before me, a violent Tory of the old school."[16] Like all Tories, and like today's Trump supporters, Ruskin was deeply suspicious of the vulgar economism that assumes that material welfare is an all-encompassing proxy for personal well-being and that free market price theories provide the touchstone of all political and social issues.

Among the delusions which at different periods have possessed themselves of the minds of large masses of the human race, perhaps the most curious – certainly the least credible – is the modern soi-disant science of political economy, based on the idea that an advantageous code of social action may be determined irrespectively of the influence of social affection.[17]

If you call Disraeli and Ruskin populists, you don't know what you're talking about.

It was in Canada, however, that progressive conservatism really took hold, and this became the name of the official Tory party from 1942 to 2003. The 1942 name change came when the Tories offered the party leadership to the leader of the western agrarian Progressive Party. The current Conservative Party, created in 2003, was formed on the merger of the Progressive Conservatives with the Canadian Alliance Party, whose roots lay in another western progressive movement. There, as here, the west saw itself as an open society, egalitarian, and untainted by eastern privilege and corruption.

The similarity between the Canadian progressive conservatives and parties further to the left gave rise to the term "Red Tory" to describe a conservative movement that is left-of-center in its acceptance of the welfare state and in its belief that an organic society is more than an agglomeration of competing and self-interested individuals.[18] In part, that was dictated by geography. The improbable country to our north, stretched across thousands of miles and hugging the American border by reason of its climate, is a revolt against economics. Canadian conservatives, if they are nationalists and wish to preserve their country, must resist the drift to continentalism and absorption by the United States and perforce are Red Tories.

That is progressive conservatism in the two countries we most closely resemble. We are presidential in our system of government and they are parliamentary, but all three have a tradition on the Right that wins elections when it defaults to progressive conservatism.

CHAPTER FOUR

The Four Turnings

PROGRESSIVE CONSERVATISM is one of America's oldest political traditions. Its origins lie in the west, the land of democracy and fresh starts. While it supported free markets, it never asked the economist to solve all our social problems. It recognized the need for a welfare safety net but did so out of a sense of fraternity with fellow Americans and not in service of some abstract theory. It thought that all lives mattered and left racial politics for the Democrats.

There has always been a progressive conservative constituency in Republican politics and during moments of true nobility. One came when Sen. Margaret Chase Smith (R-ME) spoke up to oppose Sen. Joe McCarthy (R-WI). Another was when Sen. Everett Dirksen (R-IL) brought his caucus around to vote for the 1964 Civil Rights Act. We saw it again when a quietly decent Jerry Ford (who called himself "a Ford and not a Lincoln") threw away his chances of election by pardoning a deeply depressed Richard Nixon. More recently, there were Senators Bob Dole (R-KS), Orrin Hatch (R-UT), and Alan Simpson (R-WY), and many of us saw the same republican virtues in John McCain (R-AZ), who was not afraid to take on his party over campaign finance reform.

While the Goldwater movement sought to supplant progressive conservatism, it never succeeded in doing so, and with Trump's nomination and election, that era came to an end, and progressive conservatism became the new face of the GOP. This was only the most recent of four progressive conservative moments in the party, when it was led by Abraham Lincoln, Theodore Roosevelt, Dwight Eisenhower, and Trump, with each man adding his own imprint to it.

Lionel Trilling wrote that each poet's invocation of a tradition changes the tradition itself, so it is never fixed,[1] and the same is true of the American tradition of progressive conservatism. For Lincoln, it meant the American Dream, a society where artificial barriers were removed and everyone was permitted to rise. For Theodore Roosevelt, it meant a return to republican virtue and an end to corruption. For Eisenhower, it meant a safety net for those who through no fault of their own were unable to rise and a liberal nationalism that was on the right side of the civil rights revolution. For Trump it was all of that as well as a determination to take on a corrupt establishment that had made America immobile. At each turning, progressive conservatism renewed itself in defense of the common good.

The First Turning: Lincoln

Just about every American politician has tried to wrap himself in the mantle of the sixteenth president, but Lincoln is best seen as a progressive conservative. He came to politics as a Henry Clay Whig who supported "internal improvements" (federal support for infrastructure projects) and high tariffs to pay for them. In office, he backed an income tax, a Legal Tender Act that created paper money (the "greenback") backed by government credit, the transcontinental railway, land grant colleges, and free land for farmers under the Homestead Act. Quite apart from the Civil War, his domestic policies made him one of the most consequential of American presidents. These were all progressive conservative themes, but what makes him the movement's American founder was his invention of the American Dream.

Lincoln's law partner, William Herndon, once gave him a copy of George Fitzhugh's *Sociology of the South* and reported that no book angered him more.[2] Fitzhugh was an antebellum Virginian who defended slavery and in doing so advanced an aristocratic vision of fixed social classes that came to be called the mudsill theory. The mudsill is the lowest floor of a building, placed directly on the ground, and was a metaphor for society's natural slaves. Without the mudsill, we'd not have a great civilization composed of the superior people who inhabited the mansion above it. "Every social structure must have its substratum," wrote Fitzhugh.

> In free society this substratum, the weak, poor and ignorant, is borne down upon and oppressed with continually increasing weight by all above. We have solved the problem of relieving this substratum from the pressure from above. The slaves are the substratum, and the master's feelings and interests alike prevent him from bearing down upon and oppressing them.[3]

Fitzhugh was a racist, of course, but he was also something more than that. He simply liked slavery and thought it inevitable. He wasn't even that much of a racist. Whites made good slaves, too, he thought, and he would not discriminate on the basis of race or color. His was an equal opportunity slavery.

Fitzhugh thought that slavery was good all-around for everyone. In the south it had produced a leisured class of slaveowners, and leisure was the basis of culture. It was slaveholding, not getting and spending, that had given us the ancient world's art, literature, and philosophy. The slaveowner was also a paternalist who, lacking the capitalist's mercenary incentives, was bound by ties of affection to his slaves, whom he treated well. That was why the true philanthropist would buy slaves, said Fitzhugh.

Fitzhugh denied the possibility of social and economic mobility in both the north and the south. The industrialized north had created its own mudsill, with the difference that callous Northern wage slavery was so much worse than the paternalistic slavery of the south.[4] Today the mudsill lives on in the Left's meritocrats who think that the Trump deplorables are doomed to permanent inferiority by their broken homes and drug dependencies, as portrayed in *Hillbilly Elegy*. An older Left had allied itself to America's underclass, to the coal miners of Harlan County and the Joads of *The Grapes of Wrath*, but the modern Democratic Party has abandoned them in favor of policies that serve its elites. If tens of millions of Americans were left behind, history was simply unfolding as it should and as Fitzhugh would have predicted.

Fitzhugh put to pen what many of his contemporaries thought, but the mudsill theory infuriated Lincoln, and he responded to it in an 1859 speech at a Wisconsin Agricultural Fair. In so doing he gave us a new understanding of American conservatism by identifying it with the American Dream and its promise of economic and social mobility. The mudsill theory assumed that workers must be uneducated, that the perfect worker would be no better than a blind horse. "But free labor says no!" thundered Lincoln.

> The prudent, penniless beginner in the world, labors for wages awhile, saves a surplus with which to buy tools or land, for himself; then labors on his own account another while, and at length hires another new beginner to help him. This, say its advocates, is free labor – the just and generous, and prosperous system, which opens the way for all – gives hope to all, and energy, and progress, and improvement of condition to all.[5]

Lincoln didn't just believe this. He lived it. Through his own efforts he had risen from a hardscrabble farm, read voraciously, and became a lawyer and then the president, and from his personal rise he took an understanding of society that led in time to the Emancipation Proclamation and the Thirteenth Amendment's abolition of slavery. That was how, he told Congress on July 4, 1861, the fight to preserve the Union should be seen. It was about a principle more encompassing than slavery.

> This is essentially a people's contest. On the side of the Union it is a struggle for maintaining in the world that form and substance of government whose leading object is to elevate the condition of men; to lift artificial weights from all shoulders; to clear the paths of laudable pursuit for all; to afford all an unfettered start and a fair chance in the race of life.

He revered the founders, especially Jefferson, and told a gathering at Independence Hall in Philadelphia that "I have never had a feeling politically that did not spring from the sentiments embodied in the Declaration of Independence."[6] Jefferson had introduced an abstract truth about equality applicable to all men and all times. What Lincoln had done, however, was to give new meaning to the Declaration. First, and most obviously, Lincoln understood that Jefferson's egalitarianism was incompatible with the institution of slavery. In addition, Lincoln had a different understanding about why equality mattered. More than an abstract truth, it was also a guarantee of social mobility.

> This progress by which the poor, honest, industrious, and resolute man raises himself, that he may work on his own account ... is that progress that human nature is entitled to, is that improvement in condition that is intended to be secured by those institutions under which we live, is the great principle for which this government was really formed.[7]

Jefferson spoke of a natural aristocracy in which the most gifted and able might rise to the top, but this was simply a happy by-product of equality. For Lincoln, however, it was more than that. Rather, the central idea of America, as expressed in the Declaration, became through Lincoln the promise of social and income mobility and a faith in the ability of all people, black or white, to rise to a higher station in life. There was nothing base about labor, as Fitzhugh had thought. Instead, what was ignoble was the disdain for work by a leisured, aristocratic class and the failure to better oneself. That was what America meant to him, and his ideal of self-improvement and mobility has come down to us as the American Dream.

The Second Turning: Theodore Roosevelt

Historians Arthur Schlesinger Jr. and Heather Richardson identified a cyclical pattern in Republican policies. After a period of liberalism (which is better regarded as progressive conservatism), the party reverts to right-wing dogmas and an alliance with big business. That in turn is followed by a return to progressive conservatism, and so it was in the period between Lincoln's assassination and the rise of Theodore Roosevelt at the cusp of the American Century.

The post-Lincoln Republican Party quickly abandoned the work of racial justice in the south. Immediately after the war, congressional Republicans such as Thaddeus Stevens (PA) sought to defend the interests of African Americans, but President Andrew Johnson vetoed Republican bills that would give them the voting rights that "Black Codes" in the south denied them. That prompted his impeachment, which sadly failed to remove him. Then, with the compromise that elected Republican Rutherford B. Hayes in 1877, Reconstruction and the attempt to bring the American Dream to African Americans was halted.

This was also the Gilded Age period, one of great fortunes and enormous wealth inequalities, when the Republicans abandoned Lincoln's progressive agenda and saw every government effort to regulate business as suspect. It was also a period of massive civil unrest, with the Haymarket Riot, the Pullman strike, and the assassination of President James A. Garfield. Republicans saw the specter of communism behind the disturbances, and Hayes sent in federal troops to suppress a railway strike.[8]

The Democratic Party was equally conservative during the period, and the administration of Grover Cleveland (1885–89 and 1893–97) is remembered as one of the most right-wing in American history. A progressive movement nevertheless arose, born in the urban workers' unions and the agrarian Grange and Farmers' Alliance parties.[9] The agrarians argued that the government should regulate the monopoly rates railways charged to carry grain and produce, and in 1892 the People's Party ran on a progressive platform and won 22 electoral votes from farming states in the west. Then in 1896, the Democrats embraced a progressive platform under William Jennings Bryan and won 196 electoral votes in farming states and the south.

Republicans pooh-bahs called this class warfare and un-American, but a younger group of liberal Republicans, including Theodore Roosevelt, began to embrace more progressive policies. This included an attack on the corruption that, from the time of the Grant administration (1869–77) had tarnished the party. Roosevelt began his political career as an anti-corruption, "good government" urban reformer who opposed the Democratic patronage machines[10] and ran (unsuccessfully) against a Democratic Tammany Hall candidate for mayor of New York in 1886.

Roosevelt was a larger-than-life figure. The ardent conservationist and big-game hunter, the man who invited Booker T. Washington to dine at the White House and the exponent of Manifest Destiny, the man who won the Nobel Peace Prize and stormed San Juan Hill, and the man who insisted on giving a ninety-minute campaign speech after he had been shot in the chest remains an enigma for us. Henry Adams described him as pure act, "the quality that mediæval theology ascribed to God."[11] Nevertheless, he had one big idea, which was that progressives had correctly identified a pathology of the Gilded Age.

The progressives thought that, in an age of rising economic inequalities, America had become immobile, and they blamed this on large monopolistic holding companies ("trusts") and the way in which their money had corrupted our politics. Radical reformers such as Louis Brandeis wanted to break them up, but conservatives such as Roosevelt thought the answer lay in prudent campaign finance reform laws and safety regulations, not in trust-busting. In his 1905 Message to Congress, he wrote:

> This is an age of combination, and any effort to prevent all combination will be not only useless, but in the end vicious ... We should, moreover, recognize in cordial and ample fashion the immense good effected by corporate agencies in a country such as ours, and the wealth of intellect, energy, and fidelity devoted to their service.

After successfully breaking up the Northern Securities railway holding company, Roosevelt backed away from an aggressive anti-trust agenda, and the best history of the progressive movement called it "the triumph of conservatism."[12]

Roosevelt called himself both a progressive and a conservative.

Those of us who believe in Progressive Nationalism are sometimes dismissed with the label that we are "radicals." So we are; we are radicals in such matters as eliminating special privilege and securing general popular rule, the genuine rule of the democracy. But we are not overmuch concerned with matters of mere terminology. We are not in the least afraid of the word "conservative," and, wherever there is any reason for caution, we are not only content but desirous to make progress slowly and in a cautious, conservative manner.[13]

His successor, William Howard Taft (1909–13), continued and expanded Roosevelt's antitrust agenda. Nevertheless, Roosevelt felt that Taft had abandoned Lincoln's policies and made economic and social mobility a principal theme of his 1910 "New Nationalism" speech in Osawatomie, Kansas.[14] Roosevelt quoted from Lincoln's Wisconsin Agricultural Fair speech and said that "in every wise struggle for human betterment one of the main objects, and often the only object, has been to achieve in large measure equality of opportunity." He spoke of the "conflict between the men who possess more than they have earned and the men who have earned more than they possess" and condemned the crony capitalism that entrenched a well-connected elite.

Then, when he failed to secure the Republican nomination in 1912, Roosevelt bolted the party to run as the Progressive ("Bull Moose") candidate for the presidency. He warned of the party's tendency to fossilize, "to become mere ultra-conservative reactionaries, to reject and oppose all progress."[15] The new party's platform pledged "to dissolve the unholy alliance between corrupt business and corrupt politics" and proposed an ambitious social welfare agenda, including safety and health standards, a ban on child labor, an eight-hour working day, and a national old age security and health system.

The split in the Republican Party doomed it to defeat in 1912. The two progressive candidates, Roosevelt from the Right and Woodrow Wilson from the Left, polled 10 million votes between them to Taft's 3.5 million votes. Had the Republicans managed to stay united as a single progressive conservative party, they would have defeated Wilson, but when the conservatives were divided among themselves, the party lost. The same thing would happen again in 1992 when a progressive Ross Perot siphoned votes away from a conservative George H. W. Bush.

The Third Turning: Eisenhower

After the First World War, the Republican Party turned right again with leaders such as Calvin Coolidge, whom historically minded right-wingers regard as the ne plus ultra of conservatism. Thereafter the New Deal hardened Republicans into a right-wing party in opposition to what they saw as a socialist Franklin Roosevelt administration. That was short-sighted since it relegated the Republicans to minority status until the party learned to live with the New Deal.

Franklin Roosevelt can be seen as a progressive conservative, and in 1932 he was endorsed by four progressive Republican senators, Robert LaFollette (WI), Hiram Johnson (CA), George W. Norris (NE), and Bronson Cutting (NM).[16] For that matter, brain trusters Henry Wallace and Harold Ickes joined the administration as progressive Republicans. They knew, as did the rest of the country, that the economic crisis required drastic change, which only Franklin Roosevelt would provide. He did so not as a socialist but rather as a crisis manager and in preserving the economy saved the country from far worse alternatives.

That was how he saw himself, complaining to Felix Frankfurter that he was the best friend the profit system ever had.[17] He had a point. Free market systems depend for their survival on the bourgeois virtues of industriousness and a willingness to delay gratification, as Daniel Bell pointed out in *The Cultural Contradictions of Capitalism*. Those virtues, in turn, are parasitic on an economy in which the gains are shared with the workers. That is something today's right-wingers forget when they fail to ask whether their free-market principles will survive in a radically unequal economy. When millennials and Zoomers find themselves too strapped to get married, buy a house, and have children, don't be surprised if they give up on capitalism.

That was how things looked when FDR first took office. On March 4, 1933, the Dow Jones Industrial Average had fallen 90 percent from its 1929 high. New capital investments had declined by 95 percent. There had been five thousand bank failures, wiping out nine million individual bank accounts. Thirty-two states had closed their banks, and farm income had fallen by 50 percent. Local governments couldn't pay their teachers, and nearly half the country's homes were in danger of foreclosure. The best estimate put the unemployment rate at 30 percent.[18] When the Soviet Union's trade office in New York invited six thousand skilled workers to go to Russia, a hundred thousand Americans applied.[19]

Americans wanted radical change, and Coolidge's free market policies weren't on the table. What was were the darker alternatives offered by Huey Long and the anti-Semitic Father Coughlin as well as the full employment polices of fascism and communism. If we didn't go there, we can thank FDR and not the Coolidge Republicans of the period.

To meet the crisis, Roosevelt threw a mishmash of policies at the wall to see which would stick. Some of these, such as the National Recovery Act and perhaps the Securities Act, were misguided forms of crony capitalism, but enough of them worked to help get Americans back to work. Fourteen million Americans were unemployed when he took office, but by the summer of 1934 the number was down to 9.5 million.[20] The GDP had declined by 12.9 percent in 1932 but from 1934 to 1936 grew an average of more than 10 percent each year.

The president enacted laws that Republican found impossible to repeal and presided over an astonishing economic recovery. Then, in the greatest act of American presidential statesmanship, he brought his country out of its deep isolationism and provided the leadership that saved democracy. On December 7, 1941, there only twelve democracies in the world, and smart people thought it a failed American invention. They said that authoritarianism was the wave of the future. But in the Second World War, Americans proved them wrong.

Franklin Roosevelt was a world-historical figure, and it's not surprising that the Republican Party lost four straight presidential elections after 1932. After the last defeat, Senator Henry Cabot Lodge (R-MA) was moved to ask, "Does the Republican Party Have a Future?"[21] Lodge's answer was yes but only if Republicans returned to their progressive roots as the party of Lincoln and Theodore Roosevelt.

The Republicans did just that in nominating and electing Dwight Eisenhower. To do so, moderate leaders such as Lodge and Tom Dewey had to defeat conservatives who sought to undo the New Deal and who thought that their candidate, Senator Robert Taft (R-OH), had wrapped up the nomination.[22] Taft lost, and Eisenhower went on to win 55 percent of the vote in 1952 and 57 percent in 1956. We're asked to remember his opponent, Adlai Stevenson, as a liberal intellectual, but he never won a state north of the Mason-Dixon line and only nine of them in 1952 and seven in 1956.

Eisenhower called himself a "modern Republican," but the progressive label is more apt. He wrote in his diary that the GOP would be sunk if it weren't progressive[23] and resisted calls to eliminate New Deal programs. In some cases, he saw them expanded. He created the Department of Health, Education, and Welfare and extended the coverage of Social Security by 10.5 million people, including farmers, the self-employed, domestic workers, and state and local officials. He staved off the threat of unemployment with the Interstate Highway System, the greatest internal improvements program in American history, and together with Canada opened the St. Lawrence Seaway, which permitted Great Lakes tankers to reach ports across the world.

In 1954 Eisenhower sought an expanded federal role in health care but was rebuffed by a Republican Congress. He didn't want "socialized medicine," he said, but worried that the rising cost of health care would bankrupt many Americans. What he proposed was a government reinsurance program to encourage private insurance companies to guarantee policies for low-income and high-risk groups. Where the primary insurer would deny coverage, the reinsurance fund would take over and bear the cost. It was a sensible proposal, but it was killed in the House by conservative Republicans who didn't want any federal role in health insurance, and in consequence the party lost control of both House and Senate in 1954.[24] After the defeat, an angered Eisenhower told his press secretary that he wanted to create a progressive party and that "if the right wing wants a fight, they're going to get it.... Either this Republican Party will reflect progressivism or I won't be with them anymore."[25] If it did become progressive, he wrote, "the party would grow so rapidly that within a few years it would dominate American politics."[26]

He despised Senator Joe McCarthy (R-WI) and wanted nothing to do with the man or his smears. He did not attack McCarthy directly lest he give the man undue prominence[27] but went out of his way to signal his revulsion. Eisenhower defended the men McCarthy attacked, and when the senator's chief counsel, Roy Cohn, complained about left-wing books in America's overseas libraries, Eisenhower asked students "not to join the book burners."[27] He forbade his administration from responding to requests for information from McCarthy's subcommittee, and during the Army-McCarthy investigations it released information that discredited the senator and ultimately destroyed him.[29]

There were no wars on Eisenhower's watch. He also saw how wasteful the arms race was and bemoaned the fact that a modern heavy bomber cost as much was thirty new brick schools. "Every gun that is made, every warship launched, every rocket fired signifies, in the final sense, a theft from those who hunger and are not fed, those who are cold and are not clothed."[30] He sought an arms deal with the Soviet Union and told the United Nations of his willingness to put the American nuclear arsenal under the supervision of an international agency.[31] The proposal went nowhere, but during his presidency Eisenhower continued to seek a test ban treaty. Memorably, in his farewell address, he described the way in which the military and the arms industry pressured the government for more arms spending and called them the "military-industrial complex."

Eisenhower also had very a progressive record on civil rights. In his first State of the Union Address, he announced that he would end segregation in the District of Columbia, the federal government, and the armed forces. Truman had remarked that "poor Ike" didn't know what he was up against. "He'll say, 'Do this! Do that!' and nothing will happen." But that's not how it turned out. Harry Truman had ordered the military desegregated, but Eisenhower was the person who made it happen.[32]

The Supreme Court's 1954 decision in *Brown v. Board of Education* ended judicially sanctioned segregation, and Eisenhower deserves much of the credit, both for appointing Earl Warren as chief justice and for letting his assistant attorney general argue that public segregation was unconstitutional.[33] Eisenhower's subsequent Supreme Court appointments would vote to uphold the *Brown* decision, and the federal judges in the south who bravely enforced the civil rights laws were often Eisenhower Republicans, such as John Minor Wisdom and Frank M. Johnson. Then, when state and local officials resisted a federal court order, Eisenhower sent in the Army to desegregate Little Rock's Central High School, and the rioters retreated before the drawn bayonets of the 101st Airborne Division.

Eisenhower didn't share the racial prejudices of his time. Jesse Owens, the hero of the 1936 Olympics, was snubbed by Franklin Roosevelt, who met with all the white Olympians but not with Owens. It would take almost twenty years before Owens visited the White House – when Eisenhower named him America's "Ambassador of Sports." Then, when the sit-in demonstrations began, Eisenhower took the side of the protestors.[34] If Woolworths invited African Americans to shop at their stores, he said it should also seat them for lunch.

At Eisenhower's strong urging, Congress passed the first civil rights legislation in eighty-two years in 1957. African Americans were disenfranchised in most of the southern states, and the statute banned the suppression of voting rights in federal elections. Eisenhower wanted judges to rule on whether this had been done, but Lyndon Johnson (D-TX) and his fellow southerners scuppered the bill by giving the accused the right to a jury trial. They knew that a jury of white southerners would never vote to convict one of their own. Eisenhower was furious about the change and threatened a veto, but African American leaders persuaded him to sign the bill as better than nothing.[35] They knew that the Republicans were the civil rights party, and Eisenhower earned the public support of people such as Adam Clayton Powell Jr. and Jackie Robinson.

While Eisenhower's progressive credentials are undeniable, he was also a conservative whose 1956 Economic Report was a staunch defense of free market principles. He recognized that welfare programs cannot sustain themselves without the money to pay for them. In the long run, low wage earners benefit more from a faster growth rate in national income than from redistributing existing national wealth in their favor.

Eisenhower staked out what Arthur Schlesinger Jr. called the "vital center" in American politics, the place where free market principles are tempered by a safety net for those left behind. And that was the secret of his popularity.[36] As a spokesman for Eisenhower Republicanism put it, "in politics – as in chess – the man who holds the center holds a position of almost unbeatable strength."[37]

Eisenhower was America's most admired man from 1951 to 1960 and in office enjoyed a 65 percent average approval rating.[38] It was also a period of enormous prosperity, the Fabulous Fifties. Wages were up, inflation was down, and Americans went out and bought things – homes, cars, consumer appliances – that their parents could never have afforded. They returned home from the wars and moved into dream homes with plate glass windows and dream cars with fins in the driveway. By 1960, 90 percent of homes had a TV set, and what people watched were shows like *Father Knows Best* and *Leave it to Beaver*, shows we're supposed to scorn today.

John Kenneth Galbraith told us that the pursuit of private wealth was wasteful, but no one missed being poor. Intellectuals called it the age of anxiety, but everyone else felt good about America. We had become a rich middle-class country with a great deal more income equality and mobility than exists today, and if racial and gender differences were greater then, we had what we lack now, the sense that things were getting better for everyone. The social problems people complained about were laughably trivial: lurid comic books, juvenile delinquents in black leather jackets, and Elvis the Pelvis. The real pathologies of today, the crime and the broken homes, were far less troubling then. Families were stable and divorce rates were low. Births to unmarried mothers, which are now at 40 percent, were only 5 percent in the 1950s.

In office, Eisenhower balanced the budget and presided over eight years of peace and prosperity, the only president to do so since George Washington. But when a hip John Kennedy was elected, we were asked to forget how great the fifties had been. Those dream homes were made of ticky-tacky, and the dream cars were *Unsafe at any Speed*. The 50s were a time of soulless conformity and dull repression, of inauthentic men in gray flannel suits. It was nothing of the sort, of course, and it did not take long before the limits of hipness were evident in Vietnam and the era's assassinations, drugs, and riots. The sixties did indeed transform America, but not always for the better, and we're permitted to remember Eisenhower's presidency as a halcyon time before it all went south.

The Fourth Turning: Trump

Right-wing conservatives such as Barry Goldwater and William F. Buckley were also happy to see the Eisenhower era behind them. They decried "me too" liberal Republicanism and with Phyllis Schlafly wanted the party to offer "a choice, not an echo." That's what Barry Goldwater gave them in 1964, and while that was a crushing electoral defeat, it was also the birth of a new conservative movement. The libertarian Goldwaterites had shown how right-wingers could defeat GOP moderates such as Henry Cabot Lodge for the nomination.

What Goldwater offered was the promise of purity in a single word: liberty. We were naturally self-righting, self-correcting, he said, and all our ills derived from constraints imposed on us by the government. Little wonder that he inspired a generation of young Americans eager to take on the world but with little experience about how things work. Over time, however, we learned that a one-word touchstone wasn't going to answer, that it gave us a cynical Southern Strategy, trade and immigration policies that impoverished the most fragile of Americans, and endless wars inspired by the idea that liberty was written on everyone's heart. Instead of purity, we found ourselves rubbing shoulders with Lee Atwater, Charles Koch, and Donald Rumsfeld, the right-wing version of the Altamont rock concert.

It took some time to understand all this, and in their think tanks and magazines the Goldwaterites were permitted to present themselves as the intellectual voice of the Republican Party. They didn't take Republican presidents along with them, however. Over the course of the next forty years, the Republicans elected four presidents, and while all were right of center, none wanted to take on the Democrats over welfare policies or the New Deal. Their election had made them the leaders of the free world, and they were content to trade away domestic policies to the Democrats in return for a free hand in foreign affairs. For Nixon this meant an honorable exit from the Vietnam War. For Ronald Reagan and G. H. W. Bush, it meant defeating the Soviet Union and its allies. For George W. Bush it meant prosecuting the war on terror. Since the Democrats were more interested in domestic than foreign policy, they saw this as an attractive bargain, and so it remained until it all came apart in the disaster of the second Iraq war. The only Republican president whose head wasn't turned by the idea of being the leader of the free world was Donald Trump, who was chiefly interested in domestic issues and who was evidently bored out of his skull by his NATO allies.

Nixon's first message to Congress as president implied that he'd retain most of Lyndon Johnson's war on poverty programs in exchange for a free hand in foreign affairs.[39] That was Nixon's métier and would in short order result in three foreign policy triumphs: the winding down of American involvement in the Vietnam War, Nixon's stunning 1972 visit to China, and the rescue of a faltering Israel in the 1973 Yom Kippur War. On domestic matters, Nixon admired Disraeli and permitted Daniel Patrick Moynihan to compare him to the great English progressive conservative.[40] At Moynihan's urging Nixon proposed to reform America's welfare laws with a negative income tax scheme called the Family Assistance Program.[40] That went nowhere, but Congress did enact the Supplemental Security Income (SSI) program, which provides a guaranteed income for the elderly and disabled. The Environmental Protection Agency was also a creation of the Nixon presidency.[42]

Nixon was also the president who ended school segregation in America.[43] On racial matters, the right-wingers had aligned themselves with the south, and in explicitly racial terms Buckley's *National Review* wanted the 1957 Civil Rights Act weakened.[44] Republicans soon learned not to talk like that, but like Goldwater, Ronald Reagan opposed the 1964 Civil Rights Act, and his appointees watered down the affirmative action programs that Nixon had instituted.

Reagan was not the second coming of Barry Goldwater, however. His great issues were lowering the tax rates and winning the Cold War, and he was content to leave the New Deal programs in place. The progressive conservative impulse was stronger still in George H. W. Bush's "kinder, gentler" conservatism and his Americans with Disabilities Act. George W. Bush's "compassionate conservatism" might have come down to the same thing but for the fact that his two terms were consumed by the war on terror and the second Iraq war.

And then came Trump. In 2016, seventeen serious candidates sought the Republican presidential nomination, some as right-wingers, some as religious conservatives, but only Trump ran as a progressive conservative. It very early became clear that, unlike the others, he wasn't an orthodox right-winger and wasn't going to trench on government entitlement programs. Like Disraeli, he reached out to a forgotten class of voters who had not shared in the gains of a rising economy. Like Disraeli, too, he argued that the duty to care for fellow citizens arose from the logic of nationalism and a sense of fraternity with them. He didn't call it the common good, but that's what it came down to. Finally, like Disraeli, Trump looked beyond abstract principles to see how people really fared. Both men parted company with free market orthodoxy and created a new party that was explicitly progressive in its concern for those left behind and conservative in its nationalism.

That's where the similarity ended. In their personalities, the two could not have been less alike. The Victorian dandy who wrote amusing novels and remained faithful to his wife had little in common with the twice-divorced real estate magnate. As for Theodore Roosevelt, both men shared what Arthur Schlesinger Jr. charitably described as an "incurable delight in self-dramatization,"[45] but that was about it. They were all wholly different from each other apart from their pragmatism, concern for their fellow citizens, and love of country. It is policies, not personalities, that makes someone a progressive conservative.

Besides, no one ever said that a progressive conservative had to be a milquetoast. Disraeli wasn't above mocking Gladstone. Teddy Roosevelt thought the man in the arena should be a bold risk-taker. And truth be told, Eisenhower had a temper. The pallid, official Republican Party could use a measure of their audacity and impudence.

Trump became a progressive conservative when he realized that the Republican Party had taken too narrow a view of American politics. It had seen issues along a single left-right economic divide, where the Democrats were socialists and the Republicans were the right-wing growth party. But there's more going on than a single economic axis can capture. Along a different axis, voters can be divided according to their views about a variety of other issues: a classless versus a class society, honesty versus public corruption, and nationalism versus globalism. Grouping all such concerns together, our politics can be portrayed along two axes, economic and noneconomic, according to the preferences of the two-dimensional men who voted for a two-dimensional progressive conservative party in 2016.

That's what emerged from a survey Lee Drutman conducted after the 2016 election. He asked voters whom they had voted for and how they had felt about various economic and social issues. Then he mapped this on a diagram, red dots for a Trump voter, blue for Hillary Clinton, and yellow for other candidates, as seen in the diagram in the photo insert. Economic preferences were portrayed on the horizontal axis, left wing on the left and right wing on the right. Social preferences were shown on the vertical axis, left wing at the bottom and right wing at the top.

This divided voters into four quadrants, where the winning one was the upper left. Its voters were left of center on economics, as were the overwhelming majority of Americans (73.5 percent versus the 26.5 percent of unelectable Republican right-wingers). They were also conservative on social issues, as were the majority of Americans (51.6 percent versus 48.4 percent). It was the sweet spot Trump staked out and the home of progressive conservatives. In a 2017 *Wall Street Journal* op-ed, I wrote that the diagram identified the path the GOP must take to become a winning party.[46]

Figure 4.1   The Four Quadrants of American Politics

Progressive Conservatives	Right-Wing Conservatives
Secular Left-Wingers	Secular Right-Wingers

What this will require is a pivot from the upper-right quadrant inhabited by Republican right-wingers. Economically and socially conservative, they dream of a return to Ronald Reagan and the 1980s. They're a minority voting bloc, however, largely composed of Boomers, and they're outnumbered by millennials (1981–96) who have no personal memories of the Reagan years and by the rising generation of Zoomers (1997–2012) for whom 9/11 is simply something they read about on the web.

The bottom-right quadrant is composed of libertarians who are right-wing on economics and left-wing on social issues. Before the 2016 election, some Republicans spoke of a "libertarian moment." But the election revealed how empty those claims were. The libertarian candidate garnered only 3.3 percent of the vote, and those who identified as libertarian and voted for the two major candidates split their votes between Trump and Hillary Clinton. Then in 2020 the libertarian candidate received little more than 1 percent of the vote.

The bottom-left quadrant is the home of the economically and socially left-wing Democratic Party. Before Trump, our political battles were a contest between the upper-right and the larger lower-left quadrants, which the latter would win. It took Trump to recognize that progressive conservatism could break the logjam and create a winning coalition.

Progressive conservatism is the secret code to American politics, and if it didn't work in 2020, it's because it wasn't on the ballot. It was a plague year with riots in the streets, a year not to be repeated. In addition, while Trump ran as a progressive conservative in 2016, he didn't entirely govern like one. For two years, the Republicans controlled all three branches of government, but the unity was illusory, and the Trump agenda was blocked by a right-wing Congress led by libertarians such as Speaker Paul Ryan. All Trump got out of Congress was the 2017 amendments to the tax code. These were welcome and helped spur an economic recovery, but they were the product of free market orthodoxy and left in place the loopholes of a seventy-five-thousand-page tax code, behind which America's wealthy could shelter their income. Trump wanted them dropped but was rolled by a right-wing Republican Congress and had to content himself with a cut in the corporate tax rate. He had campaigned on a pledge to repeal Obamacare and replace it with something "beautiful," but that didn't happen either. A modest start was made with regulatory cutbacks, but in the end all that happened was a reduction in their rate of growth. If we were expecting Trumpism from him, Trump was a failed president and progressive conservatism was a cause, interrupted.

The Four Quadrants in 2016

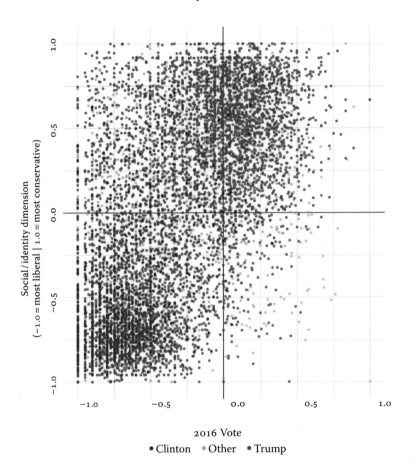

2016 Vote
● Clinton   ● Other   ● Trump

Source: Lee Drutman, "Political Divisions in 2016 and Beyond: Tensions Between and Within the Two Parties," Voter Survey Group (June 2017).

Edmund Burke
Studio of Sir Joshua Reynolds
National Portrait Gallery, London

Benjamin Disraeli

Men of mark: a gallery of contemporary portraits of men distinguished
in the senate, the church, science, literature and art, the army, navy,
law, medicine, etc. Photographed from life by Lock and Whitfield,
with brief biographical notices by Thompson Cooper.
Wellcome Collection. Public Domain.

Abraham Lincoln in Illinois, 1858

Abraham Lincoln, head-and-shoulders portrait, facing front.
T Painter Pearson, photographer. Between 1885 and 1911,
from ambrotype taken Aug. 26, 1858.
Library of Congress. Prints & Photographs Division.

The "damned cowboy" in 1885

Theodore Roosevelt. George Grantham Bain, photographer.
Presidents of the United States: Selected Images from
the Collections of the Library of Congress.
Prints & Photographs Division.

Dwight Eisenhower in Kansas, 1907
National Archives, Eisenhower Presidential Library, Abilene, Kansas

Sen. Margaret Chase Smith
Image courtesy of the U.S. Senate Historical Office. Public Domain.

Gouverneur Morris

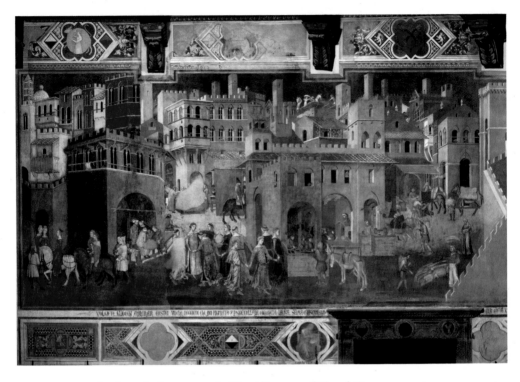

Ambrogio Lorenzetti, *The Allegory of Good Government*,
Palazzo Pubblico, Siena. Fresco (1338–1339).

CHAPTER FIVE

A Cause, Interrupted

WHILE TRUMP HAS DEPARTED the scene, the ideas he brought to the party will remain and provide the road map for successful Republicans who adopt the threefold progressive conservative agenda of a defense of the American Dream, republican virtue and a corruption-free government, and nationalism. What remains is to finish the job that Trump promised and failed to carry out. He was an outsider and when handed the levers of power didn't know which to pull. Even if he had, no president had ever faced stronger headwinds. He was despised by Democrats who recognized him as an existential threat and spurned by Republican politicians who hadn't signed on to the Trump agenda. If Trump remains popular among Republican voters, that's because they want to see the policies he favored enacted.

The American Dream

The American Dream defines progressive conservatism, whose followers support free market capitalism not as an abstract theory but because that's the best way to promote the common good and social and economic mobility. We want to live in a society where people can make their own way and where entrenched and illegitimate elites don't block our paths. America has been the greatest money-making machine the world has ever known, and we'd simply like everyone to be able to share in the wealth.

Progressive conservatives aren't ascetics who scorn wealth. Free market capitalism has given us a world in which people live longer, eat better, and buy homes and household goods their ancestors only dreamed of. Two hundred years ago, 90 percent of the world's population lived in extreme poverty (in today's dollars, $1.90 a day or less). Thirty years ago, more than a third of people did so. Today it's less than 10 percent.[1] It's wonderful progress and was the dream of Theodore Roosevelt's progressives. The factory worker and the farmer who voted for Roosevelt didn't think money smelled but only that it should be better shared. They wouldn't have had much use for rich celebrities who ask the rest of us to practice voluntary simplicity. People with too few things don't need advice about decluttering from people with too many things.

From Lincoln on, America's progressive conservatives supported policies that would permit free men to rise and knew that the American Dream didn't happen by itself, that it required progressive reforms, things like good schools and the rule of law. We had thought, however, that America was the one place where this had happened. But in recent years, we've begun to wonder whether the American Dream has faded and moved offshore.

Obama seized on this anxiety in a 2011 speech in Osawatomie, Kansas. That was where "Osawatomie" John Brown fought a pitched battle against proslavery forces in 1856, and it's where Theodore Roosevelt gave his New Nationalism speech. And like Roosevelt, Obama described income inequality and immobility as the defining issue of our time. America's grand bargain, he said, was that those who contribute to the country should share in its wealth. That bargain had made the country great, the envy of the world, but now it was betrayed by the "breathtaking greed" of the superrich.

> Look at the statistics. In the last few decades, the average income of the top 1 percent has gone up by more than 250 percent to $1.2 million per year.... And yet, over the last decade the incomes of most Americans have actually fallen by about 6 percent.

The problem was worsened, he said, by a tax system whose shelters and loopholes gave the superrich lower rates than the middle class. "Some billionaires have a tax rate as low as 1 percent. One percent.

That is the height of unfairness. It is wrong." Worse still, he said, the promise of income mobility, that a child born in poverty might through his own efforts rise to the middle class, had been broken.

American wages had stagnated, and the evidence began to mount that we had become unequal and immobile, that the American Dream was a thing of the past. What rankled wasn't so much the growing inequalities as the lack of mobility between parents and children – *inter*generational immobility. There's still a lot of *intra*-generational mobility (mobility during our lifetimes), in which people are born poor and die rich. Boomers are sometimes surprised to find that they'll die as millionaires given the way they've salted away retirement funds in houses and pension plans. But even if we personally move up the ladder during our lifetimes, we'll still be upset if we think our children won't have it as good as we did. And that's what many Americans had begun to fear. A 2014 CNN poll reported that six in ten Americans believe that the American Dream is out of reach, that their children will be worse off than they were.[2]

That should have signaled a demand for transformative change. To Republican leaders, however, it sounded like class warfare, and they wanted no part of it. The 2012 Republican platform, chaired by Gov. Bob McDonnell (who shortly afterward was indicted on federal corruption charges), defined the party as one "of maximum economic freedom" and condemned the Democrats for failing to pursue a free trade agenda. The Romney campaign also produced a fifty-nine-point manifesto with the message that there was nothing wrong with the country that a return to classic libertarian principles wouldn't fix. It was a bloodless and technocratic essay written by and for Republican insiders and to which only they paid any attention. If voters had read it, they'd have seen that the lead-off issue was a reduction in the corporate tax rate.

Here's what the voters noticed instead: a talk Romney gave to some right-wing donors about "makers" versus "takers." The takers were people who don't pay income tax and "who are dependent upon government, who believe that they are victims, who believe the government has a responsibility to care for them, who believe that they are entitled to health care, to food, to housing, to you-name-it."

They constituted 47 percent of Americans, and they were going to vote for Obama no matter what. "My job is not to worry about those people," he said. "I'll never convince them they should take personal responsibility and care for their lives." It sounded dreadful, but Romney was simply parroting what people at right-wing think tanks say to each other when they think no one is listening.

When the talk became public, it was the defining moment of the campaign,[3] the death rattle of the old Republican Party. Apart from telling us what he thought of welfare recipients, Romney seemingly conceded the election by saying that nearly half of the voters would never support him. Obama's policies had given the country stagnant growth and a jobless recovery, but voters felt that he had their back, while Romney came across as the boss about to hand you the pink slip. And so Obama won.

That is where things stood in 2015 when Trump announced his candidacy. During the campaign, my wife Esther Goldberg and I, along with Bob Tyrrell of the *American Spectator*, helped write speeches for him and his family. I visited New York and talked to Jared Kushner about the need to make income immobility and the decline of the American Dream a central theme of the campaign. For the 2016 Republican Convention I prepared a well-received speech for Donald Trump Jr. that laid the blame for income immobility on the Democrats.

> The other party also tells us they believe in the American Dream. They say we should worry about economic inequality and immobility. You know what? They're right. But what they don't tell you is that it was their policies that caused the problem.

Then in August Trump spoke on the need to restore the American Dream in what the *Washington Post* called his best campaign speech.

> I refuse to let another generation of American children be excluded from the American Dream. Our whole country loses when young people of limitless potential are denied the opportunity to contribute their talents because we failed to

provide them the opportunities they deserved. Let our children be dreamers too.[4]

The eclipse of the American Dream was the sleeper issue in the 2016 campaign and the omen of a political revolution. It would have been a key issue for the Democrats of old. The new Democrats were a different party, however. Their Keynesian economic prescriptions had failed them, and they had moved on to embrace the policies favored by highly educated urban elites. Hillary Clinton boasted that she'd throw the coal miners out of work, and Obama told a union leader that manufacturing jobs "are just not going to come back."[5] Working class voters had been abandoned by both the Romney Republicans and by Hillary Clinton's Democratic Party. Only one person stood up for them, and they elected him president in 2016.

What happened next is what we'd expect when income inequality hardens into income immobility. The old Democratic Party, which had told us that its reforms had saved free market capitalism, gave way to a party that was socialist in all but name. True, Bernie Sanders lost the nomination, but after defeating the man, the party stole his ideas. It's what Marx would have predicted.

As the most advanced capitalist country, America should have been the first place where socialism triumphed, according to Marxist theories of history. First feudalism, then capitalism, then socialism. If it didn't work out like that in America, this was a bit of an embarrassment, which Marx tried to explain away by pointing to the country's social mobility. "True enough, the classes already exist, but [they] have not yet acquired permanent character, [and] are in constant flux and reflux, constantly changing their elements and yielding them up to one another."[6] That's why *It Didn't Happen Here*, said Seymour Martin Lipset and Gary Marks in 2000. America was the only country without a socialist party because we were mobile and wouldn't support socialism. Except what happens when the classes become fixed, as they have here? We're willing to accept inequality so long as our kids have an equal shot at getting ahead, and when that stops happening, people vote for socialists. Unless progressive conservatives offer something better.

Machiavellian Moments

Over the years, American politics has centered on a few major issues: war, the economy, and race. But there were two times when public corruption – the corruption of public officials – took center stage. The first was in 1776. The second is now.

Historian J. G. A. Pocock called the first occasion a Machiavellian Moment.[7] In the Renaissance people rediscovered classical Roman historians, and Machiavelli praised the public-spirited Lucius Junius Brutus, who had expelled the corrupt last king, Tarquin the Proud. Then, during the American Revolution, the Patriots read their Livy, and republican virtue became a way of showing how America was superior to the mother country. With their courtiers and placemen, monarchies were necessarily corrupt, the Patriots thought, and to answer this we'd need a republic, one from which selfish dealings and wasteful bargains would be banished, a government founded on republican virtue, the virtue shown by people such as George Washington who champion the general welfare in a personally disinterested manner.

Over the last several years we've had another Machiavellian Moment in which Trump made public corruption a campaign issue. In 2016 the greatest scandal concerned Hillary Clinton and her family and the charge that their foundation had sold off American foreign policy to the highest bidder.[8] Even the *New York Times* concluded that "it was hard to tell where the foundation ended and the State Department began."[9] It looked like pay-for-play, and when she had nothing left to trade away, after Trump defeated her, contributions began to dry up. As for the way it was run, the foundation seemed like a slush fund for the Clintons themselves, according to a nonpartisan watchdog group.[10]

Democratic corruption was a winning issue for Trump. Here's how he put it in a campaign speech.

When we talk about the insider, who are we talking about? It's the comfortable politicians looking out for their own interests. It's the lobbyists who know how to insert that perfect loophole into every bill. It's the financial industry that knows how to regulate their competition out of existence. The insiders also include the media executives, anchors and journalists in Washington, Los Angeles, and New York City, who are part of the same failed status quo and want nothing to change.

For the seventy-four million people who voted for Trump in 2020, corruption remained a major issue. For everyone else, the media did its best to hide it. While Hunter Biden's father was vice president, his firm received millions of dollars from foreign sources, including a Russian friend of Vladimir Putin's and Chinese businessmen connected to the Communist Party. When Joe Biden was chosen to oversee our relations with Ukraine, Burisma, a very corrupt Ukrainian gas company, quickly hired Hunter at $50,000 a month even though he had zero experience in the oil industry or familiarity with the country. Hunter then brought a Burisma executive to meet with his father, who falsely denied that any such meeting took place.[11] US officials said this made it difficult to push an anti-corruption agenda in Ukraine and told the vice president's staff to get Hunter to resign, but this didn't happen till 2019. The story heated up just before the 2020 election, when Hunter Biden's laptop turned up with a trove of emails backing up a story about his father's collusion with the Ukrainians. When the *New York Post* reported on this, however, its stories were censored by Facebook and Twitter and ignored by the mainstream press. A partisan, left-wing media lied by omission while spreading actual lies about Trump's collusion with Russia.

It became clear that the real Ukraine scandal had Biden's name on it and that Trump was impeached for what the Democratic nominee had done. The greater scandal, however, was the attempt by the Democratic Party to bring down the Trump administration with baseless charges about collusion with the Russian government. The story originated with Hillary Clinton in 2016, who did so to deflect attention from her use of a private mail server. While charging that Trump had colluded with the Russians, it was she who had relied on the sketchiest of Russian sources for her opposition research, and Obama and Joe Biden knew this. But at their urging, the government's spy agencies ran an investigation targeting one political party to assist another.

Republicans learned that Democrats were not to be trusted. If they could deny the legitimacy of the 2016 election, if they could live in a fantasy world of Russian collusion, if they could credit every baseless smear of conservatives while ignoring the evidence of their own corruption, it became easy to think they would steal an election. They no longer merited our trust, and this became a national crisis after the 2020 election when 70 percent of Republicans thought the Biden victory was tainted by fraud.[12] Before long, it became clear that Biden had won, but the left-wing media had lost all credibility and weren't to be believed. Democracy depends on guardrails, on the sense of trust that everyone will observe the rules of the game, and the guardrails had been pulled down. Those who for four years spread a conspiracy theory about Russian collusion aren't in a good position to lecture anyone else about conspiracy theories.

All this contributes to a sense of conservative despair. Democrats can do what they want and will never be held to account while Republican complaints are mocked as mere populism. If what that word means is a concern for corruption, however, then the Patriots of 1776 were populists too.

The Unknown Country

In his inaugural address, Trump said his presidency would be defined by a sense of national identity. "A new national pride will stir our souls, lift our sights, and heal our divisions." Then in an October 2018 rally he explicitly defined himself as a nationalist. "You know what I am? I'm a nationalist."

Trump isn't the first nationalist in the White House. George Washington was a nationalist who made a nation out of quite dissimilar colonies. And Lincoln's defense of the union made him the greatest of our nationalists. Theodore Roosevelt gave a new meaning to the word by asking that the national government provide for those unable to care for themselves. That was what his New Nationalism meant, and he also called it the "Square Deal." Franklin Roosevelt's New Deal was simply an extension of this, a form of nationalism for a suffering people during an economic crisis.[13]

Some right-wingers have rediscovered nationalism but without recognizing its leftward gravitational force. The nationalist is loyal to America and therefore wants to see the national government given the power to remedy national ills. And because he is bound by ties of sympathy and fraternity to his fellow citizens, he will recognize that the federal government is charged with a duty to promote the common good and to ensure a minimal standard of welfare for all Americans.

That makes him a progressive conservative, both in his love for his country and in his support for a national safety net. By way of example, progressive conservatives such as senators Everett Dirksen (R-IL) and Margaret Chase Smith (R-ME) bucked Republican right-wingers to support the 1965 Elementary and Secondary Education Act, which authorized sending federal funds to poor states. They also backed federal civil and voting rights legislation that the party's right-wingers and Southern Democrats opposed.

Right-wing nationalists have also failed to recognize that American nationalism is a liberal nationalism since it's based on the liberal values to be found in the Declaration and the Bill of Rights. Our country was born in the noble ideals of our founders, and that has served to correct illiberal departures from them – as Trump discovered, to his cost. Those ideals became the sentiments expressed in the 1848 Seneca Falls Declaration and the promissory note presented by Martin Luther King Jr. in his "I Have a Dream" speech. The Declaration was a sealed car speeding through our history, darkened in obscurity on departure but emerging in sunlight on arrival.

The American nationalist can therefore look at our history and still love his country. But when he saw what some of his countrymen said about it, he began to feel like a stranger in a strange land. The signposts had been turned about, the fences were torn down, the roads were unfamiliar. For half of his countrymen, their nation was not his nation, and America had become the unknown country.

II · RESTORING THE AMERICAN DREAM

To criticize inequality and to desire equality is not,
as is sometimes suggested, to cherish the romantic illusion
that men are equal in character and intelligence. It is to hold
that, while their natural endowments differ profoundly,
it is the mark of a civilized society to aim at eliminating
such inequalities as have their source, not in individual
differences, but in its own organization, and that individual
differences, which are a source of social energy, are more
likely to ripen and find expression if social inequalities are,
as far as practical, diminished.

RICHARD H. TAWNEY, *Equality*

CHAPTER SIX

Inequality – and Why It Matters

BY FAILING TO RECOGNIZE how natural a thing aristocracy is, modern political theory is impoverished. Traditional legal scholars distinguish between different forms of government, different constitutional structures, as if that's all there is. If things are out of whack, a little adjustment, perhaps over the Electoral College, will fix it. They assume that inequalities are naturally self-correcting, that with a small turn of the dial we'll revert to an egalitarian Eisenhower era. But that was a brief interval between the aristocracy that preceded it and the aristocracy that followed. More recently, radical scholars dissent and tell us that racism is at the root of everything. That's doesn't explain aristocracy, however. If race were all there is, we'd expect to find inequalities between the races but equality within each race. And that doesn't describe America, not for whites, not for blacks.

Family bonds are stronger than racial ones, and in Chapter 9 I explain how genetic imperatives can account for aristocracy and why in every period and in every society a small group of people has, by its efforts, political connections, or luck, climbed to the top of the heap and sought to keep their children there. The egalitarian 1950s was a brief interlude, and aristocracy is nature's default position. To displace it requires the concerted and continual efforts of progressive conservatives to level the playing field.

In America, it's been that way from the start, although one aristocracy in time has always given way to the next. In a dynamic economy, the sources of wealth change, and Schumpeter's creative destruction churns those on top. In the founders' time, the tidewater planters created what Gordon Wood described as the strongest aristocracy that America has ever known.[1] The Civil War ploughed them under, and the new men were the captains of industry made wealthy by the factories and steel mills or by the streetcar mergers Theodore Dreiser's *Titan* put together. Theirs was an Edith Wharton era of Fifth Avenue mansions and Newport estates, a Gilded Age where by 1910 the top 10 percent owned 80 percent of the country's assets and the top 1 percent owned 45 percent.[2]

In time their new money was blessed as old money, but today they've been replaced by a new class of high tech entrepreneurs. Each year *Forbes* magazine lists the four hundred wealthiest Americans, and only a tenth of the people on the 1982 list remained on the list thirty years later. When Steven Kaplan and Joshua Rauh looked at the Forbes 400 list of the richest Americans, they found that most had pulled themselves up by their bootstraps. Nearly 70 percent had built their businesses by themselves, up from 40 percent in 1982.[3] At the very top end, among the 0.0001 percent, America has never been more open to advancement. That is why the true egalitarian and the progressive conservative must support free market capitalism.

The Evidence

Free market capitalism doesn't describe today's economy, however. When you descend from the high tech gazillionaires to the top 1 or 10 percent, a different picture emerges. Now we're looking at the country's managerial class and a professional class of executives, lawyers, and lobbyists. Below them, we've placed a stumbling block in the path of the Ragged Dicks who seek to rise from poverty. The broken educational system, the absurd immigration policies, and the regulatory barriers aren't a hindrance to the elite, meritocratic new class at the top of the heap but have shipped the American Dream offshore for everyone else.

Since the Eisenhower era, we've returned to a period of stark income inequality, as seen in Table 6.1. The 1950s and 1960s were periods of wage compression and economic equality, and the top 1 percent didn't earn more than the bottom 50 percent. The factory worker didn't live much differently than the company executive. One drove a Lincoln, the other a Ford, but the lifestyles were similar. In recent years, however, the share of the bottom 50 percent has cratered while that of the top 1 percent has almost returned to the historic highs before the 1929 stock market crash.[4]

The figures in Table 6.1 even understate what has happened since they don't include earnings from unrealized capital gains. Taking them into account would likely increase the top 1 percent's earnings by an additional 4–5 percent of the total. Today the lives of the factory worker and the executive have diverged in the holidays they take, the restaurants they frequent, and the schools their kids attend. What had been a united country in the 1950s has become Disraeli's Two Nations.

What about the middle class? After the Great Recession, its share of the national income flatlined. The mean earnings for households in the 50–75 percent income range increased from $41,757 in 2007 to $42,210 in 2016, a 1 percent increase.[131] For the 1993–2018 period, the average income gain for all Americans was 30 percent, but the top 1 percent increased their earnings by 100 percent while the figure for the bottom 99 percent was 18 percent. The rich got a lot richer.[5]

Table 6.1   Income Inequality:
Percent Share of Pre-tax National Income

	1929	1959	1969	2019
Top one percent	22.3	13.2	11.6	18.8
Top ten percent	47.1	36.0	34.4	45.5
Bottom 50 percent	13.5	18.0	20.2	13.3

Source: World Inequality Database, accessed July 29, 2021

That's not to discount our generous safety net. We spent $1.5 trillion, or a third of the 2019 federal budget, on welfare programs such as Medicare, Medicaid, the Children's Health Insurance

Program (CHIP), the Affordable Care Act marketplace subsidies, the Earned Income Tax Credit, Supplemental Security Income, food stamps, school meals, low-income housing assistance, and other programs, and that doesn't include the poverty programs run by state and local governments. That's served to reduce inequalities, and our Gini ratio, measuring income inequality, falls from 0.51 to 0.39 after taxes and welfare transfers are taken into account.[6] But that has not propped up our middle class,[7] and however you measure it, we're still the most unequal country in the First World.[8]

Apart from inequalities in income streams, there are stark differences in American wealth holdings, as seen in Table 6.2. The Federal Reserve reports that the top 10 percent own more than $90 trillion in assets out of a total of 130 trillion. During the Trump years, the bottom 50 percent saw an increase in their wealth holdings, but the top 10 percent still held 70 percent of the nation's wealth, and Emmanuel Saez puts that number at nearly 80 percent.[9] It's down from Gilded Age heights, but it's still a remarkably unequal split in wealth.

Table 6.2   Wealth Holdings, in $ Trillions

	2006: Q1	2017: Q1	2021: Q1
Top 1%	18.9	28.8	41.5
90–99%	22.4	35.5	48.8
50–90%	20.3	37.2	36.5
Bottom 50%	1.4	1.2	2.6
Total	62.0	92.7	129.5

Source: Distribution of Household Wealth in the U.S. since 1989, Federal Reserve, June 21, 2021.

Under Trump, things had begun to turn around before the pandemic hit. Median real incomes grew 5 percent from 2016 to 2019, and the gains were at the bottom end of the income distribution. Families at the top end experienced very little if any growth, while families near the bottom experienced substantial gains.[10] Real median income grew 9 percent for people without a high school degree and 6.3 percent for those who had only completed high school, and it declined 2.3 percent for those with a college degree. We began to see a revival of the American Dream, which is plausibly attributed to Trump's policies: the tax cuts that restarted the economy, the insistence on fair trade deals that kept blue collar jobs in America, and the attack on job-destroying regulations. If that's populism, we need more, not less of it.

Why Inequality Matters

Should inequality matter? Right-wingers say it shouldn't and that people who care about it are just envious. But the founders thought that extreme wealth inequalities would corrupt America and sap republican virtue. Progressive conservatives agree and believe that the right-winger's ideology can mask a callous lack of empathy to the poor. They also think that when you parade your indifference to poverty as Romney did, you lose elections.

Call it envy if you will, but the fact is that we all have relative preferences. We'd all want more money in absolute terms, but we also care about how we rank relative to our peers. I'd feel happier if I got a $1,000 raise but not if everyone else in the office got a $10,000 raise. Relative preferences are part of our DNA, and they're no bad thing if they nudge us out of a slothful supineness. But they also make very unequal societies unhappy.

There's a second reason why egalitarian countries are happier than very unequal ones, and it's the economist's diminishing marginal utility. Utility is simply what economists call happiness. Marginal refers to the change in happiness from one level of consumption to a higher one. What diminishing marginal utility means is that the increase in happiness from one level to another gets smaller as it increases. I'm always better off with more things, but going from zero to one scoop of ice cream will make me happier than going from ten to eleven scoops. Similarly, giving me $10,000 will make me happier than giving the same amount to Bill Gates. That's why our tax laws are meant to redistribute wealth from the rich to the poor and not the other way around.

Figure 6.1   More Inequality, More Unhappiness

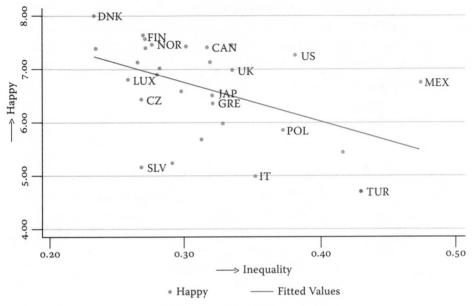

• Happy   —— Fitted Values

Happy = 8.91−7.20 Inequality. Adj. Rsq. = 0.18

Source: Gallup World Poll.

This isn't an argument for wealth-destroying polices that make everyone equal and poor, but it does explain why, as between two liberal and free market states, people will be happier in the egalitarian one. Imagine two countries, one richer than the other. In the richer one, a single person holds nearly all the wealth and everyone else lives in penury. In the poorer one, the wealth is more equally shared. What diminishing marginal utility tells us is that people in the egalitarian society will be happier than those in the richer country. Money isn't the ultimate good – happiness is – and as I found in Figure 6.1, more inequality means more unhappiness.[11]

Apart from relative preferences and diminishing marginal utility, there's a third reason why egalitarian societies are happier than unequal ones. As seen in Figure 6.2, unequal countries are low-trust countries. People sense that the game is unfairly stacked against them. And low-trust counties are unhappy ones. Deprived of trust, people are friendless, lonely, and depressed. They lack the sense of solidarity or community that is one of the most basic of human goods.

Simone Weil called this "the need for roots," and it's sadly missing in today's America. In *Bowling Alone*, sociologist Robert Putnam reported that the percentage of people who agreed that "most people can be trusted" fell from 55 in 1960 to 34 in 1998.[12] Between 1985 to 2004, the number of Americans who told a friend something of personal importance to themselves during the prior six months fell from 73 to 51 percent, while the number of people who had no such confidants rose from 10 to 25 percent.[13]

Figure 6.2   More Inequality, More Distrust

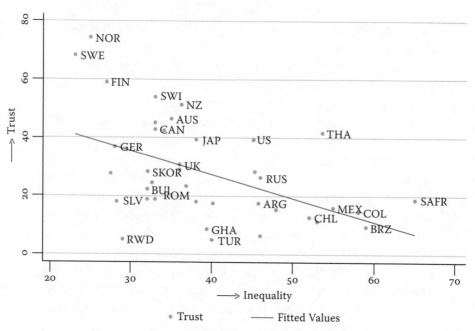

Trust = 59.46–.81Inequality. Adj. Rsq. = 0.21

Source: World Values Survey,
at http://www.wvsevsdb.com/wvs/WVSAnalizeQuestion.jsp.

With the Covid pandemic, it's gotten worse. Social distancing kept us from meeting people, and Zoom meetings never took the place of real-life encounters. A recent Harvard University study reported that 36 percent of respondents felt lonely frequently or almost all the time. Loneliness is associated with depression and physical illness, and Surgeon General Vivek Murthy calls it a public health crisis.[14] Lonely people are more likely to kill themselves, and more people have done so in recent years. The suicide rate increased by 35 percent between 1999 and 2018,[15] and for men in their fifties, suicide rates have increased by nearly 50 percent.[16]

We've also become divided by the heightened partisan divisions in our politics and by a cancel culture that invites us to rat out friends and neighbors. A casual comment, told in jest but preserved on video, can cost you your job and ruin your life. It's even happening in high school. Teenagers are naturally susceptible to peer pressure, and they're often jerks. We all went through that and survived, but today's teenagers are being called out by fellow students for racism.

In one example, a fifteen-year-old cheerleader sent a friend a three-second Snapchat video after she received her learner's permit. "I can drive, [racial slur]," she sang. That's a word she had heard everywhere in rap music videos. Her Snapchat video would have quickly disappeared except that another student saved it to use it when the time was right. That time came three years later, after the girl had been accepted to the University of Tennessee with its nationally recognized cheer team. It was her dream college, but when her fellow student shared it and it spread on social media, the college asked her to withdraw. She's now taking online classes at a local community college. As for the person who ratted her out, he's proud of what he did. He taught someone a lesson. The *New York Times* sympathized. The deeper story was about "a complex portrait of behavior that for generations had gone unchecked in schools in one of the nation's wealthiest counties, where Black students said they had long been subjected to ridicule."[17] The message to be taken from this is that you really have no friends but you probably do know some social justice sociopaths who'd like to weaponize your idle comments in order to cancel you.

Something extraordinarily disturbing has happened to us and produced a deeply lonely society. We make friends by sharing vulnerabilities, but that can't happen when the pandemic keeps us apart and when things we thought innocent can get us fired. And so we learn to hunker down apart from saying hello and making anodyne remarks about the weather. Shorn of liberalism's free speech protections, we've descended into a state of nature, where man is a wolf to man.

The rise of loneliness and decline in trust costs us in economic as well as in psychological terms. Right-wingers think there's a wealth-equality trade-off, that we have to choose between wealth and equality. But that's not what the evidence shows. As countries become more unequal, they became poorer and not richer.[18] That's because inequality makes people mistrustful, and mistrust makes it difficult to deal with others and extract the gains that come from bargaining and joint cooperation.

Deeply unequal countries are also more likely to restrict the economic freedom that is the engine of growth. The Chavismo movement in Venezuela, which impoverished the country and outlived Hugo Chávez, wouldn't seem possible in countries with Swedish-style income equality. Chávez rose to power with the support of a poor underclass that was willing to trade off political freedom for the promise of economic equality. Once in power, he embarked on an attack on the rule of law that destroyed the economy, and under his successor it has become worse.[19] That should be of concern in America since the rise in inequality has led to the demand for wealth-destroying socialism.

Income inequality can also weaken the economy when the wealthy manipulate the rules in their favor. In the next section, we'll see how large corporations can tilt the economy in their direction through wasteful governmental subsidies and tax loopholes bought by campaign contributions.[21] Mitt Romney had a point about makers vs. takers except that the takers include crony capitalists and a professional class that owes its jobs to the regulatory state that employs them. We've become an interest group plutocracy, and this has magnified the loss of trust that comes from living in an unequal country.

CHAPTER SEVEN

Immobility – and Why It Matters

WEALTH INEQUALITIES don't make us an aristocracy. A country with huge differences in wealth isn't aristocratic when the wealth is churned, when old money falls and new money rises. Shirtsleeves to shirtsleeves in three generations isn't an aristocracy. What makes an aristocracy is not inequality but intergenerational immobility, where rich parents raise rich kids and poor parents raise poor kids, where an elite upper class has stolen the future of an underclass.

We can tolerate inequalities if we think that our children can get ahead. What we can't abide is an aristocracy, where children are locked into the same economic and social class as their parents. That, we thought, was what we had left behind in the countries from which our ancestors came. It wasn't supposed to happen here, in the country of the American Dream.

So just how much mobility is there in America? Historically, a lot. The nineteenth century was a golden age for income mobility. When jobs were lacking, a person could strike out for Frederick Jackson Turner's frontier until that closed in 1890. In the 1950s and 1960s, more people than ever before went to college, and on graduation they found good jobs waiting for them and better homes than the ones they grew up in. Women and minorities still faced discriminatory barriers, but these receded with feminism and the civil rights movement. For more people than ever before, we were the land of opportunity. More recently, however, income mobility has slowed, and today there is much less chance for a family to move up the ranks.

The Evidence

There are two kinds of economic mobility: absolute and relative. Absolute mobility measures whether a person will earn more than his parents, while relative mobility measures which rung of the income ladder he lands on compared to that of his parents. On both measures we're not very mobile today.

Children born in the 1940s who came of age in the 1960s and 1970s fared very well on absolute measures, with 90 percent of them earning more than their parents. However, absolute mobility stalled for millennials born in the 1980s, and only 50 percent of them earned more than their parents.[1] At 50 percent, a society is in stasis, neither improving nor regressing, and that's not the American Dream.

From the perspective of relative mobility, intergenerational mobility was substantially higher for cohorts born in the early 1950s compared to those born a decade later.[2] For the latter, the Pew Economic Mobility Project reports that 40 percent of children born into the lowest income quintile remain there as adults and that 70 percent born into the middle quintile remain there when they grow up.[3]

All this happened at a time when the federal government had embarked on Lyndon Johnson's War on Poverty and his Great Society programs. They were meant to lift people out of poverty, but they're widely regarded as failures, particularly for black families. In a study of how children born between 1942 and 1972 fared during their lives, black families had an especially low rate of upward mobility. While only 17 percent of whites born to the bottom 10 percent of family earners remained there as adults, the figure for blacks was 42 percent.[4] Improving economic mobility for disadvantaged families, black and white, should be a top priority for policy makers, but things we've done so far haven't worked. That's why we should look at how other countries became more mobile than we are.

Those on the Right who deny that we're immobile are seemingly unaware of the existence of other countries, which takes chauvinism a bit far and isn't very helpful if people are more mobile elsewhere. As indeed they are. Among economists the consensus is that, compared to other countries, we're immobile.[5]

Table 7.1, taken from the Pew Economic Mobility Project 2011, ranks countries on an immobility scale, where a higher score means less mobility (a closer correlation between the incomes of fathers and sons).[6] At zero there is no correlation and the society is perfectly mobile. Denmark has a ranking of .15 and is relatively mobile, while a relatively immobile Britain has a ranking of .50. Remarkably, the US is one of the least mobile societies in the First World. Our ranking of .47, high as it is, might even be too low. Bhashkar Mazumder would put it at .60,[7] and the most recent Pew Economic Mobility report puts it at .52 for men.[8]

Table 7.1   Cross-country Immobility Rankings

COUNTRY	IMMOBILITY
UK	0.50
Italy	0.48
U.S.	0.47
France	0.41
Spain	0.40
Germany	0.32
Sweden	0.27
Australia	0.26
Canada	0.19
Finland	0.18
Norway	0.17
Denmark	0.15

Source: http://www.economicmobility.org/assets/pdfs/PEW_EMP_US-CANADA.pdf.

On Table 7.1 the country to emulate on a politics of mobility is Denmark. In part that points to a conservative agenda: tight immigration restrictions, good K–12 schools, lower regulatory barriers, and a strong rule of law. But there are also things the Left would like: free college tuition, universal health care, and bicycles. Put all this together and you have a progressive conservative agenda, possibly without the bicycles. And if that's what makes for mobility, the comparison with Denmark shows how both Democrats and right-wing Republicans have become the parties of immobility and aristocracy, how they both employ their ideologies to veil illegitimate class privileges. America needs a party of mobility, which is what Republicans will be when they adopt progressive conservatism.

We can't turn ourselves into Denmark, but what about Canada? It has about the same household wealth,[9] economic productivity,[10] and degree of economic freedom as the US.[11] People's tastes are so similar that Hollywood previews its films at the Toronto International Film Festival to see whether they'll be a hit in the North American market. But Canada's social and economic policies resemble those of Denmark, and Canada is highly mobile and we're not.

Figures 7.1 and 7.2 compare the mobility rankings for the two countries for families at the bottom and top ends. With perfect

Figure 7.1   Earnings Deciles of Sons born to Bottom-Decile Fathers: US and Canada

Son's Earnings Decile

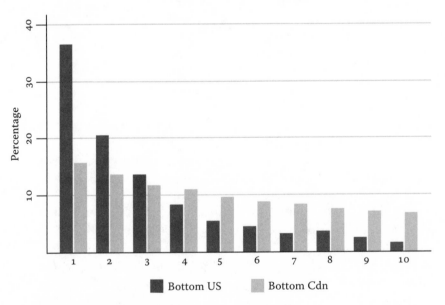

Sources: Corak, Curtis and Phipps (2011); Hertz (2005).

mobility, each column would be the same height, at the 10 percent level across the figure's ten deciles. The greater the deviation from this, the greater the immobility.

Figure 7.1 shows how children of parents in the bottom 10 percent of the income streams of the two countries fare. More than half of US children will end up in the bottom two deciles of their cohort, and very few will reach the top decile. In Canada, by contrast, far fewer children will find themselves in the bottom two deciles, and many more will reach the top decile. Poverty is heritable in America and much less so in Canada.

Figure 7.2 shows how children of parents in the top 10 percent fare in the two countries. Canadian children are much more likely to descend toward the mean (downward economic mobility is a form of mobility). By contrast, if your father was in the top 10 percent

Figure 7.2   Earnings Deciles of Sons born to Top-Decile Fathers: US and Canada

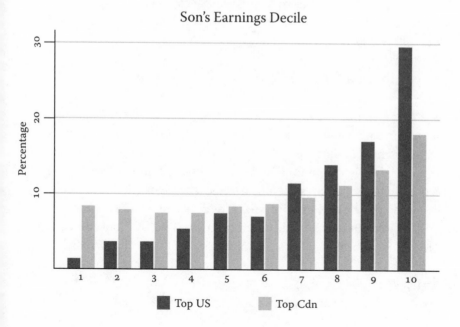

Son's Earnings Decile

Top US   Top Cdn

Sources: Corak, Curtis and Phipps (2011); Hertz (2005).

in the US, you'll likely end up in the top 20 percent. You might be an academic and not the executive that he was, but the likelihood that you'll be in the bottom 10 percent is vanishingly small. Even as a drug abuser, there's hope for the Hunter Bidens.

The American Dream isn't dead. It has just fled to other, more mobile countries, and that's going to hurt since it's so at odds with our self-image as Americans. We thought we were uniquely the land of opportunity, and it turns out we're not. Somehow, things have gone south, and we'd like to know why so we can fix it. What's not going to satisfy us are right-wing calls to complacency.

Accounting for Immobility

The comparison with Canada is useful because it's like the control group in an experiment. Since the two countries are so similar, looking north of the border helps identify the causes of American immobility. It permits us to dismiss faulty explanations trotted out to explain American intergenerational immobility and to focus on the differences that really matter.

a. Skill-Based Technological Change

We've moved to an information economy that favors high-tech people in a high-tech world.[12] Poorly skilled workers used to expect that decent middle-class jobs would be waiting for them, but now they've been left behind. It's therefore been assumed that recent technological changes shift jobs from low to highly skilled employees and that this explains rising economic inequality. What this doesn't explain is American immobility, however. Canada and the other First World countries that are more mobile aren't exactly living in the Stone Age. They're as technologically advanced as we are, and skill-biased technological change (SBTC) theories are therefore unable to explain why they're mobile and we're not.

b. Genoeconomics

Neo-Darwinians study how psychological traits might be inherited, and the new field of genoeconomics suggests that individual and national incomes are related to genetic factors. From smart and rich parents, smart and rich kids. That was the message of *The Bell Curve* by Charles Murray and Richard Herrnstein twenty-five years ago.[13] The two authors warned of a coming class society, where people are divided by their IQs. Intelligence is a heritable trait, they found, and in an information economy, the children of the wealthy will be wealthy themselves.

There are several problems with this, however. If it's big brains that make you wealthy today, formerly it was big muscles, and genoeconomics should have worked equally well back then. From brawny parents, brawny kids. In addition, we'd expect genetic advantages to dissipate in a couple of generations because of the well-known phenomenon of regression to the mean. The children of tall parents will be taller than other children, but on average they'll be shorter than their parents, and the same is true of the children of intelligent parents. That's not a recipe for aristocracy. Finally, genetic explanations of immobility piggyback on SBTC theories since they assume that we've become less mobile in an information economy that favors big brains. As such, they can't explain why we're immobile while other technologically advanced First World nations are mobile. It's not as if there's a uniquely American gene.

c. Globalization

The trend to globalization, with free trade in goods and increased cross-border trade, has moved low-tech jobs to countries with lower labor costs. It brings developing countries into the middle class but shrinks the First World's middle class. In this way, globalization has made the US less mobile. But it doesn't explain why we're less mobile than other First World countries. By definition, globalization is a worldwide phenomenon, and we'd expect it to affect the Canadas and Denmarks as much as us. Indeed, it should affect them more since their economies depend more on foreign trade than ours does. Because of its size, the US is the lowest exporting country in the First World.[14]

d. The Great Gatsby Curve

Inequality hardens into immobility when rich kids inherit their wealth from rich parents. That's the message to be drawn from Figure 7.3, which shows a nearly one-to-one relationship between inequality (the Gini coefficient) and Table 7.1's measure of intergenerational immobility. On the lower left, Denmark is an egalitarian and highly mobile society. Brazil, on the upper right, is an unequal and immobile society. The United States is in the upper-right quadrant, closer to Brazil than to Denmark. The straight line has been called the Great Gatsby Curve, with a nod to F. Scott Fitzgerald's tycoon.

That's a story about inertia, and it got a major boost in 2014 when Thomas Piketty's *Capital in the Twenty-First Century* was published in English. Piketty argued that capitalism tends inexorably toward inequality because of capital's tendency to grow more quickly than the economy as a whole. Growth comes from capital income, said Piketty, not labor income. Great fortunes accumulate from generation to generation thanks to the magic of compound interest, and to those who have, more is given.

It was an elegant if very simple theory, but any theory stands or falls on the evidence, and in Piketty's case it simply wasn't there. As Daron Acemoğlu and James Robinson noted,[15] Piketty did not engage in hypothesis testing or statistical analysis of causation or even correlation. When Acemoğlu and James Robinson did so, what they found was just the opposite of what Piketty's theory would have predicted.

Piketty's error was in assuming that the wealthy would reinvest all their money and save it for their descendants. But people spend their money on themselves over their lifetimes, and if that's where it all goes, it's the equivalent of a 100 percent inheritance tax and makes us less of an aristocracy. In what economist Thorstein Veblen derided as "conspicuous consumption," the rich throw away their money on expensive baubles rather than saving it for the kids. Then

Figure 7.3   *Income Immobility Tracks Income Inequality*

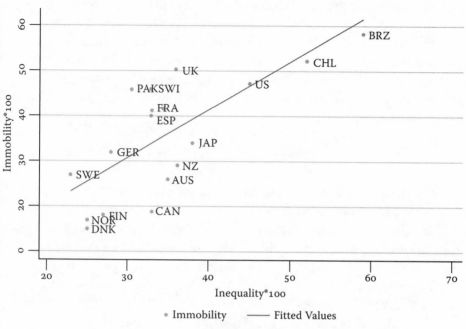

Immobililty*100 = 1.06*Inequality*100 – 0.93. Adj. R-sq. = 0.49

Sources: Miles Corak, "Inequality from Generation to Generation: The United States in Comparison," in Rycroft); CIA Fact Book.

there are the trophy wives. Nothing breaks up an estate more quickly than a few messy divorces, which is perhaps why we're always on the side of the gold diggers.

One might have expected that America would be especially immobile because it is more unequal than other First World countries. But a diagram about a host of countries in general needn't tell us very much about the United States in particular, and Piketty himself walked back the suggestion that his theory explains inequality here.[16] In America, the extremely rich have gotten to the top through the meritocratic sorting and the cultural factors discussed in the next section, that is through labor income and not from capital income and daddy's money.[17]

Whatever the Great Gatsby Curve might tell us about other countries, then, it might not say much about American immobility.

In addition, there's a hidden ambiguity in its message. To see that, recognize that the curve can be seen to move in both directions, up and down. That is, one might argue that we're necessarily immobile because we're unequal. But perhaps it's just the opposite. Perhaps we're unequal because we're immobile. It's a chicken and egg problem, with causation working in both directions. Had we Canada's mobility, our economic elites would be less entrenched, and we'd become more equal.

e. Demographics and Culture

As Figures 7.1 and 7.2 show, the children of America's least and most advantaged are likely to remain in place. That's not the case in the country we most resemble. There are important legal and institutional differences that explain why the American Dream fled to Canada, which we'll see in the next chapter. Before we get there, however, we need to examine whether cross-country demographic and cultural factors might account for the difference.

At the top end of the income distribution, parents try to ensure that their children will do well, and culture matters. The rich resist impulse gratification, and their children go to college, don't do drugs, and don't have children when they're unwed. Children in professional families are also more likely to hear words describing abstract thoughts that stimulate mental processes and become better prepared to deal with tasks performed by people in the highest income brackets.[18] But there aren't any great cultural differences between us and Canada at the top end, so that can't explain why they're mobile and we're not. What does matter at the top end are the legal and structural differences discussed in the next chapter, where we entrench our elites and Canada doesn't.

The cross-country cultural differences are more significant at the bottom end of the income distribution, particularly when it comes to race. It's not as if the United States is multiracial while Canada is white. Both countries are 73 percent white. However, Canada is 8.5 percent black or native (autochthone) Canadian, while the comparable American figure is 14 percent. The difference matters because blacks and native people in America have much lower rates of upward mobility than whites.[19] To some extent the same is likely true of Canada,[20] but a big difference is that the black and native population is smaller in that country.

There are several ways in which this might matter. One might want to blame historic American racial prejudice for the difference, but I'm not sure that Canadians today are less racist than Americans. One difference that stands out, however, is that between the unwed birth rate in the United States (40 percent) and Canada (30 percent). In particular, the black unwed birth rate in the US is over 70 percent, while the black unwed rate in Canada is half that at 37 percent.[21] That, with the difference in the size of the black population in the two countries, might explain much of the cross-country difference in Figure 7.2 for the bottom 10 percent earners.

There is a broad consensus that fatherless homes are associated with other social ills. The strongest predictor of upward mobility is a stable, two-parent family structure,[22] and children born to unwed mothers are more likely to drop out of school and commit crimes.[23] Not only are children more likely to succeed if they come from a two-parent family, but it helps if their neighborhood is composed of two-parent families. Within America, there are important social capital spillover benefits for people who live in counties with lower crime rates and a larger share of two-parent families.[24] Cultural explanations of economic immobility have been condemned for "blaming the victim," but there's too much evidence of their explanatory power to ignore them.[25]

Sociologist William Julius Wilson offered a persuasive economic explanation for black unwed birth rates. Black families were weaker than white ones because black unemployment levels were much higher than those for white families, particularly in the inner cities from which the jobs had fled. Add to that the racial and cultural prejudices of white employers, and it's not hard to see why black unemployment rates were double those of whites. In particular, failed left-wing welfare policies had ignored the need for two-parent families by restricting child support payments to single mothers. Taking this all together, black families were more dependent than whites on welfare checks and more likely to be affected by welfare's perverse incentives.

Cross-country differences in incarceration rates also matter since America locks people up much more than Canada does. About 2.2 million Americans, or 0.6 percent of the population, are in jail, while the Canadian figure is about 40,000, or 0.1 percent of Canadians. More a third of the US prison population is black, and 21 percent of black men born to the lowest-income families are in custody on a given day as compared with 6 percent of white men.[26]

In sum, there are things we can't change about American immobility, and some of them we wouldn't want to change. We'd want to see a return to stable two-parent families if we cared about kids. But then how do we legislate cultural change? David Hume wasn't far off the mark when he observed that "all plans of government, which suppose great reformation in the manners of mankind, are plainly imaginary."[27] Today the principal moral rearmament crusade we need from the government is one that gives people real jobs. After that we mostly can take care of ourselves.

But that's not the end of the matter. The self-serving excuses a comfortable elite trots out to explain the demise of the American Dream don't explain why it's moved offshore. Our upper classes haven't just climbed to the top of the heap. They've done so through the artificial means by which an aristocratic society hobbles lower-class children, and if that happened here and not in Canada, we need to look northward for a progressive conservative mobility agenda. In part, that would mean the progressive reforms such as cheap college tuition and a national health program for catastrophic medical illnesses, issues I discuss in the last chapter. More than anything, however, we should seek to emulate the ways in which Canada is a more conservative country in its immigration laws, K–12 education system, regulatory regime, and adherence to the rule of law. None of that would be permitted to continue but for the overlord class it benefits in the US.

CHAPTER EIGHT

The Left's Betrayal

I F WE'RE MORE ARISTOCRATIC than other countries, the Red
Queen hypothesis explains why. In Lewis Carroll's *Through the
Looking Glass*, Alice is puzzled to find that, while she keeps running, she always stays in the same spot. The Red Queen tells her
why. "Here, you see, it takes all the running you can do, to keep in
the same place. If you want to get somewhere else, you must run at
least twice as fast as that!" On education, immigration, and regulations we ran a good race, then stalled and watched everyone else
catch up and pass us.

The public school system was supposed to be an elevator that
brought students into the middle class, but now it's stalled. Our
grade school students are captives of a mediocre K–12 system and
perform far worse than similar students in Canada and other First
World countries. Our demented immigration laws import immobility with entrants whose children and grandchildren will earn less
than native-born Americans. Add to this our burdensome and
wasteful regulations and departures from the rule of law, and it's
easy to see why we've become more aristocratic than other countries. The good news is that, unlike the difference in cultural norms,
these are things that can be remedied by progressive conservatives
who want to restore the American Dream.

What is maddening is that while the Democrats purport to
champion equality and mobility, it's their policies that hold us back.
Progressive conservatives must take ownership of the issue and
denounce the self-serving hypocrisy of our elites, who employ a
left-wing ideology to protect an unjust aristocracy that keeps them
on top.

Bad Schools and Failing Universities

We boast about how good our education system is, but people are better educated in other First World countries according to the OECD, which ranks adults in different countries according to their skill levels.[1] For the top level of literary skills, where one can search for and integrate information across dense texts, synthesize ideas, and make high-level inferences, we're below average. On numeracy skills we're near the bottom. And all of this was before the teachers shut the schools for the pandemic and used Zoom classes to push critical race theories. It's gotten worse.

Part of the problem is the willingness of America's left-wing elites to tolerate mediocrity in our public K–12 schools. Their kids can get a good education in America, but we send poor kids to substandard schools. Expanding school choice would make everyone better off, but for a variety of noxious reasons we reject this. The Democrats are aligned with the teachers' unions, and the elites are better off when there's no competition from below.

As for higher ed, the world's best universities are found in the United States, but that's mostly because dollars count. We attract premium scholars from the rest of the world and benefit from the brain drain. That works for the top schools, but the rest of them fail to produce students who are better educated than those in other First World countries. Rigorous academic teaching is in retreat, with tendentious, politicized courses taking its place. We've also saddled our college graduates with mountains of student debt that can't be discharged in bankruptcy with the result that millions of them are debt slaves with no hope of emerging into solvency. Then we're surprised when they are radicalized.

a. K–12 Schools

During the twentieth century, we invested heavily in education. Our public schools were free, and our state colleges were inexpensive. The teaching was both academic and practical, and we also benefited (unfairly) from the glass ceiling that made schoolteachers rather than lawyers and doctors of smart young women. All this paid off when our economy increased twenty-fold from 1900 to 2000 during what economist Claudia Goldin calls the "human capital century."[2] It was also the American Century.

What was special about the twentieth century was technological change, which asked for employees with higher skill levels. What that in turn required was a match between education and technology with well-educated workers trained in reading and math.[3] More than most other countries, our schools stepped up to the plate and gave students a solid grounding in the skills they'd need. The American high school diploma was a badge of quality that signaled that graduates were sufficiently educated for most of the available jobs, and this powered the country's extraordinary economic growth during Goldin's human capital century. But that was then. Today math skills have declined, and we've fallen behind other First World countries.

The quality of a country's educational system is measured by an international test: the Program for International Student Assessment, or PISA. The test, which was first administered in 2000, covers fifteen-year-old student learning in three subjects: mathematics, science, and reading. Since the test was first given, we've not moved up the ranks. Currently we're thirty-seventh in math, eighteenth in science, and thirteenth in reading. Table 8.1 gives the results. Overall, we're thirty-first in the world. Canada is sixth.

The OECD also ranks adults by skill level. The results, seen in Table 8.2, show that we score below average in literary skills and well below average on numeracy skills. Shockingly, more than half of American adults are unable to read at a sixth-grade level,[4] which is what it would take to read an instruction manual or a simple business letter. Understand that we're not talking about people who are mentally slow. We're talking about ordinary Americans who have been cheated by the Left's K–12 public schools.

So how do we improve? First, you have to want to do so. The Left mostly doesn't. It has given up and says that what's behind the school reform movement is racism. Oregon blames its contemptibly low scores on racial prejudice and has scraped the requirement that high school graduates prove their math and literacy skills. This had become an "unfair test for children who don't test well."[5] Meanwhile,

Table 8.1   PISA Student Performance Scores

	MATH	SCIENCE	READING
Australia	491	503	503
Canada	512	518	520
Denmark	509	493	501
France	495	493	493
Germany	500	503	498
Japan	527	529	504
Netherlands	519	503	485
Norway	501	490	499
Sweden	502	499	506
U.K.	502	505	504
U.S.	478	502	505

Source: OECD PISA 2018: Insights and Interpretations.

Table 8.2   OECD Proficiency Levels, Literary (native language) and Numeracy

	LITERARY MEAN	NUMERACY MEAN
Netherlands	284	280
Australia	280	268
Sweden	279	279
Norway	278	278
Canada	274	266
Denmark	271	278
Germany	270	272
UK (England)	272	262
US	270	253
OECD Average	273	269

Source: OECD Skills Outlook 2013: First Results from the Survey of Adult Skills, Tables A2.4, A2.6 (2013).

some California schools will tackle the problem of underperforming students by eliminating psychologically damaging F grades.

If you do want to make things better, spend more money on teachers, says the Left. There's little by way of evidence that this would do much more than transfer money to a Democratic interest group, however. Internationally, spending more on schools correlates with better PISA scores,[6] but American teachers are already among the best paid in the world. We spend 38 percent more per pupil than the OECD average and a third more than Canada does.[7]

Among American states, there are sizable differences in per-pupil expenditures, but that doesn't explain why some states succeed and others don't. Differences in per-pupil spending and spending increases haven't been found to affect American test scores.[8] Spending differences also can't explain the significant black-white achievement gap since we spend as much or more on education for minorities than we do for white children.[9] We've not seen any bang for our buck, and that's not an argument for spending more bucks. We've also tried any number of top-down bureaucratic fixes over the last twenty years – No Child Left Behind, Race to the Top, Common Core – and they've not made a difference either.

Immigrant children represent a special challenge for teachers, but then Canada has a larger immigrant population. About 20 percent of Canadians are foreign-born compared to 14 percent here, and children of immigrants in Canada perform at the same level as native-born students. Where the foreign-born population is highest, it has not been a handicap on Canadian PISA scores. Nearly 30 percent of Ontarians are immigrants, and the province's students scored sixth in the world in reading and science and thirteenth in math.

If pressed about why we rank poorly compared to Canada, the Left is apt to allude delicately to demographic differences. There are in fact very substantial racial differences in American PISA scores. In 2015, the average mathematical literacy scores were 419 for blacks, 446 for Hispanics and 499 for white Americans. But *all* Canadians on average outperform white Americans, and as we've seen Canada, isn't an all-white country. Canada doesn't collect PISA data by race, and its global score of 516 in math was 17 points higher than that for America's white students. Only 41.8 percent of white American fifteen-year-olds were proficient in math, compared to 49.5 of all Canadians.[10] Quite apart from the substandard performance of white American children, it's a little disquieting to hear the Left suggest that one-third of our students, the minorities, are less than fully American.

So why does Canada do a better job of educating its K–12 students? A big reason is school choice in Canada. When parents can choose the school their child attends, schools have to compete with each other to attract students and the money that follows them. State monopolies, which aren't very good when it comes to making cars, aren't much good either when it comes to K–12 schools. Yet ostensibly free market America paradoxically resists school competition.

Students do better when they are offered financial assistance to switch schools and are given a choice between public and private schools. More than three quarters of high schoolers in the Netherlands and more than 60 percent in Belgium and Ireland attend state-supported private schools, and the difference in test scores is huge. Going from a nonprivate school system to one where half the schools are privately operated increases the achievement level in math by substantially more than a grade in math and three quarters of a grade in science.[11] In America, when students won a school choice lottery or used a scholarship to attend a private school of their choice, their test scores went up and they were more likely to graduate from high school and enroll in college.[12] Even the children left behind in public school benefit from the competition since their schools will find it harder to ignore the needs of students.[13]

So why there and not here? One reason is because many of those countries have established religions. In England, Anglican schools received state support, and when religious prejudices softened, Catholic and Jewish schools were permitted to follow. Canada didn't have an established religion, but the right to state-supported education for religious minorities (Catholics in Ontario, Protestants in Quebec) was guaranteed in the country's founding constitution.[14]

That's not what happened in America, where Catholic and Jewish parents who drop out of public schools have to pay twice to educate their children: once in property taxes to pay for public schools and once for tuition to a parochial school that doesn't get state funding. Ironically, when it comes to school choice, there is more religious freedom in First World countries with established churches than in wall-of-separation America.

That's how we ended up with our mixed K–12 school system, with (1) state-supported public schools, (2) state-supported charter schools, (3) privately supported parochial and private schools, and (4) homeschooling. The greatest number of children, about fifty million of them, attend state public schools.[15] About three million attend state-funded charter schools that operate independently of the established school system. A further five million kids attend private or parochial schools, and another two million are homeschooled.

Charter schools are religiously neutral and typically are founded by parents whose children would otherwise be consigned to a failing public school. A meta-analysis of more than fifty empirical studies reported that charter schools had higher achievement gains in math as well as higher high school and college graduation rates.[16] They are nevertheless under attack from public school teachers' unions, which try to block or underfund and micromanage them. In major cities, public schools get a third more public funding than charter schools.[17]

You'll not find charter schools in other countries, and the reason is simple. American charters too often lack the institutional resources and reputational advantages of established religious schools like those of the Jesuits. Real school choice means state aid for sectarian schools, not just charter schools. So why not here? Anti-Catholic bigotry used to explain why parochial schools weren't state funded. There's little of that left today, but what's replaced it are the country's heightened political and cultural differences over issues such as same-sex marriage and abortion. The dominant political culture thinks parochial schools are on the wrong side on those issues, which is why it opposes state funding for them.

There was a revealing expression of this in the media's attack on Nick Sandmann, a sixteen-year-old who attended a right-to-life rally in 2019 with his Catholic high school classmates. Sandmann was approached by a sixty-five-year-old Native American provocateur who locked eyes with him inches from his face. When Sandmann responded with smiling imperturbability, this was taken to reveal his racism. Progressive celebrity Reza Aslan tweeted, "Have you ever seen a more punchable face?" The *New York Times* described the incident as "a throng of cheering and jeering high school boys, predominantly white and wearing 'Make America Great Again' gear, surrounding a Native American elder."[18] Catholic, white, and Trump! That was a trifecta for the *Times*, which had seen what it wanted to see in an ideological enemy. However, for those who wanted to look, a longer video of the same incident told a different story, and the *Washington Post* and CNN were forced to settle lawsuits alleging that they had falsely libeled Sandmann.

School choice would give us better schools, but that's of small concern to leftists such as Harvard Law Professor Elizabeth Bartholet. Homeschooled kids do better on standardized tests and then do better in college,[19] but that doesn't cut it with her. The problem is that the majority of homeschooling parents are Christians who "are committed to homeschooling largely because they reject mainstream, democratic culture and values and want to ensure that their children adopt their own particular religious and social views."[20] They're often "extreme religious ideologues" who reject woke culture, and we obviously can't have any of that. Ironically, Bartholet claims that she's on the side of moral autonomy and against authoritarianism when she's the real authoritarian who wants to indoctrinate the children of dissenting parents.

Bartholet took some flak for her intolerance, but there was nothing exceptional in her message. She was merely repeating what the left-wing media – NPR, *The Atlantic*,[21] *The New Yorker*[22] – has been telling us about the need to instruct students in an approved set of beliefs. Compared to other countries, our public schools do an abysmal job teaching English, math, and science, but they make up for this with lectures on systemic racism. The Left is willing to hobble our children provided it can shape their politics.

A second reason why America has resisted school choice is because teachers' unions seek to evade monitoring and competition.[23] They've made our public K–12 schools resemble the old Soviet department stores whose mission was to serve the interests of the salesclerks and not the customers, and they're able to get away with this because of their political clout. During the COVID-19 pandemic, the unions refused to send the teachers back to work even though the risk of catching the disease from the kids was extremely small. In Fairfax Country, Virginia, the union demanded that its members get the vaccine ahead of the elderly and having gotten it still refused to return to the classroom. The parochial and charter schools had stayed open, so the unions demanded that charter schools be defunded before they returned to teaching.

The two biggest unions – the National Education Association (NEA) and the American Federation of Teachers (AFT) – have a combined membership of 4.5 million members, or 2.9 percent of the working American population. In Canada, by contrast, K–12 teachers and school employees make up only 1.4 percent of the total workforce. Somehow Canada beats the US hands down on K–12 education with less than half the teaching staff per capita.

The political power of American teachers' unions is legendary. In Woody Allen's movie *Sleeper*, set in the future, we're told that the old world was destroyed when American Federation of Teachers President Albert Shanker got hold of a nuclear bomb. Teachers staff Democratic campaign committees, bring their members to the polls, and are one of the biggest campaign donors, with nearly all of their support going to the Democratic Party.[24]

A third reason why we resist school choice is the "suburban veto" of upper-class parents who vote it down. The Supreme Court has blessed school vouchers for religious schools provided there are adequate nonreligious schools for parents to choose from.[25] States don't have to subsidize sectarian schools, but if they do so for private schools, they can't exclude parochial schools. But that doesn't mean that sectarian schools are going to get funded. That would require political support in local communities, and when it is put to a vote in wealthy suburbs, school choice is defeated.[26]

Upper-class parents vote down school choice because they're served by the status quo. Access to good public schools is largely a matter of how much you're able to pay for your house, and higher home prices reflect well-funded local schools. Fixing inner-city public schools would mean that suburban housing prices would decline since you'd no longer have to pay a premium to live in a good school district. In addition, suburbanites would be worse off in relative terms since their children would be faced with increased competition from below. That's a zero-sum game in which it's necessary that poor children fail if rich children are to succeed.

If there is such a thing as structural racism in America, look no further than the smug left-wingers who support our two-tier K–12 school system. In the lower tier, we send inner-city black students to public schools that don't educate them and exist to provide jobs for a mostly white work force of teachers. In the upper tier, rich white parents can escape to a better school system either by sending their children to expensive private schools or by buying a pricey house in a racially segregated suburb. In all of this, it requires an enormous amount of cognitive dissonance for rich leftists to maintain the self-serving belief that they're on the side of racial justice. If they took the red pill and faced up to their hypocrisy, they'd have to abandon their allies in the teachers' unions, and they'll not do that. Much easier to condemn systemic racism in the abstract as this requires nothing more than putting up a sneering yard sign on a well-manicured lawn in a racially segregated neighborhood to express contempt for their conservative neighbors and solidarity with people they'll never meet.

In sum, fixing America's schools isn't rocket science. What is needed is real parental choice in the form of vouchers and state aid for parochial schools. More than other First World countries, we've resisted this and for a variety of smelly motives have forced children into mediocre public schools. And if we're economically unequal and immobile, one reason is that our K–12 education system ensconces an aristocracy. That's the message from a study that mapped the dispersion of literacy scores against a measure of cross-country earnings inequality. What the study found was a nearly one-to-one relationship between the two, with the United States leading the pack: highest earnings inequality and highest test score inequality.[27] And that's how we've produced a society of peers and peasants like that of seventeenth-century France.

b. Higher Education

Left-wingers who seek to deflect attention from the state of our K–12 schools will often point to our university system. America's higher ed is a $500-billion-a-year industry, and our elite universities are the best anywhere. But there's a simple reason for this. We pay premium salaries for academics and import talent from all over the world. Half the science Nobel laureates in the last sixty years have come from American universities, but 30 percent of them were born outside the United States.

What's not so clear is what this has done for the average American university student. The top US schools are better than the top Canadian ones, but the average Canadian grad is better educated than the average American one if Table 8.2 tells us anything. In America, it matters greatly if you can get into a top university, but the credential value of the degree is less important in Canada. McGill University, the University of Saskatchewan – they're all about the same. They're all pretty good, and they're probably better than the average American university. The spread between the best and the worst school is greater in the US, and that's what you'd expect in an aristocracy.

College is a fun experience for American students, but there's little evidence that much learning goes on. Richard Arum and Josipa Roksa report that 36 percent of students showed *no* improvement in analytic abilities and writing skills after four years in college.[28] They had stood still at a time when we'd have expected major improvements if for no other reason than that the students were four years older. There's still a salary premium paid to people who've acquired the credential of a university degree, but that doesn't tell you much about what they learned while at college. Rather, it signals the worthlessness of a mere high school degree.

After high school only 35 percent of students are prepared for college-level math and reading,[29] and universities find themselves picking up the slack with course offerings on things that should have been taught in grade school. Other subjects that should be relegated to on-the-job training (hospitality management, parks and recreation) are treated as serious academic disciplines. Take a look at the course offerings (civic leadership, comics studies, pre-chiropractic) at Portland State University and ask whether it has any reason to exist. There is no recognition that in an era of globalization we are competing against students in other countries who receive a serious university education.

Problems with American higher education help explain our income inequality, according to Claudia Goldin and Lawrence Katz in *The Race Between Education and Technology*.[30] Salaries at the top end have pulled away from average salaries, as we saw in Chapter 6, and some have argued that this was because we moved to a high-tech, STEM economy. Goldin and Katz disagree, however, and tie the rise of income inequality to the decline of US higher education. The rise in income inequality occurred after 1980, and if this was because of a STEM economy, we should have seen major technological improvements at that point. But that didn't happen, the two authors argue. There was technological change both before and after, but that wasn't driving the run-up in top incomes. Instead, the change happened at the supply side and not the demand side. There was a demand for STEM workers, but our colleges had stopped producing the number of skilled workers to keep up with the demand. The wage premium for highly skilled workers increased because there was a smaller supply, not because there was a greater demand for them.

Our colleges admit people who don't belong there, teach them worthless things, and saddle them with impossible debt loads. We've produced more college grads, but the value of a university degree has declined, and students aren't being trained for the jobs that might await them. Sometimes it's just the opposite. An employer looking at a transcript full of courses on critical race studies might think that, in hiring the applicant, he'd be getting a lawsuit and not a productive worker.

How Our Immigration System Imports Immobility

America prides itself on being the country of immigrants, but as we saw there's a bit of puffery in this. We're 14 percent foreign born, and there's a higher percentage of foreign-born residents in other countries, especially our sister settler nations of Australia (30 percent) and Canada (20 percent). There, immigration isn't the kind of political issue that it is here, and the difference lies in the kind of immigrants the three countries admit. Australia and Canada screen immigrants on the basis of whether they're likely to make native Australians and Canadians better off, and if people are generally happy with immigration in those countries, it's a sign that those policies are working. Here, however, the costs and benefits of immigration are far less clear, and that's one of the principal reasons why it's a hot political issue and why Donald Trump was elected in 2016.

No other country in the world would tolerate our open border policies, which as everyone knows are simply meant to import people who'll eventually vote for Democrats. But it's our legal immigration policies that are of greater concern and which actually help make America immobile. We accept immigrants who'll earn less than the average native-born American, and the difference persists over two generations. US immigrants earn 20 percent less than native-born Americans, their children will earn 10 percent less, and their grandchildren 5 percent less.[31] By contrast, Canadian immigrants are more skilled than their American counterparts and assimilate more quickly into the national economy.[32] As compared to Canadians whose parents were born in Canada, second-generation Canadians are as well-educated and as likely to be employed.[33]

Whether our legal immigration policies help or hurt America's native-born citizens is a matter of dispute. It'll help some natives because they can buy goods and services more cheaply. That will be true of the farmers who hire migrant workers during harvest time and the homeowners who get their houses cleaned by foreign-born maids. New arrivals also need to buy stuff, and that will benefit merchants. On the other hand, the cheap farm worker or maid or gardener might be taking a job away from the native-born. The

most respected immigration scholar, George Borjas, ran the numbers and concluded that it was a wash.[34]

In 2015, the economy increased by about $2 trillion through
immigration, but almost all of this went to the immigrants themselves.[35] To the extent that they contribute more than this (perhaps
$50 billion), that's likely erased by the public services they con-
sume. The National Academy of Sciences calculated the cost of
providing schools, hospitals, the justice system, and welfare to legal
immigrants less the taxes they pay and concluded that they and
their dependent children create a net fiscal burden ranging from
$43 billion to $300 billion a year.[36]

Even if immigrants paid their way, however, we need to recognize how immigration creates winners and losers because the losers are the most fragile of Americans. Relative to other countries,
we admit low-skilled immigrants, and they compete away jobs and
income from low-skilled and poor Americans while benefiting the
richer Americans who profit from the cheaper services immigrants
provide. Quantifying this, Borjas reported that immigration
amounts to a redistribution of about half a trillion dollars from
America's poor to its rich. Increasing the immigrant flow by 10 percent depressed the earnings of native-born American workers by
4 percent between 1960–2010,[37] and black Americans were especially hard hit. A 10 percent increase in immigrant workers in a
particular skill group was reported to reduce black wages by
2.5 percent and to lower their employment rate by 5.9 percentage
points.[38] That doesn't much look like social justice.

If increased immigration makes the poorest among us worse off,
taking in fewer immigrants would have the opposite effect. We're
told that immigrants work at jobs that Americans don't want to do.
Pay Americans more, however, and we'll do the work. California
garlic farmers found that they had to hire native Americans at $13
an hour when there weren't enough undocumented aliens to fill the
demand at $11 an hour and complained that in the future they
might even have to pay $15 an hour.[39] Consumers would have to
pay a bit more for their garlic, but that's not the end of the world.
All the farmer would have to do is pay what the Left regards as a
suitable minimum wage.

That's not the end of it either because we're forgetting one thing: *opportunity costs*. We've been comparing immigrants to native Americans, and as we've seen in the previous section, that's not the highest of bars. Telling us that immigrants are as well educated as native Americans isn't exactly high praise. We're also one of the most crime-ridden countries in the First World, and we shouldn't be satisfied if immigrants are no more law-abiding than the rest of us. What this ignores is the opportunity cost of *not* admitting more qualified immigrants. We're the world's premium immigration destination, and we should be competing for the highest-skilled immigrants. Instead, we're sending them to other countries such as Australia and Canada.

In sum, our immigration policies represent an enormous wealth transfer from poor to rich Americans. We admit unskilled immigrants who compete jobs and income away from low-earning Americans but who provide cheap nannies, maids, and gardeners for the rich. That's nobody's idea of social justice, but the Left nevertheless preens in its pretended virtue.

Our immigration system also weakens our collective sense of national identity. Screening for language skills would be especially useful because without the ability to communicate with natives, the immigrant is likely to live in one of the large ethnic enclaves in the United States. He'll settle into a community of people like himself and will be less likely to acquire English proficiency or assimilate to the majority culture. He'll not learn how to deal with people from the majority culture, how to bargain with them, or how to join with them in encompassing social groups. That's going to impoverish the immigrant and also the native who is deprived of contacts with culturally remote neighbors.

If you're a left-winger who thinks America is an essentially flawed and racist society, the loss of a national identity isn't a problem. If you think that half of Americans are deplorable or parasitical "takers," you don't start with much of a sense of national identity to begin with. But for everyone else, the idea that our immigration system divides us is troubling. It also results in a loss of trust that impoverishes all of us. Robert Putnam explains how this hurts us.

> Immigration and ethnic diversity tend to reduce social soli-
> darity and social capital. New evidence from the US suggests
> that ethnically diverse neighborhood residents of all races
> tend to "hunker down." Trust (even of one's own race) is lower,
> altruism and community cooperation rarer, friends fewer.[40]

In our divisions, the sense of solidarity has never been weaker, and
that helps explain reports that a third of us are clinically depressed.
We've permitted ourselves to hate our fellow citizens and preen
with a sense of virtue for doing so. We've left our country behind
but never calculated the emotional cost of doing so.

The Regulatory Briar Patch

We all benefit from environmental protection and safety regulations but are apt to overlook the disproportionate burden this
places on poorer Americans. Building in more safety raises the unit
costs of products and costs consumers more. If we all had the same
desire to avoid risk, that wouldn't impose a burden on one economic class over another. But we don't have uniform preferences
about risk, and the rich are more risk averse than the poor.

If we're overregulated, that's because the rules are designed for
the benefit of the richest and not average Americans. The rich will
disproportionately demand extra protection from risk, and their
voices are more likely to be heard than poor consumers. Regulations add over $80,000 to new home prices,[41] and that makes the
homes safer, but it also squeezes poor people out of the housing
market. By mandating safety standards that only the rich want,
we're not doing the poor any favors.

There is a class divide in the rules set by the regulatory state.
Political scientists Martin Gilens of Princeton and Benjamin Page
of Northwestern University have calculated that policies supported
by at least 80 percent of affluent voters passed into law about 45
percent of the time, while policies opposed by at least 80 percent of
those voters passed into law just 18 percent of the time. The views
of poor and middle-class voters had little influence.[42]

There's a further reason why we're overregulated. The regulatory state is the briar patch in which many of our elites live. It provides direct employment for many of them as civil servants and indirect employment for the lawyers, lobbyists, and economists hired to navigate around it and shape its rules. This includes the outside lawyers, the human relations team, and the government relations departments that find easy passageways around regulatory rules.

In addition, the regulatory state protects the biggest firms by insulating them from competition. The new entrant is asked to bear the costs of a mind-bending number of rules, and breaking them can land him in jail. By contrast, established firms, with their compliance experts, will be happy to bear the costs of excessive regulations for their anticompetitive effects. If we've grown an aristocracy, the rise of the administrative state is one of the reasons.

We've also been made immobile by our departures from the rule of law. Until fairly recently, that wasn't on people's radar screen. When it comes to what makes a country rich, the Left talked about its infrastructure (e.g., its highway system) while conservatives pushed privatization. But none of that matters as much as a legal regime that protects property rights, enforces contracts, and doesn't fetter us with excessive regulation. Together, this comprises what we call the rule of law, and it accounts for 44 percent of a country's total wealth, according to the World Bank.[43] Daniel Kauffman reports that an improvement in the rule of law from relatively poor to merely average performance would result in the long run in an estimated fourfold increase in per capita incomes, a reduction in infant mortality of a similar magnitude, and significant gains in literacy.[44] Going in the other direction, the example of Venezuela shows how quickly a country can descend into miserable penury when it abandons the rule of law.

America isn't the poster child for the rule of law.[45] Other countries have begun to notice how politics creeps in to affect how crimes are prosecuted. Local biases affect contract law enforcement, and woe to the out-of-state defendant in a state court. Fifty years ago, we were looked to as a model jurisdiction, one from which foreign courts sought guidance. No longer. The courts of Canada,

Britain, Sweden, Germany, and Israel now look to each other for direction, not to our courts.

The World Justice Project (WJP) ranks countries on the rule of law and reports that we come in at twenty-first (with Canada coming in at sixth). And it's not because we don't have enough law. That's how failed states like Afghanistan fail. America's problem is just the opposite: too much law, an uncountable number of federal crimes, a humungous set of administrative rules, and a confused tangle of private law rules that transfer wealth to the trial lawyers from the rest of us. America gets high marks for the ease of starting a business, but thereafter the new firm must confront a vague and uncertain set of criminal and civil liability rules as well as regulatory hurdles that can turn honest businessmen into unwitting felons. That's great if what you want is an aristocracy.

By contrast, the rule of law promotes mobility by making it easier for the new man to get ahead. He can rely on laws that are neutral as to race, gender, and class, such as the rules of offer and acceptance in contract law. Legally enforceable contracts were the ally of the newly freed slave, the emancipated woman, and the foreigner who came to America. Without them, we're left with the state of nature, which is the old boy's network where connections matter and the new man never breaks into the club.[46]

* * *

Progressive conservatives are the mobility party. That makes them progressives in their support for policies right-wingers oppose: a national health care system that protects Americans from catastrophic medical conditions and relief from the crushing burden of a costly college education. These are reforms I discuss in the book's last chapter. More than anything, however, the progressive conservative is a conservative and opposed to the ways in which the Left has made us immobile.

If we really want to make America mobile again, the way back is simple enough. Fix our broken schools. Reform our immigration laws. Relax the regulatory burden, and return to the rule of law. And yet those who boast of their concern about immobility are members of an economic elite who oppose all such reforms, who for self-interested reasons would keep things just as they are, unequal and immobile. In place of reforms that would help the underclass of every race, they offer the trinkets of merely symbolic reforms and the delicious sense of justified hatred. Ignore your bleak prospects, they say, and see how we tear down statues and rename schools. Look, now we capitalize the word "Black"! It's a swindle, and it's made worse by the Left's cruel hypocrisy. They can write entire books on inequality without recognizing their own complicity.

In the Black Lives Matter era, the Left took to heart a message from Ibram X. Kendi's *How to Be an Antiracist*. Kendi's central argument was that it's policy outcomes, not personal intent, that matter. The lofty preamble to a bill, the legislator's fine speeches – none of that counts if you collaborate on policies that in fact harm black people. If a leftist really wants to call himself an antiracist or a social justice warrior, therefore, he'll have to ditch his white allies in the teachers' unions, the entrenched professoriate in our mediocre universities, the open borders crowd, and the lawyers who staff our bloated bureaucracies. The hypocrisy is contemptible and made worse if the leftist prefers not to know how his policies are so self-serving.

CHAPTER NINE

Why Aristocracies Never Really Go Away

W E'D LIKE TO THINK that there's something natural about social mobility, that the Ragged Dicks are always bound to climb the ladder, that nothing need be done to make it happen. That's not what Lincoln thought, and it's not what a casual knowledge of history would tell us. Instead, what's natural is aristocracy, a society of stable classes, never wholly fixed yet never entirely open either.

Parents have always done what they could to ensure that their children would rise to the top. In traditional aristocracies, they sought titles that their eldest son would inherit as a peer or baronet. This was a thing of value, and a corrupt ministry could finance its expenditures by selling them off. James I created the new order of baronets, hereditary knighthoods, for just this purpose with a going price of £1,000 for each new title. In the eighteenth century, Sir Robert Walpole's ministry (1721–42) was notorious for selling peerages, and the practice continued even into the twentieth century. Burke's Peerage is often nothing more than a record of centuries-old corruption that is not ennobled by the passage of time.

Apart from hereditary titles of nobility, parents could provide for their children by passing on their wealth. When land was the chief source of value, the great aristocrats were also the greatest landowners. The laws of primogeniture, under which all of an estate's property passed to the first-born son if the deceased died without a will, served to keep great estates together and preserved an aristocratic society,[1] and that was why one of Thomas Jefferson's first acts as a rising politician was to abolish the presumption of primogeniture in Virginia. What he sought, he later recalled, was a republican code of laws, one in which "every fibre would be eradicated of ancient or future aristocracy."[2]

Land mattered less when great merchant fortunes arose in the nineteenth and twentieth centuries. In Britain the great land-owning aristocratic families never fully recovered from the Second World War and the punitive estate duties levied by the Labour government of Clement Atlee. Like Jefferson, the point was to break up an aristocracy, which in the case of Britain was already fading. Apart from the royal family, only life peers are created today.

In today's information economy, the source of wealth isn't land or even capital assets. Instead, it comes from entrepreneurial labor, which has put paid to Thomas Piketty's fears of a patrimonial capitalism in which money is inherited. But the desire to see our children do well abides. Now, however, parents seek to give their children a leg up through the educational resources we saw in the last chapter. We live in a meritocratic society, but it's one in which merit has become heritable and in which an aristocratic new class at the pinnacle of our society places stumbling blocks in the path of middle-class children. In this way, the elite has succeeded in passing on their advantages to the Hunter Bidens and overcoming the law of regression to the mean.

We shouldn't be surprised, for nothing is more natural than an aristocracy. For it to arise, only two things are needed, common to all of us: a bequest motive and relative preferences. The bequest motive is simply the desire to see our children do well. We are hardwired to seek to pass on our genes, and this means that, as in Deuteronomy, we distinguish between strangers and brothers. We'll be willing to incur enormous sacrifices for children and near relatives, but for strangers to whom we are not related we have only a constrained sympathy. What that will leave us with is a world of family ties, thick with nepotism, where sons succeed fathers in politics, business, and Hollywood.

The second needed thing for an aristocracy is the relative preferences we saw in Chapter 6. We have absolute preferences when we want something and relative preferences when we also want more of it than the other fellow. And as we wish well for our children, given the bequest motive, we would want them to fare better than other people's children, given relative preferences. We would be willing to accept a poorer world so long as our children end up on top. We might even prefer a world that leaves our children worse off so long as everyone else fares worse still.

The Bequest Motive

The desire to protect our children is so strong that those who lack it seem like moral monsters. On Twitter one reads stories about feminists who say they'll abort their child if he's a boy. One lady said she'd call her boy Adolph. The name will be a curse, and employers won't hire him, but that's fine because he'll be white, and punishing him for his skin color will strike a blow for racial justice.

Unlike them, the rest of us prefer our own children over those of others, and evolutionary biologists tell us that this is because of our desire to pass on our genes to our descendants. That in turn explains how aristocracies arise. We want our kids to be the nobles and other kids to be the serfs. That's not egalitarian, but then evolutionary biology is not egalitarian.

The person who explained why this is so was W. D. Hamilton (1936–2000), one of the twentieth century's towering scientists, a biologist who trained under a statistician and who brought his mathematical learning to bear in studying the laws of inheritance.[3] Darwinian natural selection shouldn't be seen at the level of individuals, argued Hamilton, but rather from the perspective of our genes. On this arresting hypothesis (which Richard Dawkins subsequently labeled the selfish gene[4]), the gene is the decision-making principal, and the individual whose body the gene inhabits is merely its agent. We might think we want children, but we're genetically hardwired to feel that way. The gene is really in charge. It gives the command, and the individual follows it. And the command is be fruitful and multiply.

Genes are transmitted when the individual passes on his genes to his children. In addition, we also share genes with our relatives, as geneticist Sewall Wright noted in 1922. Wright gave a mathematical formula for the probability that two individuals shared a common gene, which he called the "coefficient of relatedness" or r. Between father and daughter, for example, r is 0.5, and between father and grandchild it is 0.25. That's how, by taking swabs taken from children or grandchildren, courts can identify heiresses or long-dead murderers.

Hamilton recognized that we share our genes with siblings and cousins as well as with direct descendants. Identical twins share 100 percent, and nonidentical twins share 50 percent of their genes with each other. I share 12.5 percent of my genes with my first cousins. If the gene is thought to be endowed with the desire to maximize its copies, it will realize that this might occur through relatives as well as through children.

From this, Hamilton arrived at a theory of "inclusive fitness" to explain how we might sacrifice for our relatives. Fitness refers to the ability to maximize copies of one's genes, and Hamilton made a cost-benefit rule of out of this. The cost arises when a person incurs risks that threaten his life and capacity to reproduce, and the benefit is from the increased copies of the gene provided by children and other relatives. Under Hamilton's Law, the decision-making gene gives the following order to its body when considering whether to bear a sacrifice in order to help a relative:

$$(1) \quad \text{Be altruistic if } rB > C$$

Here, r is Sewall-Wright's coefficient of relatedness, B is the relative's fitness benefit (increased probability of the gene's reproductive success), and C is the individual donor's fitness cost (reduced probability of the individual's reproductive success). J. B. S. Haldane had earlier intuited the same idea by saying that he would lay down his life for two brothers or eight first cousins. For one brother, $r = 0.5$, and for two of them $r = 1.0$. For one cousin, $r = 0.125$, and for eight of them $r = 1.0$. When the donor sacrifices himself for either two brothers or eight cousins, it's an even trade.

When it's all tied up like this, the selfish gene is indifferent when choosing between the body it inhabits and those of its kin. But could it ever be more than an even trade? Yes, and this explains the intensity of a parent's feelings for his child and the desire for an aristocracy. To take one well-known family, the coefficient of relatedness between George VI and Princess Elizabeth was 0.5. But then she had four children, and they had two each, and each of them had two more. For the king, the daughter represented not merely an r of 0.5 but a sum of 2.5 over only three generations, and at that point a father is impelled to sacrifice for his child. That is why the social contract takes this form: we take from our parents and, without repaying them, give to our children. There is always an asymmetry in the relationship, one biased toward future generations and aristocracy.

Relative Preferences

To pass on our genes, we'll want our children to be attractive mates in marriage markets. That means we'll want them to be rich and well-educated. The bequest motive may thus explain why aristocracies arise. But for a full explanation of aristocracy and immobility, one more thing is needed. Why might the aristocrat be willing to impoverish future societies so long as his children end up on top? Why might he prefer to live in seventeenth century France rather than in Ragged Dick's much wealthier America?

The answer is relative preferences. We don't care about how wealthy we are solely in absolute terms. We also care about how wealthy we are relative to other people. That means a society where elite parents want their children to be better off, middle-class kids worse off, and possibly everyone poorer.

That's called spite, and it's one of the nastiest of human motivations. But we see it all around us, and Hamilton's Law helps explains why. Suppose that I imagine my child in competition with another child. I'll want my child to do well, and he'll do better if the other child is handicapped. Let's call my child x and the other child y and imagine we're in a zero-sum world where y's fitness loss $-B$ equals x's fitness gain B. The spiteful donor z is related to x but not to y, and he might be willing to bear a personal fitness cost C_z in order to impose a fitness cost $-B$ upon y if this would confer a fitness benefit B upon x.

$$(2) \quad \text{Be spiteful if } (r_y - r_x)(-B) > C_z$$

Donor z will then be spiteful so long as $(r_y - r_x)(-B)$ exceeds his fitness cost C_z.[5] The donor in this second inequality is an altruist, like the donor in the first inequality above. He does care about other people, just not in a good way.

Table 9.1   Choosing Future Worlds

	PRESENT	WORLD I	WORLD II
Top Quintile	$150,000	$160,000	$140,000
Second Quintile	$75,000	$150,000	$50,000
Median	$50,000	$140,000	$40,000

To see how spite might shape our political choices, consider Table 9.1, where top-quintile people are given a choice between moving to World I or World II. If they wished well for everyone, they'd prefer World I, where everyone is made better off and income inequalities are reduced. World II is a poorer society all around, but a spiteful altruist might nevertheless prefer it if he could ensure that he and his children will be in the top quintile. In World II his children will be less wealthy in absolute dollars, but they'll be better off in relative terms than they would be in World I.

World I is a society of income mobility where everyone is permitted to advance, while World II is a spiteful, beggar-thy-neighbor, aristocratic society where national wealth is sacrificed to preserve the relative wealth of an aristocratic class. It is seventeenth-century France, where a centralized and *dirigiste* administration stifled the economy. That made the country poorer than it might have been but served to protect aristocrats from competition from below. And that is where we are today.

A Cyclical Theory of History

Hamilton's Law is both a theory of evolutionary biology and a rebuttal to Whig theories that see history moving in a single direction. In restating the Whig theory in a 1989 essay, Francis Fukuyama argued that we had arrived at history's end point in the triumph of Western liberal ideals. That meant free markets, free trade, and democracy, and it came to be called the Washington Consensus. Repressive societies would recognize that they'd be unstable unless they provided for the material needs of their citizens, and to do this they'd have to move to a free market economy. Having done so, they'd grow a middle class, which in turn would demand democracy. That was what happened in Chile under Pinochet, and it was expected that China would follow the same path.[6]

Fukuyama's essay hasn't fared very well, however. Fukuyama himself backed away from it in two more recent books that describe a sclerotic society of special interests that enact wealth-destroying laws.[7] That's what has happened here, and it's made America immobile. Meanwhile, a rival set of policies called the Beijing Consensus gains traction. While its government is dictatorial, China has made itself rich by embracing free markets and promoting economic mobility. Forty years ago, 835 million Chinese people lived in extreme poverty (earning less than $1.25 a day).[8] Today no one does, according to its government,[9] and that's an expansion of wealth and gain in mobility unmatched in history. If you're a poor country and you're offered a choice between the Washington Consensus as practiced in America today and the Beijing Consensus, which would you choose?

The rise of China invites us to reimagine all political disputes from the perspective of social and economic mobility. In nineteenth-century Europe, socialists could pass themselves off as the party of mobility when they were ranged against class-ridden, aristocratic conservatives. Now China has shown how a socialist country may promote an extraordinarily high degree of mobility by adopting free bargaining and private enterprise. Whether this will prove stable remains to be seen, however. China might grow its own aristocracy, as communist societies did in the last century. The very term "new class" came from an ex-communist, Milovan Djilas, who argued that the party's ideals had been betrayed by an elite *nomenklatura* that had installed itself in the leadership positions of the Soviet Union and Tito's Yugoslavia.

Perhaps that's inevitable. Gaetano Mosca (1858–1941) thought so in any event. In every society, he said, an elite will rise to power and breed an aristocracy that persists over generations. "All ruling classes tend to become hereditary in fact if not in law."[10]

In contrast to the European socialists, America offered a free market politics of mobility, and while this was enormously successful in the nineteenth and twentieth centuries, it didn't repeal Hamilton's Law. Because of the bequest motive, the elite of the day will always seek to ensure that its children end up on top. They are also prepared to hinder wealth creation for everyone, to give us a poorer economy, if this leaves their own children better off relative to everyone else. That is what has happened here for reasons we saw in the last chapter, and so we find an immobile America surpassed by the more mobile societies of Europe and even by China.

Our political labels are impoverished and need to be recast in terms of mobility versus immobility. The white American Left, which forms America's overclass and defends open borders, bad schools, and the regulatory state, has become the party of aristocracy. So too are the elite right-wingers who support open borders and reflexively oppose every effort to redistribute wealth in favor of the underclass.

History is never linear, moving always toward the heavenly end state of a modern, mobile, and egalitarian society. Instead, it's cyclical, balanced between the opposing forces of mobility and immobility, egalitarianism and aristocracy, efficiency and inefficiency; and oscillating unevenly between them. History is driven by contradictory impulses, between the bequest motives of the rich and poor and the demand to avoid the waste that social stagnation can impose on an economy. In time, a hierarchical society invites a social or political revolution that overthrows its elites, and that is how the election of 2016 should be seen.

So it has always been, an endless cycle of genetic struggles that pit an overclass against an underclass, in battles without final victories but in which progressive conservatives have always sided with the underclass.

Genopolitics

What then should progressive conservatives do, to advance a politics of mobility? What they won't do is copy the policies of the two major parties. Unlike right-wing Republican progressive conservatives will oppose open borders, and unlike the corporate branch of the GOP, they'll not want an immigration system whose goal is simply to provide firms with cheap labor. Like Lincoln, the progressive conservative will want a state-supported public education system that trains students to take their place in the economy, and like Theodore Roosevelt and Dwight Eisenhower, he'll break with right-wingers to back a national welfare system.

Unlike the Democrats, progressive conservatism is a pro-growth party and on the side of free enterprise. It will oppose burdensome regulations and departures from the rule of law that serve little purpose apart from entrenching a left-wing elite. It will want future generations to enjoy a benign climate but will oppose anti-growth extremists who pose as experts to shut down energy industries and kill jobs on the basis of fanciful doomsday predictions.

While he is a conservative, the progressive conservative is not a reactionary. He supports economic growth and has little patience for the right-winger who blames social ills on what he calls neoliberalism. What such people have missed is that pro-growth policies are pro-family and that we'll want to pass on to our descendants an economy that doesn't ask them to eat nuts and berries in the forest.

The progressive conservative is pro-natalist. *Non omnis moriar*, he thinks. I do not wholly die, nor does America, and we are bound in a compact with our descendants. He will therefore fault the Democrats for failing to exorcise the Zero Population Growth movement from their party. A preferential option for homosexuals and the celebration of abortion and euthanasia have made them the party of infertility and death. The progressive conservative doesn't harbor ill-feelings towards gays, but his preferential option is for the next generation. At the same time, there are Democratic policies which, while burdened by wasteful special interest favors, are pro-natalist, and they deserve to be emulated, particularly the favorable tax treatment accorded to families with children.

The progressive conservative believes, with the founders, that good government requires something more than an intelligently designed constitution, that it's going to take a virtuous citizenry as well, and that there's a role for the state in promoting virtue. It's true that when the government does interfere with our choices, it's often in the wrong way and at the wrong time. Mostly, we can sort ourselves out so long as we have solid jobs. But then the government is properly charged with creating a jobs economy and policing corruption, and it's often failed to do that.

What pro-natalism requires are parents who raise families, and that in turn will require more jobs that employ fathers. With the pandemic, our labor participation rate, measuring the number of adults with jobs, fell drastically, and people are coming back to work very slowly. They're staying at home, in front of their computers. It's called the Big Resignation and it's not healthy. So too, paying people not to work and a universal basic income are profoundly demoralizing. What's missing are the virtues of Theodore Roosevelt's man in the arena, the strenuous person who dares and takes chances and who picks himself up if he falls.

These are virtues sometimes lacking in younger American males, supine, gender-confused, and coddled with the thought that all must have prizes. They're ill-suited for permanent relationships, and many have become drop-outs in marriage markets. That's a form of genetic suicide, and we'd expect it to be self-correcting. But genetics is not enough and needs to be bolstered by a progressive conservative jobs economy.

III · DRAINING THE SWAMP

If I was in a town where there were twelve fountains, and I
knew with certainty that one of them was poisoned, I would
be obliged to warn everyone to stay away from that
fountain, and to name the poisoner.

BLAISE PASCAL

CHAPTER TEN

American Corruption

W E BEGAN, as a country, with the idea that we'd free ourselves of corruption, and yet we're one of the most corrupt countries in the First World. That costs us and makes us poorer than we would be with honest public officials. Right-wingers have foolishly let the Left assume ownership of the issue, but it's one that calls for a progressive conservative response.

The Republic of Virtue

Without the fear of corruption, we would never have had a country. America was born in J. G. A. Pocock's Machiavellian Moment, when the patriots of 1776 sought to create a republic free of monarchical corruption. What corruption meant to them were the positions or "places" the king handed out to his courtiers and hangers on. By contrast, a republic would be populated with disinterested citizens who put their country's needs above their own interests.

At the 1787 Constitutional Convention, James Madison thought we might cure corruption through what he called "filtration,"[1] where what would be filtered was democracy. The voters would elect the House of Representatives, which in turn would choose the senators, and both bodies would pick the president.[2] Such a system would "extract from the mass of the Society" those who "feel most strongly the proper motives to pursue the end of their appointment, and be most capable to devise the proper means of attaining it." In that way, the most senior places in government would be occupied by "the purest and noblest characters" in society.[3]

What Madison proposed was something close to parliamentary government, where the MPs choose the prime minister. His ideas went nowhere at the Constitutional Convention, however. On July 16, 1787, the delegates voted for the Connecticut Compromise, under which the states would have equal representation in the Senate and state legislatures would decide how to choose senators. There would still be filtration, but now the states would do the filtering, and as a strong nationalist Madison hated this. The next morning the dispirited nationalists from the large states of Virginia and Pennsylvania met over breakfast to consider their options. Some thought they should make the best of it. Others argued for a walkout, and since he was the strongest and most inflexible of nationalists, Madison was likely of this number. The Connecticut Compromise had caused "serious anxiety,"[4] he wrote, and he seems to have wanted to bring the Convention to an end without a new constitution and with perhaps a breakup of the country. He had lost, and he knew it.[5]

If there wasn't a walkout, the credit goes to Gouverneur Morris, who was the first to recognize that the nationalists might still win the trick if the president were popularly elected, for he would then draw power to the national government. The president is the only person voted on by the nation as a whole, and when Congress is in gridlock, a president can get things done through executive orders and his guidance of the administrative state. The president is also the head of state, the symbol of the country, the person who gives his name to the period in which he governs. We live under a presidential constitution, and for that we can praise or blame Gouverneur Morris.

All this Morris realized within a few hours after Madison proposed a walkout and said so in a speech he made about corruption. In proposing a popularly elected president, he knew that in time he'd bring nationalists like Madison around. But that wouldn't give him a majority of the votes, and Morris had to appeal to other delegates and specifically to their fear of corruption. They had wanted a congressionally appointed executive, he said, but:

If the Legislature elect, it will be the work of intrigue, of cabal, and of faction: it will be like the election of a pope by a conclave of cardinals; real merit will rarely be the title of the appointment.[6]

By August 24, the delegates had voted seven times for a president chosen by Congress, and they thought the issue had been settled. It wasn't, though. Gouverneur Morris returned to the attack to warn of corruption were the president were chosen by Congress. "Cabal & corruption are attached to that mode of election."[7] He proposed a popular election for the president, and while this gained three more votes, it still failed, six to five.[8] That was as close as we came to a popularly elected president at the Philadelphia Convention.

On August 31 the delegates created a Committee on Unfinished Parts, with one delegate from each state. They were supposed to fine-tune what they had agreed to, but instead the Committee produced a very different document with a plan for electing presidents very similar to what we have now in Article II. The task of persuading the other delegates to accept the new plan fell to Morris, who had been a member of the Committee. The new system for choosing a president was designed to address the possibility of corruption, he explained. "The principal advantage aimed at was that of taking away the opportunity for cabal," which the delegates would have taken to mean corruption. A legislative appointment would have introduced "the danger of intrigue & faction."[9]

The delegates never knew that they had created a presidential form of government. They didn't anticipate the rise of democracy, the extension of the franchise, the party system, the telegraph, the railways and highway system, the internet, and all the features of modernity. But what they gave us was a country united under our strong presidential form of government.

It all began with Morris's speech on July 17, and it was the fear of corruption that carried the day.

How Did That Work Out?

The dream of a corruption-free republic didn't last very long. At the 1787 Convention, democracy had been a dirty word, but in the age of Andrew Jackson it was the barriers to democracy that were seen as illegitimate. At his rowdy inauguration, his supporters came to cheer their hero and also to find a job in the new administration. The government had been staffed by his opponents, and Jackson replaced 10 percent of them with people loyal to him. That was the beginning of the "spoils system," the idea that a president was entitled to replace the prior administration's civil servants with his own men. That's why Abraham Lincoln spent much of his first months in office worrying about who the postmasters were to be. And it's how Tammany Hall was able to fill up police and fire departments with loyal Democrats.

That began to change with civil service reform and the 1883 Pendleton Act. The Act banned the pay-for-play practice of federal politicians who solicited campaign funds from job seekers. It also required that certain appointments be based on merit through competitive exams.[10] But like water that seeps to find its level, the corrupt always find means to evade anti-corruption laws, and today America isn't a poster child for purity in government.

So just how corrupt are we? What we're interested in is public corruption, where public officials misbehave, and not the private chiseling where one person cheats another. We're also looking for something more than the number of criminal indictments for bribery. The truly corrupt state might be captured by corrupt officials and prosecute no one. Corrupt leaders might even insulate themselves in office by accusing their opponents of corruption. That's what happens in Russia, where the Anti-Corruption Foundation found itself charged with money laundering after it exposed the corruption of Vladimir Putin's political allies. Even when the police go after the right people, corruption is sometimes caught, sometimes not. The evidence of wrongdoing is often hard to come by without the kind of FBI sting operation that brought down Congressman Michael Myers (D-NJ) in the Abscam scandal portrayed in the film *American Hustle*.

Even if no laws are broken, a country can still be corrupt. Corruption is mostly a game played under the radar screen through pay-for-play cooperation and back-scratching that isn't criminal but that really amounts to corruption. Hunter Biden traded on his father's name to make money from corrupt foreign companies, and smelly as that was, it wasn't a crime. It was only criminal if there were a quid pro quo and if Joe Biden favored the firm in exchange for the gift to his son, and that's next to impossible to prove. It's not even a crime if it's just the kind of logrolling where one favor is traded for another.

> A political logroll ... is the swap of one official act for another. Representative A agrees with Representative B to vote for milk price supports, if B agrees to vote for tighter controls on air pollution. A President appoints C as an ambassador, which Senator D asked the President to do, in exchange for D's promise to vote to confirm E as a member of the National Labor Relations Board. Governance would hardly be possible without these accommodations, which allow each public official to achieve more of his principal objective while surrendering something about which he cares less, but the other politician cares more strongly.[11]

That's how the wheels are greased in politics, and everyone does it.

Before convicting an official for corruption, federal courts want to see money cross hands. And even when it does, that might not amount to bribery. So the Supreme Court held in reversing the conviction of former Virginia Governor Bob McDonnell.[12] Star Scientific, a Virginia drug company, wanted the FDA to approve its signature product, Anatabloc. That would require expensive testing and clinical trials, however, and Star Scientific couldn't afford to do this by itself. So the Star Scientific CEO, Jonnie Williams, asked McDonnell to get Virginia's public universities to do it for free.

Williams was a highly persuasive individual. He took the governor's wife to New York on a $20,000 shopping spree. There was also a $50,000 "loan" to McDonnell's company, a Rolex watch, a set of golf clubs, holidays, and dinners, $175,000 in all over a two-year period. There was no question about the size of the gifts, but had the governor really taken official action to repay the favors or agreed to do so? That's what is needed to prove a charge of bribery.[13]

There wasn't official action in the sense of McDonnell ordering Virginia officials to help Williams and Star Scientific. Short of this, however, McDonnell did everything he could to get them on board. He hosted an event with Williams, even popping an Anatabloc pill and announcing that it was working well for him. His conduct might have been "distasteful," ruled the Supreme Court, but it didn't add up to bribery. All he had done was give Williams the routine courtesies that all politicians provide for their constituents, and if it didn't take, that was because everyone in Richmond knew that their governor was dirty and should be ignored.

The favors elected officials confer on campaign donors aren't crimes either, according to the Supreme Court. Campaign contributions will get the donor's phone calls returned, and there's nothing wrong with that, ruled Justice Anthony Kennedy in *Citizens United v. FEC*. "Ingratiation and access ... are not corruption."[14] Subsequently Chief Justice John Roberts took it one step further.

Table 10.1   Transparency International's Corruption Perceptions Index 2020

COUNTRY	RANK	SCORE	COUNTRY	RANK	SCORE
New Zealand	1	88	Australia	11	77
Denmark	1	88	Hong Kong	11	77
Finland	3	85	Austria	15	76
Switzerland	3	85	Belgium	15	76
Singapore	3	85	Iceland	17	75
Sweden	3	85	Estonia	17	75
Norway	7	84	Japan	19	74
Netherlands	8	82	Ireland	20	72
Luxembourg	9	80	Uruguay	21	71
Germany	9	80	UAE	21	71
Canada	11	77	France	23	69
UK	11	77	US	25	67

Not merely will campaign donors gain access, but they can expect that the officials they support will respond to their interests. So far from that being a problem, said Roberts, it's "a central feature of democracy."[15]

So objective measures of corruption, in terms of criminal convictions, don't tell the whole story. They don't catch the pay-for-play favors which, if not criminal, look like corruption. What is needed is a more subjective measure of the kind provided by a highly respected German NGO, Transparency International, in its Corruption Perceptions Index (CPI). On a score of 1 to 100, the CPI ranks countries based on reports from respected observers, including businessmen, lawyers, and experts from the country in question.[16] People are asked questions such as the following:

- Has the government been captured by special interests?

- Is corruption a problem in the court system? The tax bureau? Inspection bodies?

- Are misbehaving public officeholders prosecuted or penalized?

The CPI is the most widely followed measure of public corruption. It has been criticized for its lack of objectivity,[17] but objectivity is overrated, and any subjective ranking system must inevitably rely on judgment calls. On it, the US is tied with Chile at 25, behind many of its First World competitors. We score moderately well on competitiveness and country-level risk and not at all well on the rule of law.

The Cost of Corruption

That's going to hurt. Figure 10.1 estimates a country's 2019 per capita gross domestic product from its 2019 CPI ranking for 138 countries, from the corrupt and poor Democratic Republic of the Congo to the honest and rich Luxembourg and Singapore. The (ordinary least squares) straight line estimates how public corruption is correlated with poverty and accounts for more than 60 percent of the relationship between the two variables. Corruption makes a country poorer, and that's consistent with the other empirical studies that report that public corruption impoverishes people.[18]

Figure 10.1   Less Corruption, More Wealth

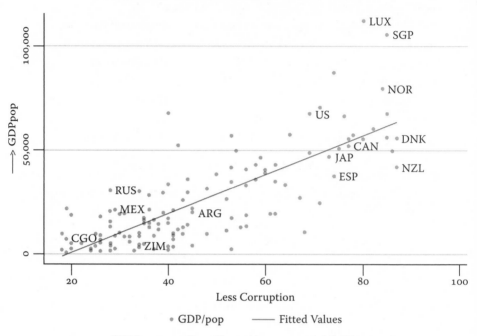

GDP/pop = 934*Less Corruption − 17,736. Adj. R-sq. = 0.62

Sources: World Economic Outlook − GDP per capita. International Monetary Fund, Oct. 2019 (retrieved March 30, 2020; Transparency International Corruption Perceptions Index, 2019.

The US's CPI score of 67 is nothing to brag about. We're richer and less corrupt than developing and undeveloped countries but more corrupt than many of our First World competitors. Figure 10.1 is just a model, of course, and models don't necessary say much about an individual country. Within the United States, however, there's evidence of the cost of corruption at the state level. As we saw, cross-country prosecutions might not tell us much since the truly corrupt state might not prosecute anyone or might prosecute the wrong people. But when the feds prosecute corruption at the state level, the problem of tainted prosecutions is minimized because the federal Justice Department can be presumed to employ uniform standards across the country. And what such studies have found is that more federal prosecutions for corruption means less economic growth in a state.[19]

As a matter of common observation, Louisiana and Mississippi (first and second, respectively, in federal corruption prosecutions per capita) aren't exactly economic dynamos. Another study found that corrupt states have lower bond ratings, which means they'll pay higher interest rates on their public debt, where the burden will fall on the taxpayers.[20]

The fraudulent or criminally irresponsible firm that escapes prosecution harms everyone touched by it. It will flourish while the honest and efficient firm might fail in the market. Even if not actually corrupt, the crony capitalist who milks the system will waste money in lobbying and draw resources from better firms that fail to invest in politics. In sum, public corruption rewards the undeserving and imposes a cost on everyone else.

CHAPTER ELEVEN

Where Did We Go Wrong?

As seen in Table 10.1, Denmark beats us hands down on public corruption and government integrity. But while Francis Fukuyama said that "getting to Denmark" should be the goal of public policy,[1] that might seem an impossible dream given that country's homogeneity. Societies that are ethnically similar are more trusting[2] and less corrupt.[3] As for America, we're not especially homogenous, and we can't turn ourselves into Denmark. As a self-styled "nation of immigrants," America prides itself on its diversity, and we're not about to change that and wouldn't want to even if we could. On the other hand, other countries that beat us in the CPI rankings, such as Australia and Canada, are far more welcoming to immigrants and just as diverse. Evidently, ethnic diversity isn't an excuse to throw up our hands at corruption.

Bigness

There's another difference between Denmark and us. It's a small country, we're a big one, and big countries have a corruption problem. We're the third-largest country, both in size and in population, and it's the latter that matters most. Geographic barriers were the more pressing question at our founding, when modern means of transportation and communication had not been invented. Now, however, population is the more relevant factor, and in a study of 140 countries I found that more people meant more corruption even after taking other relevant factors into account.[4]

The question of the optimal size of a country greatly divided the delegates at their 1787 Constitutional Convention. Madison warned about the corruption of special interests that bleed the public purse and said we'd see more of this in small states. The bigger the country, the less likely that one group would find itself in a majority and be able to oppress minority groups. We'd have Episcopalians and bankers and tobacco farmers, but none of them would amount to a majority of the whole country. They'd also be dispersed and unable to unite at the national level. That, said Madison, was an argument for a strong national government, but few of the other delegates agreed with him.

Madison's ideas now look very dated, given technological changes. In the eighteenth century, with all its barriers to travel and communication, interest groups weren't able organize at the national level. What Madison hadn't foreseen was how the revolution in transportation and communication along with the expansion of the federal government would change the cost-benefit equation. Today it's about as easy to form a national interest group as a state interest group, and there's much more bang for your buck if you legislate from Washington, DC, than from Dover, Delaware. Because of this, the greater concern today is the influence of concentrated interest groups at the national level, which is to say oppression by minorities, not majorities. And that's an argument for smallness, not bigness.

Mancur Olson described minoritarian misbehavior as a collective action problem in *The Rise and Decline of Nations*. We'd all be better off if we could band together and prevent interest groups from wastefully directing public spending their way. But when the benefits of combining together are dispersed across all American citizens, it's easy to free ride and do nothing. The interest group doesn't have the same problem because its numbers are far fewer.

A classic example is government protection of the sugar industry, where tariff barriers raise sugar prices 64 to 92 percent above the world average.[5] Poorer Americans spend a disproportionately greater amount of their earnings on food, and a sweet tooth will hurt them more than it will hurt rich Americans. But they're no match for the lobbyists employed by America's sugar producers. It's 120 sugar producers on one side versus 340 million American consumers on the other side, and it's harder for the dispersed, nationwide consumer group to organize on a collective basis against the smaller, concentrated group of sugar producers.

So Madison did have a point, but it wasn't the way he thought. He said that in an "extended republic," a majority faction would find it hard to get organized. That's correct when it's a dispersed majority of consumers up against a minority group like the sugar manufacturers. In a large country, wasteful interest groups get formed, not benign ones.

At the 1787 Convention, the other delegates weren't buying Madison's argument for bigness. He was from the biggest state, Virginia, and the other delegates were from smaller states. They didn't want a country dominated by the largest states, and echoing Montesquieu they thought that small is beautiful. Like Madison, the French author feared the influence of factions or interest groups. In small states, however, he thought there would be fewer of them. People would know each other better and wouldn't need to organize into groups. "The public good is better sensed, better understood, closer to each citizen."[6]

That's probably true today in smaller states such as Denmark, where people have similar tastes and interests. The Danes like bicycling and pickled herring, and if they go to church it will likely be a Lutheran one. Nearly 100 percent of them speak Danish, a language nobody else speaks unless they're from Greenland. They have a stronger sense of the common good and find it easier to unite to promote it. What they have going for them is a small population. If the country were twenty times bigger, it would be more diverse and less unified. Its leaders would be more remote from the people and their policies tainted more by interest group corruption.

That's what happened to us as we grew in numbers. By the 1830s, interest group corruption became a serious political issue with the Second Bank of the United States, which Andrew Jackson refused to recharter. Then during the Progressive Era, the honest storekeeper on Main Street denounced a corrupt Wall Street. We saw the same clash in the 2008–09 bank bailouts, which were said to have rescued our financial system but which led to a jobless economic recovery and shifted wealth from a large number of dispersed and disorganized losers to a small number of powerful, concentrated financial winners.[7]

If bigness is badness, that's an argument for federalism and the devolution of authority from the federal government to the states. That would permit us to sort ourselves out according to the kind of government we want and free us from one-size-fits-all policies ill-suited in a divided country. It would also permit people to exit corrupt states, and that would make for a more honest country. States would compete with each other to provide honest government in the manner suggested by Frederick Jackson Turner in his frontier thesis.[8]

Corrupt states would have an incentive to clean up their acts because they'll be losing citizens and the tax base that goes along with them. But jurisdictional competition by the individual states might not do the trick. Corruption can become so deep-seated that a state won't police dishonest local officials, and that was an argument for the FBI in the era of Al Capone. What this argues for is a mixed regime in dealing with corruption: decentralization but with federal oversight of local corruption.

That's a message we learned in 1964 when local officials conspired in the murders of three civil rights workers in Philadelphia, Mississippi. James Chaney, Andy Goodman, and Michael Schwerner had come to the state to promote black voter registration and were arrested by Deputy Sheriff Cecil Price for speeding. He soon released them but not before organizing a lynch party that killed the three.

At the time, there wasn't a federal statue against murder, but the Department of Justice charged them with the lesser crime of conspiring to deprive the victims of their rights under a Reconstruction-era statute. A local Mississippi judge subpoenaed the FBI agents investigating the crime to reveal their sources, but Acting Attorney General Nicholas Katzenbach refused to allow this, thinking the Mississippi court system so corrupt and tainted with racism that the information would be turned over to the murderers and their lawyers.[9] Before the jury, Doar explained why the case was being argued in federal court.

I am here because your National Government is concerned about your local law enforcement … When local law enforcement officials become involved as participants in violent crime and use their position, power and authority to accomplish this, there is very little to be hoped for, except with assistance from the Federal Government.[10]

The case went to the Supreme Court, which held that the murderers could be prosecuted under federal law.[11] Remarkably, none of the accused were tried for murder in a Mississippi state court until forty years later, after the voting rights campaign for which the three had died finally bore fruit and a different kind of electorate had cast its ballots.

Presidential Government

There are three different systems of government today, each with about the same number of people. The oldest is dictatorship, once in decline but today in the ascendant in the form of the Beijing Consensus. The other two are democratic, with about two billion people each. The presidential system, born in the United States and exported to about eighty countries, features a separation of powers, usually with the bicameral legislature we have in America. The parliamentary or Westminster system originated in England and was exported throughout the British Empire when the former colonies won their independence. It's also the most common system in Europe. It lacks the separation of powers since parliament is supreme and appoints the prime minister. Most parliamentary systems are unicameral, although some, like that of Australia, have both an effective upper and lower house in parliament.

Dictatorial countries are corrupt countries. In Transparency International's CPI ranking, the countries at the bottom of the list are Syria (13), South Sudan (12) and Somalia (9). Venezuela is sixteenth and Haiti eighteenth. Even China, which seeks to project an image of honesty, scores a lowly 41 on the CPI. As between presi-

dential and parliamentary systems, theorists have speculated about
which better polices corruption.[12] But which system does so is
really an empirical question, and when you look at the numbers, as
I did, parliamentary systems are clearly less corrupt than presidential ones.[13] And you can easily see why. The problem of corruption
is embedded in presidential but not parliamentary systems.

There are three reasons for this. First, parliamentary governments are better able to check a misbehaving and corrupt executive
than presidential governments. Instead of the no-confidence
motion in parliament, where a majority of MPs can defeat a government, we have an impeachment power with its requirement of a
two-thirds vote in the Senate to remove a president. That's a near
impossibility, and it's made impeachments a dead letter except as
an attention-getting device. Presidents also control the flow of
information from the agencies of government and can sit on scan-
dals until they fade away. When challenged, they can assert a doctrine of executive privilege to deny oversight powers to Congress,
and when congressional committees hold hearings to get to the
bottom of a scandal, they're condemned as partisan fishing expedi-
tions. There is nothing like the kind of monitoring powers an opposition enjoys in a parliamentary regime, where prime ministers are
subjected to a daily grilling in parliament.

Second, legislation often enacts corrupt interest group bargains,
and they're harder to undo in presidential regimes. Getting legislation passed or repealed in America is like waiting for three cherries
to line up in a Las Vegas slot machine. Absent a supermajority in
Congress to override a presidential veto, one needs the simultane-
ous concurrence of the president, Senate, and House. That's not a
bad thing if the heightened barriers mean that good bills will survive
and bad bills won't. But if this might prevent bad laws from being
enacted, it also impedes their repeal after they're enacted. So the
choice is between ex ante screening before a law is enacted in a
presidential regime and the subsequent ex post reversibility that is
possible in a parliamentary one, where one needs only one cherry
from the one-armed bandit and where a majority government can
do what it likes. And in general, reversibility trumps ex ante screen-

ing because it is easier to identify bad laws with the benefit of hindsight. When one parliament reverses a prior parliament, it does so with more information than the prior enacting parliament. It will know better what works and what doesn't. Easier passed, easier mended.

Third, there's a greater problem of minoritarian misbehavior under the separation of powers in a presidential regime. Enacting a law is a simple enough matter in a majority parliamentary regime, but it can be the very devil under the separation of powers of presidential government, especially when this is made worse by the filibuster's requirement of sixty votes in the US Senate. That's going to require horse trading, and the earmarks that masters of pork like former Senator Robert Byrd (D-WV) employed to give us the fifty-odd Robert Byrd centers for this, that, and the other thing in West Virginia. It's wasteful, but the costs are borne by American taxpayers in general, while the benefits are concentrated in the Congressman's state or district. It's small pennies for the former, big bucks for the latter, and because of this the former won't notice it while the latter will. It's the same collective action problem that explains why the small sugar lobby can get away with wastefully imposing costs on dispersed American sugar consumers.

To reverse this, what is needed are political parties that will support the country's general welfare rather than the narrow interest of an electoral district. That's something one's more likely to find in a parliamentary system than a presidential system. In a presidential system, national parties are weaker, and one votes for the Congressman who brings home the bacon. In parliamentary systems, however, national parties are stronger, and in two-party systems parties requires broad, national support to win an election. A prime minister won't have to bribe an MP to get his vote. Instead, the party whips can bend a member to do their bidding with the threat of denying him the party's nomination at the next election. That is unthinkable in America, but in parliamentary systems it results in national parties that seek to acquire a reputation of putting the common, national good ahead of wasteful local projects.[14]

Campaign Finance Laws

Compared to the campaign finance laws of other First World nations, our laws are permissive. They let donors do things here that they can't elsewhere. That isn't necessarily to say that other countries got it right and we got it wrong. Tackling corruption can trench on rights of free expression that we value more highly than people in other countries. All the same, this helps explain why we score poorly on Transparency International's measure of political corruption.

Other countries limit the amount that political candidates can spend on their campaigns. Beginning with *Buckley v. Valeo*,[15] however, the Supreme Court struck down limits on campaign spending. That's going to advantage a deep-pockets candidate like Donald Trump, but it also allows popular insurgents funded by small dollar donors to take on a well-financed establishment candidate. Spending limits also protect incumbents who start with name recognition and a network of supporters. It's the outside challenger who'll need to spend money to get his name out there.[16] More corruption perhaps, but more democracy too.[17]

Restrictions on campaign contributions can also boomerang and result in more, not less, political corruption. The rules are highly technical, and while that's not a problem for political sophisticates, they've tripped up naïfs and resulted in partisan prosecutions. That was the story of Dinesh D'Souza, a conservative author and felon. With his wife he contributed $10,000 to a friend's political campaign. Then he persuaded another friend and her husband to pony up a further $10,000 after promising to reimburse them. The friend was his mistress, however, and it all blew up in his face when his wife found out about the affair. Because this was a sham transaction, he was prosecuted for violating the monetary limits of American campaign finance law. He was sentenced to eight months in a halfway house, given five years of probation and a $30,000 fine, and ordered to submit to a psychiatric evaluation. All this for a first offence and for a matter that is usually the subject of an administrative fine.

Other countries limit campaign contributions, but what's different about America and makes a felon of people like D'Souza is our criminal justice system. In other countries, prosecutors are unelected civil servants with much less incentive to favor one party over another. Here they're more likely to be highly political animals with a taste for the kind of publicity that a high-profile case might generate, and they're widely thought to abuse their discretion.[18] Finally, federal prosecutors obtain a guilty plea or conviction 99 percent of the time because of criminal procedure rules tilted their way, and there's nothing like this in other First World countries. In America, therefore, stiffer campaign finance laws might give us more, not less, political corruption.

* * *

All these are things we can't or can't easily change. We're a big country, but short of secession we can't make America smaller. And if we wanted to work around presidential government, we're 235 years too late. We're also not about to undo the Supreme Court decisions that tolerate play-for-play favors by public officials. But none of this is an argument for surrender. Rather, it's an invitation to examine other ways to address public corruption. More than anywhere else, our enormous regulatory industry and our campaign finance laws have created a huge lobbying industry, and that's where to look for reforms, as we'll see in the last chapter.

IV · NATIONALISM

I have fallen in love with American names.

STEPHEN VINCENT BENÉT

CHAPTER TWELVE

Anti-Nationalism

·

PROGRESSIVE CONSERVATIVES don't need to be reminded of their country's faults. But they can take it all in, the bad and the good, from the first slave ship and Wounded Knee, and from Valley Forge to Eisenhower's crusade in Europe, and seeing it in its entirety, still love their country.

Progressive conservatives were therefore happy when Trump announced that he was a nationalist. In the past that would have gone without saying. Today, however, the word set up a firestorm of protest. There is something special about nationalism. It is a triggering word, one that provokes an angry response from scores of people.

The Libertarian

Libertarianism comes in several strains, from the anarchist-capitalist to the small-government liberal. If there's a unifying thread to libertarianism, however, it's the belief in the primacy of the individual against his enemy, the state. That can make him an anti-nationalist.

The libertarian will have noticed that the nationalist favors things he dislikes, such as a safety net to protect his more fragile fellow citizens. If the nationalist opposes open borders for immigration, that's also a problem for the libertarian. If the nationalist wants tariff walls, he exposes himself as the enemy of freedom.

Worst of all is the nationalism that throws its weight around militarily. Randolph Bourne said that "war is the health of the state," by which he meant that governments expand during wartime. Even more dangerous is the idea, found in Hegel, that a particular nation might represent the era's world-spirit and have the moral authority of the period's bearer of civilization.[1] Such a nation, said Hegel, might make war to assert its greatness and treat as barbarians the countries that lag behind it. For Hegel the Prussian state represented the vanguard of history, and something of this remained it the conceit of the George W. Bush administration that, after making war on Iraq, it could recreate a Middle East that looked like America.

Like George Orwell, the libertarian might therefore wish to distinguish between nationalism and a benign patriotism. The patriot has a sense of belonging to a particular place and being rooted in its culture. He might think this superior to what he'd find in other countries, but he'll not wish to force this on other people. He might be prepared to fight a defensive war to protect his country, but not an offensive one. By contrast, thought Orwell, a suspect nationalism will seek a nation's glory by dominating other countries.[2]

Orwell wrote that in the middle of the Second World War, when it was easy to identify nationalism with Nazi Germany and patriotism with England. But Orwell's admiration for what he saw as the national habits of the English – their kindness, their respect for the law and for people's privacy, even their love of flowers – was a kind of nationalism.[3] What he didn't like were the intellectuals who thought themselves superior to all that. When he asked what had kept a beleaguered Britain on its feet in 1941, he recognized that it wasn't the desiccated liberalism of an H. G. Wells or George Bernard Shaw. Rather, it was

> chiefly the atavistic emotion of patriotism, the ingrained feeling of English-speaking peoples that they are superior to foreigners. For the last twenty years the main object of English left-wing intellectuals has been to break this feeling down, and if they had succeeded, we might be watching SS men patrolling the London streets at this moment.[4]

That's an argument for patriotism and for nationalism, too, if you're lucky enough to live in a country like Britain or America.

In sum, nationalism can take unpleasant forms, which the libertarian rightly opposes. But he's wrong to think that nationalism must always represent primitive and illiberal sentiments from which he has freed himself. There are different kinds of nationalisms even as there are different nations, and American nationalism is among the most benign.

The Globalist

The globalist rejects nationalism because he thinks this wrongly shuts out the rest of the world. That's why Superman gave up his American citizenship in 2011. It was just too limiting. Our elites might feel the same way and think they have more in common with Oxbridge academics or Left Bank Parisians than they do with people in flyover country.

Globalism used to be called cosmopolitanism. The first cosmopolitan was Democritus. Asked what country he was from, he answered "the cosmos." Cosmopolitanism was first seen as a synonym for worldly sophistication and then as an accusation of rootlessness levelled typically against Jews. Because of its anti-Semitic connotations, the word today means a cocktail and not much else.

The cosmopolitan's place is now taken by the globalist, the person who is fascinated by what's happening in the rest of the world – the bullet trains in Japan, the bustling cities of China, and the skyscrapers in Dubai – and like Tom Friedman he'll tell us that that's the future. In books such as *The World is Flat*, Friedman argued that America had fallen behind countries such as China and that individual countries would have to sacrifice some of their sovereignty to multilateral corporations and global institutions. If we are to compete, we'd have to leave our sense of nationhood behind and open our borders to the technocratic elite.

Those kinds of ideas are catnip to our elites, who think the arc of history bends toward internationalism and themselves. Their leaders gather in Davos, Switzerland, each year at the World Economic Forum to reinforce their adherence to governance by a liberal and technocratic elite, and they've been mocked as the "Davoisie" for seeing nationalism and state sovereignty as obstacles to a better transnational future.

Sometimes the globalist has a point. The nationalist's heightened sense of loyalty to his nation might come at the cost of reducing his allegiance to more encompassing groups, such as Christendom, the working class, or humanity in general. That was the point of the film *Joyeux Noel*, which portrayed the Christmas Truce of 1914. On Christmas Eve, a German soldier begins to sing "*Stille Nacht*" and across No Man's Land is answered by a Highland regiment playing "Silent Night" on bagpipes. Eventually even the atheistic French join in, and for a day the war is forgotten. The climax of the film is a Midnight Mass, celebrated by the Scottish chaplain for the soldiers of all three armies.

The film's message was that with a stronger sense of Christian or simply of human unity and less of national pride, the madness of the First World War might have been avoided. One kind of solidarity waxes, the other wanes. But the nearer ties of nationhood will always be stronger than the remoter ones of universal brotherhood. It is a mistake to think that only the most encompassing communities count and that local allegiances are suspect because they treat the outsider as an alien. The alternative to national loyalty might be a heightened sense of duty to people in other countries, but then it might signify a cold-hearted want of sympathy to anyone outside oneself. If Davos Man has become a term of disparagement, it's because his globalism is seen to betray an indifference to those nearest him, his fellow citizens, rather than a real affection for people in other countries.

The Sophisticate

American nationalism annoys sophisticates because it reminds them that they share a country with flag-waiving Middle Americans in flyover country. If the rubes haven't gotten with the program, that's just false consciousness on their part. "They get bitter," said Obama. "They cling to guns or religion."[5] Some were "truthers" who denied that he was born in America. That was false, of course, but what really bothered the sophisticate was the thought that this should matter. You'd prefer someone from Oklahoma?

We're divided over nationalism in our politics, and it's partly a matter of money. In America's richest zip codes, Joe Biden raised $486 million compared to $167 million for Trump.[6] It's also a matter of education. Biden won 55 percent of the college-educated vote while Trump got only 42 percent.[7] Mostly it's a matter of class. Like the U-words and Oxford accent of the English upper class, there is a received American culture that defines what one is permitted to read, watch, and say. The cultural signifiers are hyper-technical and ever changing, and they serve little purpose other than to exclude the backward and politically incorrect. And so nationalism has become one of the wedge issues. It's like lunchtime in middle school, and today no one at the cool kids table is a nationalist.

That's how our elites responded to Trump's nationalism. If he was a nationalist, the Left was necessarily anti-nationalist. And the hostility to American nationalism has increased in recent years. Taking a knee during the National Anthem at a sports event was a lonely protest in 2018 but two years later was de rigueur. The Left had taken the *New York Times*'s 1619 Project to heart, one in which American history was a wretched tale of racial oppression and without redeeming features save for the contributions of African Americans. The American Revolution was the work of enslavers, and the Civil War deaths, which Lincoln in his Second Inaugural saw as divine retribution for the sin of slavery, did nothing to expiate the wrong.

The Identitarian

Identitarians divide Americans and weaken nationalism by turning every political question into one about the welfare of their racial, religious, or linguistic group. In Europe they might be white nationalists and linguistic separatists. Here in America, identitarianism is primarily the province of the Left, of Black Lives Matter and the *Washington Post*. It is what progressive conservatives have always opposed. They're identitarians, but their identity is American, and that embraces all races and creeds. Theodore Roosevelt said that "we welcome the German or the Irishman who becomes an American," but added that

> We have no use for the German or Irishman who remains such ... [W]e want only Americans, and, provided they are such, we do not care whether they are of native or of Irish or of German ancestry. We have no room in any healthy American community for a German-American vote or an Irish-American vote, and it is contemptible demagogy to put planks into any party platform with the purpose of catching such a vote.[8]

No one would put it quite so strongly today. We discovered that hyphenated Americanism need take nothing away from loyalty to country and that we can take pride in the mix of cultures that make up America. That was the theme of those old war movies and comic books about ethnically mixed platoons. There'd be a sergeant from nowhere in particular and a troop composed of a cowboy called Tex, a wiry Jewish kid from Brooklyn, an Irish brawler from Boston, and a black fellow from Chicago. The message was: We're all in this together against the foreign enemy.

That's also the sense you'll get if you visit the National Museum of African American History and Culture in Washington. The emphasis was on the African American experience – and what else should it be? But if that was the intention, the museum is in one respect a failure. While designed with solely African Americans in mind, visitors to the museum from other races and cultures will come away with the feeling that you can't understand American culture and history without appreciating how much the African American contribution is a part of it. Can you imagine American music shorn of African American influences? Or American sports without Jackie Robinson and Muhammad Ali? Same with novels, movies, you name it.

It's not about you unless you're black, and yet it is about you if you're an American. It's about a history, a shared experience that is

American to its core. It's different, however, when group loyalty excludes any sense of attachment to America, for then it amounts to anti-nationalism. If all of American history should be seen from the perspective of slavery, as the *New York Times*'s 1619 Project would have it, there isn't much to like about the country, and the riots in our cities make perfect sense.

The Anti-American

Out of error, you can support policies that harm America and not be anti-American. That's how Republicans and Democrats used to think of each other. But today there are some people who just don't like America. The 1619 Project's Nikole Hannah-Jones is obviously one of them. So are newspapers that print stories about hundred-year-old lynchings. They were horrible, but they're only newsworthy if you think that they're going to happen again, and people who do so really have problems with America. You'd have to be someone like Kamala Harris, who thought that Jussie Smollett's absurdly unbelievable hate crime hoax was a "modern day lynching."[9]

But those old stories are true, says the anti-American. Isn't truth a defense? Are you telling us to hide the truth? Now that you mention it, that might not be a bad idea, answers the nationalist. Not hide it, perhaps, so much as permit us to forget it.

Ernest Renan made the case for historical amnesia in an 1882 essay entitled "What is a Nation." For the French it's not race or religion, he said. Rather, the nationalist will remember his country's glorious moments and pay less attention to the inglorious ones. "Forgetfulness, even historical errors, are essential in the creation of a nation. If the citizens of a nation have something in common, they have to have forgotten a good many things about their origins."

If Renan was right, is America still a nation? On the Left there is a concerted effort to remember all that is shameful in American history and to suppress the great deeds done by Americans. In all the ways that matter, save for the naked force of the law and our allegiance to a set of constitutional liberties, we are divided into two nations, just as much as in 1861. So if Renan was right about what makes for nationalism, the American nationalist might ask himself if he's a secessionist.

But here's the thing. You're not much of a nationalist if you want to see the country broken up. Robert E. Lee wasn't an American nationalist when he assumed the command of the Army of Northern Virginia. The true nationalist must want the country to stay united. He'll search for something we all share in common, and if the mystic chords of memory have been erased, all that remains is our creed of constitutionally protected liberties. If the American reactionary rejects them, why he's anti-American too!

CHAPTER THIRTEEN

Liberal Nationalism

JOSEPH DE MAISTRE (1753–1821) said that he had never met a man. He had met Frenchmen, Italians, and so on, but as for a "man," he'd never met one. So, too, I have never met a "nationalist." Canadian nationalists, American nationalists, even Quebec nationalists, but never a nationalist tout court. So I can't say anything about nationalism or whether it be good or bad.

I am persuaded that there are perverse forms of nationalism, but as an American nationalist I needn't take much interest in them. There is a revival of right-wing nationalism led by "National Conservative" fans of the present Hungarian government. But if that country seems to flirt with illiberalism, what is that to me? What interests me, as an American, is American nationalism, and if I can take pride in being an American, it's because American nationalism is liberal nationalism.

The NatCons betray the spirit of American nationalism by failing to understand what makes it American: its roots in our founding documents. We don't have the reigning monarch other countries have or a state religion. Instead, the focal point for nationalist and patriotic sentiments is the sense that America has a special mission to promote liberty as promised by the Declaration of Independence and guaranteed by the Bill of Rights. Those ideals constitute our identities as Americans, and while the NatCon who rejects them might be a good Hungarian nationalist, objectively he is anti-American – which is going to be a problem if he is in fact an American.

The importance of constitutional liberty as a nationalist icon has so frequently been noted that the point might seem trivial. "The American Constitution is unlike any other," said historian Hans

Kohn. "It represents the lifeblood of the American nation, its supreme symbol and manifestation." Other countries had their common cultures or religions. What America had was an idea. Robert Penn Warren wrote, "To be American is not ... a matter of blood; it is a matter of an idea – and [American] history is the image of that idea."

That was also Lincoln's idea of American nationalism in a speech on July 4, 1858. For some in his audience, the holiday was a reminder of their ancestors' patriotism and bravery. But when he spoke, half of the country was foreign-born or the descendants of people who had lived elsewhere in 1776. It didn't matter, said Lincoln. They were still entitled to celebrate the fourth, to call themselves Americans. And what made them so was something other than ties of blood.

> When they look through that old Declaration of Independence they find that those old men say that "We hold these truths to be self-evident, that all men are created equal," and then they feel that that moral sentiment taught in that day evidences their relation to those men, that it is the father of all moral principle in them, and that they have a right to claim it as though they were blood of the blood, and flesh of the flesh, of the men who wrote that Declaration, and so they are. That is the electric cord in that Declaration that links the hearts of Patriotic and liberty-loving men together, that will link those patriotic hearts as long as the love of freedom exists in the minds of men throughout the world.[1]

That looks like a paradox. If every liberty-loving person supports the principles of the Declaration, what makes this a badge of American nationhood? On that basis, however, families and friendship don't count for much either. If nationalism is the powerful sentiment that I take it to be (at least for nationalists), then the respect for liberal principles is strengthened when they become a national symbol. John Quincy Adams understood the difference between the nationalist's and the internationalist's love of liberty in an 1821 Independence Day address. "The tie which binds us to our country is not more holy in the sight of God, but it is more deeply seated in our nature, more tender and endearing, than that common link which merely connects us with our fellow-mortal, man." We value constitutionally protected liberties not merely because they are admirable in themselves but because they are *American* liberties.

That's why it is so absurd to detect the whiff of fascism in American nationalism, and if historical perspective were needed, Jean-François Revel provided it when he observed that while the dark night of fascism is always said to be descending in America, somehow it lands only in Europe. That's because for Americans, illiberalism is self-defeating, and if some Americans have been illiberal, in time they've been seen to be un-American, and we reject them as a body rejects a foreign object. That's what happened to Senator Joe McCarthy (R-WI), and it's something Trump has discovered, to his cost.

Some anti-liberal NatCons will nevertheless tell me I've missed something. I've defined American nationalism in terms of the beliefs of the founders. They call that *credal nationalism* and tell me that we're more than a creed. We're a people. As indeed we are and easily recognizable as Americans when we travel elsewhere with a loud ebullience that masks a quiet nobility.

We show we're Americans by the things we like: baseball and apple pie, Johnny Cash and Chuck Berry. You can be an American if you don't like them. It's just that you might be a wee bit more American if you did like them. You tell me how much you like Glenn Gould and how you hate the Grateful Dead. George Eliot speaks to you, but not James Baldwin. You've forgotten where you were born, and then you tell me you're a nationalist. I get it. You love America. It's just Americans you dislike.

So yes, there is something more than credal nationalism. But what's left of it? The problem is that, the founders' creed apart, we're not much of a nation. We're as divided as we were in 1861, and if you reject the creed, perhaps you ought to be a secessionist. The only things that keep us from splitting apart are the inertia of our legal regime and the way we're united by our commitment as Americans to liberal principles.

The anti-liberal NatCon's great mistake is to assume that liberalism and what he calls credal nationalism exclude a sense of membership in a nation and a feeling of loyalty to fellow Americans. Liberals are lonely and isolated individuals, he says, with no greater attachment to anything greater than themselves than consumers have to the different brands of toothpaste at the drugstore. That's wrong, says the anti-liberal. We're not just consumers. We're also products, products of a culture that defines us as Americans.

The anti-liberal NatCon is right about that, but what he's missed is that, for Americans, our culture is also one of legal rights. We're not Hungarians, who are rescued from the dislocations of modernity by a cultural nationalism based on Christianity and a common language (which Ferdinand Tönnies called *gemeinschaft*) as opposed to a bloodless and purely legal relationship with one's state (Tönnies' *gesellschaft*). In a Hungary, said Ernest Gellner, the deserted village was reinvented in the nation-state, and "a mobile anonymous society simulated a closed, cosy community using the idiom of Gemeinschaft."[2] But it is otherwise in America, where liberal constitutional icons take the place of *la patrie*. Here gemeinschaft uses the idiom of gesellschaft, and the community is formed by its identification with legal and constitutional liberties and a history in which those rights were defended and enlarged, from Bunker Hill to Selma, Alabama. We are People of the Book, and the sense of community is no less strong for that.

A lot of things go into our idea of nationhood. They include Little Round Top and Pearl Harbor, Jackie Robinson stealing home and the Miracle on Ice, Harvard Square and Fenway Park, Mount Vernon and Fallingwater, Bourbon Street and the Golden Gate Bridge, Cab Calloway's "Minnie the Moocher" and Pete Seeger's "Which side are you on." They also include the preamble to the Declaration of Independence and the Gettysburg Address, and if the anti-liberal NatCon can read them without emotion, he's not much of a nationalist.

That's why the progressive conservative doesn't complain that he's been replaced in America. He knows that we've always been replaced and that we're none the worse for it. He doesn't feel that, without leaving America, America has left him. Instead, he lives in a country that remained America when it welcomed new arrivals who were faithful to the American creed. He doesn't care for the immigrant who rejects our liberal traditions, but then he doesn't have much use for the native-born anti-liberal either. If he blames anyone for anything, it's a left-wing educational establishment that abandoned its responsibility to teach what is honorable and noble in our liberal heritage as well as the skills students need to take their place in our economy.

CHAPTER FOURTEEN

Glory and Fraternity

NATIONALISM CAN TAKE two different forms. *Vertical* nationalism desires its country's glory, its preeminence over other countries. That's the nationalism of the right-wing Trump supporter who wants to Make American Great Again. There's another kind of nationalism, however, called *horizontal* nationalism, which the right-wing nationalist often fails to recognize. It rests on a sense of kinship to and fraternity with fellow citizens and implies a generous social safety net for those who need help.

Glory

Vertical nationalism rests on a sense of shared glory in a country's greatness. Glory is a discredited word, one we might be thought to have left behind along with the Knights of the Round Table. But it's an ineradicable part of our nature, just like self-love. We need to think well of ourselves, and with glory self-love is validated by the esteem of others.

A country's glory might be based on many different things – sports heroes, a literary and artistic heritage – and we have all of that. We're the country of Jesse Owens and Joe DiMaggio, Herman Melville and Robert Frost, Scott Joplin and Samuel Barber. We don't just have cities – we have sounds for each. We have Motown, New Orleans Dixieland, Chicago Blues, Miami Latin, Woodstock, Nashville, Memphis, and Austin. We have West Coast jazz and America's songbook on Broadway. We have John Wayne and Humphrey Bogart, Jimmy Stewart and Kirk Douglas, Marilyn Monroe and Elizabeth Taylor. We have MIT and Silicon Valley, the Wright Brothers and the Moon landing. We do great things, and we take second place to nobody.

Then there's military might, where we're still top dog. From our modest beginnings, we've become the world's big military spender. Total world spending on the military in 2020 was $1,981 billion, and of that 39 percent or $778 billion was by the United States.[2] That's more than China, Russia, and the next six countries (each of which is our ally) put together.

What this needn't imply, however, is an adventuresome foreign policy. As Charles Krauthammer noted, a realist foreign policy is neither isolationist nor imperialist, and realism defined Trump's foreign policy goals. He was entirely without George W. Bush's illusions about exporting democracy to the Middle East or Obama's naïveté about the mullahs in Iran. He took on the foreign policy establishment in moving our embassy in Israel to Jerusalem, and while the Democrats predicted disaster, he brokered a rapprochement between the Jewish state and Arab countries in the region. He presided over the destruction of the ISIS caliphate but was the first president since Eisenhower not to take the country to war. That was vertical nationalism in the Trump years.

Fraternity

The horizontal nationalist distinguishes between citizens and non-citizens. The open borders crowd, Right and Left, doesn't. The right-wing version would deny welfare benefits to both. The left-winger would extend the same benefits to both. But like Kent in *King Lear*, the horizontal nationalist says, "I'll teach you differences." He would deny benefits to noncitizens, but in doing so he'd extend greater benefits to fellow citizens.

Nationalism implies fraternity. American nationalists take the side of their fellow Americans even as they prefer their friends over people they don't know. The norm of nationality and friendship is partiality. You're not a true friend if you're indifferent between your supposed friend and a stranger. So, too, you're not a nationalist if you don't care for your countrymen any more than you do for those from other countries. But as the nationalist does care for his countrymen, he'll want his country to provide for those in need.

The true nationalist doesn't ask how long his fellow citizens have been here. Like Lincoln, he doesn't think it's a matter of blood lines. The new arrival is as much his brother as the person whose family stretches back to the American Revolution so long as the electric cord of the Declaration runs through him. By contrast, the false nationalist lacks a sense of fraternity with his fellow citizens, and if he begrudges them their right to share in the country's welfare benefits, he reveals himself to be simply another right-winger.

Historically, Republicans have been the party of vertical nationalism and Democrats the party of horizontal nationalism. Republicans wanted the biggest military in the world – and got it. But when it came to horizontal nationalism, the Republicans found this in conflict with their right-wing principles. That kind of nationalism they left to the Democrats, to people like FDR who communicated a sense of caring about all Americans, a feeling one didn't quite get from Mitt Romney.

Today, however, the Democrats have abandoned horizontal nationalism, and as Trump is a nationalist, they are anti-nationalists. If Trump wanted to "Build the Wall," they would be the other party and take up the cause of the undocumented aliens. Before long, they charged that what was behind opposition to illegal immigration was nothing more than racism. By 2020 Democrats running for president were emboldened to propose that undocumented entrants be permitted to share in federal welfare benefits, and two-thirds of Democratic voters agreed with them.[281] That's morally defensible, to be sure, but if you don't prefer your fellow countrymen to aliens in our welfare policies, you're simply not a nationalist.

What was remarkable about the 2016 Republican victory was that, for the first time since 1956, a presidential candidate ran on a progressive conservative platform that united the two strands of nationalism. Trump found the sweet spot in American presidential politics, the place where presidential elections are won, with a combination of social conservatism and economic liberalism and a slogan to make America great again that implied both the vertical and horizontal nationalism of progressive conservatism.

V · THE PROMISE OF GOOD GOVERNMENT

They desire a better country

Hebrews 11:16

CHAPTER FIFTEEN

The Recovery of Republican Virtue

IN THE EARLY FOURTEENTH CENTURY, the Italian city of Siena commissioned an artist to tell its story. The city was at peace, prosperous and happy, and its council wanted to explain the secret of its success. The result was a series of frescoes called *The Allegory of Good Government*, and the artist was Ambrogio Lorenzetti.

In one panel, set in the country, farmers reap a bountiful harvest and shepherds bring their wool to market. In another, set in the city, craftsmen ply their trades and maidens dance hand in hand. A third panel showed how all this had come about through civic virtues represented by six female figures: peace, fortitude, prudence, magnanimity, temperance, and justice. Under the figure of justice was written, "Look how many goods derive from her and how sweet and peaceful is that life of the city where is preserved this virtue who outshines any other. She guards and defends those who honor her, and nourishes and feeds them." Justice is the virtue of the common good, which balances what is owed the state and what the state owes its citizens.[1]

The fresco stood in the city's council chamber, and Machiavelli must have seen it when he was sent by Florence on a mission to Siena. The two towns were the principal city-republics in early Renaissance Tuscany, and in his *Discourses on Livy*, Machiavelli agreed with Lorenzetti that the experiment of republican government would fail without civic virtue. Monarchies demand obedience, not virtue, from its subjects, but republics require something more. Its citizens must be willing to serve the common good, for only by doing so will they preserve the state and ensure its greatness. "It is not the particular good but the common good that makes cities great," said Machiavelli. "And without doubt this common good is not observed if not in republics."[2] When republics fall, it is by over-reaching and the vices portrayed in a companion Lorenzetti fresco, *The City State under Tyranny*, where "no one is ever in accord with the Common Good."

Pre-Renaissance humanists like Lorenzetti thought that good government rests on a foundation of private virtue, of a citizenry that feels a sense of duty to something greater than itself. They took their inspiration not from Aristotle or Aquinas so much as from classical Roman authors such as Seneca and Cicero and especially the latter's description of the *bonum commune*.

> We are not born simply for ourselves, for our country and friends are both able to claim a share in us. People are born for the sake of other people in order that they may mutually benefit each other. We ought therefore to follow Nature's lead and place the common good at the heart of our concerns.[3]

That was also how the founders understood the idea of disinterested civic virtue, but today America's departures from the common good painfully evoke Lorenzetti's dystopian fresco. We sense that we began nobly but that we've lost our way. In the previous three sections, I described the way back through progressive conservatism and its threefold promises of economic and social mobility, a corruption-free country, and nationalism, and that in turn will require the recovery of a sense of purity and the founders' republican virtue. Let the Romneyite right-winger parade his indifference to his countrymen and the left-winger preen in his hatreds. The progressive conservative will triumph over both by appealing to the civic virtue of Americans.

The Common Good Requires Republican Virtue

Like Lorenzetti and Machiavelli, George Washington thought that the common good required a leader who would promote republican virtue, and what this meant for him was the nationalism and unselfishness of a person with "enlarged" or "extensive" views who could rise above beggar-thy-neighbor local leaders and exhibit "a real concern for the welfare of our whole country in general."[4] In 1787 he wrote that the government under the Articles of Confederation (1781–87) was at an end and that the disorder could be laid at the feet of the state politicians who, for want of a virtuous patriotism, were ruled by local attachments and would "not yield to a more enlarged scale of politics."[5]

We united as a country under the Constitution, and the civil rights revolution was another moment of moral purity when we recognized the need to embrace fellow citizens who had been unjustly excluded from their share in the common good. Washington's sense of extensive virtue had had a blind spot for many thousands of Americans, and we were marked by a stain of impurity, which republican virtue commanded us to cleanse.

Today, however, the common good is threatened by identitarians who seek the good of their race or sex to the exclusion of everyone else and by the bitter partisanship that bids us to see political opponents as enemies. It has also been weakened by the ways in which we've permitted interest groups to favor themselves at the expense of everyone else. That's the story of the sugar producers who persuade their friends in office to erect tariff barriers, making consumers pay more than they otherwise would. To combat this, said Mancur Olson, what is needed is a government aligned to the whole of the voters, a "super-encompassing majority" that stands in proxy for the nation as a whole.[6] It is also the idealized assembly described by Edmund Burke in his Address to the Electors of Bristol, an assembly "of *one* nation, with *one* interest, that of the whole; where, not local purposes, not local prejudices, ought to guide."

Like Lorenzetti, the progressive conservative believes that this will require republican virtue, and this distinguishes him from five groups that would dispense with it. For populists, civic virtue is nothing more than the camouflage elites employ to distract gullible people. For constitutional conservatives, no one can rise above his corrupt nature, and we'll need the separation of powers to protect us from our vices. For pluralists, disinterested virtue is a sham, and only interest group bargaining can save people from their natural self-interest. For bitter partisans and ideologues, all that matters is who one's enemies are and who has the right set of political beliefs. But the progressive conservative says no, and he insists that republican virtue is not a dream and that today it's needed as much as ever before.

The populist.   For populists, democratic participation in politics shorn of any sense of a common good is all that matters. He's on the side of the majority and wants to stick it to minorities who he thinks profit from their unearned privileges. When he opposes an unjust aristocracy, the populist might join hands with the progressive conservative. However, the populist will think that justice requires only the good of his class or tribe and not of a more enlarged group. His goals are simple: we win, they lose. Washington would have condemned him for his lack of a more extended, republican virtue, as does the progressive conservative.

In American politics, populism is a term employed to smear honest conservatives. The populists were people like Senator "Pitchfork Ben" Tillman (D-SC) who defended lynch mobs and who enacted Jim Crow laws as the Governor of South Carolina. They also included Joe McCarthy, whom progressive conservative Republicans voted to condemn for his inflammatory and baseless claims. Trump appealed to populists at his rallies, but that was one of his least attractive qualities. As for Lincoln, Theodore Roosevelt, and Eisenhower, they didn't have a populist cell in their make-ups.

The constitutional conservative.   As we saw, the framers sought a constitutional structure that would minimize the possibility of public corruption. If polled, I think a majority of them would have said that republican virtue would still be needed, but that's not how James Madison saw it. His mark can scarcely be seen in the final document, but for constitutional conservatives he is the oracle of the Constitution, and the *Federalist Papers* is its sacred text.

In "Federalist 51," Madison dismissed the possibility of republican virtue. No one could rise above self-interest, he said, and the only solution is a separation of powers in which parties seeking to advance their private interest would check each other. He called this a "policy of supplying, by opposite and rival interests, the defect of better motives." Just get the machinery right, said Madison, and it will take care of everything, and for a long time Americans believed this. What we forgot, and what Machiavelli knew, is that the machinery counts for nothing in the absence of a virtuous citizenry. And so we now have a country with a separation of powers but that scores poorly on measures of corruption. Something is missing, says the progressive conservative, and it's the republican virtue that serves the common good.

The pluralist.   Similarly, progressive conservatives reject the idea of pluralism, favored by old-fashioned Democrats, in which the best laws were thought to emerge through interest group bargains that constrain each party from obtaining more than his due. Under pluralism, politics was a Madisonian competition for power among different and legitimate self-interested groups: labor unions and big businesses, Christians and Jews, farmers and suburban consumers. There was no one power elite but instead an array of plural groups, each clamoring for political gain, and the best overall policies were thought to emerge from the competition. Each group would cut deals with all the other rival groups, and this would protect everyone.

That was a highly naïve view of the legislative process, but pluralism was an honest attempt to govern a country formed by a hodgepodge of races, religions, and political views. No group was excluded from the party's big tent – not the inner-city Catholic nor the Southern Baptist, not the racial minority nor the racist Dixiecrat. It was messy, but minorities were thought to be defended against majority oppression so long as they sought a seat at the table and entered into the bargaining process.

The pluralist thought that republican virtue was a delusion and expected powerful groups to employ every bargaining edge to extract gains for themselves. And so Democratic pluralists turned a blind eye to Tammany Hall and corruption and to unjust advantages like those of whites over blacks. After a time, the confused compromises became intolerable, and Democrats moved on. They're still pluralists in the sense that they see an America composed of different groups, but what they've given up is the idea that all parties deserve a seat at the table. Now they divide their countrymen between the elect and the damned, where the elect include teachers and intellectuals, sexual minorities and people of color, regulators and lawyers. The damned are the coal miners, Evangelicals, suburban gun owners, and the members of a "heteronormative patriarchy." They're also the traditional Democrats, the parents who take a back seat to the teachers' unions, the low-wage workers whose jobs are competed away by low-skilled immigrants, and the small business owner who has to navigate his way around a wastefully burdensome regulatory state.

The maddened partisan.   The enraged partisan, Left and Right, has moved to a country that is After Virtue. When the Left pays any attention to a person's character, a new set of virtues – righteous anger and justified hatred – replaces outdated ones such as kindness and charity to others. The Trump supporters who ignore what happened on January 6 also live in a world with little room for virtue.

The ideologue.   Finally, if private virtue no longer seems to matter, it's the ideologue who's killed it off. A signal moment came in 1998 when *Newsweek* reporter Nina Burleigh announced, in the middle of the Monica Lewinsky scandal, that she'd be happy to reward Bill Clinton with oral sex for keeping abortion legal. Since then, the me-too movement has become more censorious, but that's simply one ideology, feminism, asserting priority over another. The Black Lives Matter movement did its part as well by turning every question into one of race and demanding that we ignore fatherless homes and inner-city crime. If you should mention any of this, you're a Neanderthal. In addition, the "root causes" crowd shifts the blame for rising crime rates on the COVID-19 pandemic or on climate change. Heaven forfend that we should fault the looters.

Because he is curious about the world, the progressive conservative isn't an ideologue. At the limit, ideologies are mental shortcuts that economize on the search for evidence. If there are unpleasant data that don't fit with the model, they get discarded into a mental trash folder. In 1973, confronted with five decades of communism's slave labor, police terror, and mass starvation, Marxist historian E. P. Thompson asked, "What is fifty years to an historian?" That was an ideologue.

* * *

The progressive conservative rejects the cynicism of the populist and the constitutional conservative, the pluralist's naivete, and the moral coarseness of the enraged partisan and ideologue. We'll not advance the common good without republican virtue, he says, and that will require the sense of reverence we used to feel for the truly great figures in our history, the kind of people of whom Stephen Spender thought continually.

Born of the sun, they travelled a short while toward the sun
And left the vivid air signed with their honour.[7]

When such people are canceled, when their story is no longer remembered, we no longer seek to emulate their heroic virtues. The moral poseurs who denigrate them, who sneer at our nation builders, are no better than vandals who sack our churches, thieves who plunder our patrimony, and panderers who corrupt our children's morals. For all their tinsel likes on social media, they are the very last people whose example we should follow. The progressive conservative has a better set of influencers.

That in itself will not suffice without something more, a sense of duties that are greater than one's rights, a recognition that we're all a little self-deceived, and a feeling of gratitude for the enormous luck we had in being born in America. These are the things that the founders thought the republic would need in order to endure and that they hoped religion would supply. Without them we've come to the end of the line in a country riven by animosity and mistrust. You might think it's impossible to recover those older virtues, that we've come too far to go back, that we must surrender to despair, hatred, and revenge, and that it's silly to imagine a return to purity. But the progressive conservative disagrees, for the best of reasons: because there is no alternative.

We therefore await a revival of interest in the idea of republican virtue led by progressive conservatives. If we're to advance the common good, we need to spurn the selfishness of narrow groups and demand disinterested virtue. Progressive conservatives will reject the zero-sum mindset of today's Democrats, the idea that one group must suffer if another is to prosper. And unlike the white-shoe Republican Party of the past, progressive conservatives will reach out to all Americans with a promise of prosperity, order, and good government. If this overlaps with religious doctrines, with Jewish teachings about the need to repair the world (*tikkun olam*) and Catholicism's social gospel, so much the better, but progressive conservatism is not a sectarian movement. Instead, it's rooted in a distinct, historical tradition in American politics, one that elects Republicans when adopted.

Trump's victory in 2016 was a return to the progressive policies of an earlier Republican Party, and his call to drain the swamp was a demand for republican virtue. He called out the Democrats for their abandonment of the American Dream, their corruption, and their flirtation with anti-Americanism. And that is how the Republican Party will regain power. But this will require someone other than Trump at its head. In 2016, his supporters saw a vote for their candidate as a vote for virtue when he ran against someone who reminded them of Angela Lansbury in *The Manchurian Candidate*. However, things were different in 2020 when he ran against a candidate who was merely a dotard. And what the GOP will need in 2024 is a happy warrior who displays a smiling superiority to the Left's hypocrisy. If he personally projects a sense of republican virtue, that would help too.

I've described a leader who resembles Eisenhower more than Trump. Ike spoke to the needs of the day, over issues such as civil rights and national welfare, and didn't have to raise his voice or sound like a populist to do so. A leader like that, or like Virginia's Glenn Youngkin, would bring back the suburban Republicans who left it over Trump's personality.

Uniting the Right around the Common Good

The task for progressive conservatives is thus to unite the different strands of modern conservatism around what each lacks: a sense of republican virtue and the kind of policies that make for an electable party. The progressive conservative will recognize that each branch was founded upon a portion of the truth, of what constitutes good government. Where other conservatives misled was when they claimed to represent the whole truth. They also rejected the earlier and honorable moderate Republicanism of Eisenhower, Henry Cabot Lodge, and Margaret Chase Smith, a party that never called itself a philosophy but that won presidential elections and that more closely resembled Trump's party than anything they have to offer.

Progressive conservatives should therefore seek to bring within the fold all the conservative Republicans who left the party over Trump. But which conservatism? To conserve means to preserve, and conservatism is an act of remembrance and homage to parents who bore the sacred fire before us. Leaving progressive conservatives aside, there are several varieties of American conservatism, most prominently libertarianism, integralism, traditional conservativism, natural law theories, and neoconservatism.

Across their borders partisans try to make nice, and if it were discovered that Zoroastrians supported flat taxes, the libertarian might find himself able to make a favorable reference to fire worship. But in the end, the different camps don't play well with each other and disagree as much as they agree. What can the natural lawyer who posits an unchanging human nature have in common with the traditionalist who thinks we're shaped by changing social norms and customs? Where, moreover, is the overlap between the traditionalist and the libertarian who lauds the creative destruction of capitalism? Neither of them has much use for the neocons, particularly when they became a war party. If progressive conservatism differs in part from each of them, that's not surprising. They contradict each other.

But while each differs from progressive conservatism, the overlap is great. Progressive conservatism is an authentic conservatism, and what distinguishes it from rival conservatisms is sometimes little more than the theorist's narcissism of petty differences. Give up those differences, says the progressive conservative, and you'll simply discard policies that make you unelectable and that you could never enact.

a. Libertarianism

The libertarian branch of conservatism was the dominant form of Republicanism between 1964 and 2016. Like Albert Jay Nock, libertarians took the side of the individual against *Our Enemy, the State*, and politics for them became a competition to see who wanted to dismantle more of the government. Privatize prisons – what could go wrong? Privatize Social Security and devil take the hindmost. Privatize the FDA and let consumers figure out which drug is safe. The libertarian took a sensible insight, the presumption that the state shouldn't lightly interfere with individual choices, and forgot that good government cannot be reduced to a simple rule.

The libertarian found natural allies among right-wing economists who explored government inefficiencies and the limits of state intervention, and while progressive conservatives don't think that this damns all welfare entitlements, that's the message many libertarians took. The progressive conservative will agree with Samuel Johnson: "How small, of all that human hearts endure, That part which laws or kings can cause or cure." But small though that part may be, there are things that the state should do in rescuing the needy from catastrophic illnesses, in sheltering the homeless, and in providing for a decent system of education.

If the *progressive* conservative label offends the libertarian, he might ask himself whether he seriously objects to any of its goals. He might not like our safety net, but it's not as if anyone seriously proposes to eliminate it. There's always room for reform, but no one questions the need to provide for fellow citizens who are unable to care for themselves. That can't be changed, and when something can't be changed, it's no longer a problem.

The progressive conservative will also reject John Stuart Mill's social libertarianism, the idea that the state should abstain from any attempt to make people moral. On Mill's "harm principle," the only justification for fetters on individual choice is to prevent harm to others. Self-regarding harms, the wrongs we do to ourselves and that injure no one else should be legally permitted, he said. But progressive conservatives beg to differ and think that the state might prudently seek to enforce morality. They don't think we're made better off by permissive drug laws and pornography.

They'll observe that Mill never satisfactorily explained what should count as a harm. He was right to say that physical harm did so count, but what about the way in which immoral behavior might rub off and tempt others to follow suit? Without being dogmatic, there is no basis for distinguishing this from physical harm, and while conscious of the need for caution, the progressive conservative will nevertheless reject the social libertarian's absolutism.

The progressive conservative doesn't believe that good governance comes down to binary choices. Either the state wholly abstains from interfering with private preferences, says the libertarian, or we'll end up with the Taliban's holy fascism. That is a false dilemma, however. It's the fallacy of the excluded middle, which tells us we must choose between the extreme solutions on either side. That doesn't describe America, where the state has always sought to nudge us away from self-regarding behavior that would harm us without ever meriting the label of fascism. Sometimes those nudges made sense, sometimes not (Prohibition in the 1920s), but it's always a matter of looking at the evidence and not of unconditional rules.

I'll concede, the progressive conservative tells the libertarian, that you have some great thinkers on your side. However, they don't supply me with the kinds of answers I'm looking for. If I want to know what percentage of the federal budget to spend on welfare, the Robert Nozick of *Anarchy, State, and Utopia* will say zero. If I asked Ludwig von Mises what kinds of tariffs to erect, he'd say get rid of all of them. If I asked Milton Friedman what to do about infrastructure, he'd say "privatize, privatize, privatize." They're wonderful savants, but I have a different set of teachers and a Republican Party of Lincoln, Teddy Roosevelt, and Eisenhower, not of *philosophes*.

b. Integralism

The integralist seeks to advance the common good, and that should make him an easy convert to progressive conservatism. At a more fundamental level, however, there's a yawning divide between the two as the integralist rejects the liberalism of our founders. He joins hands with Black Lives Matter to denigrate the nobility of the men to whom we owe our existence as a country and as Americans.

What the integralists want to integrate is church and state. They'd like to unite the two, and since the barrier between them was one of liberalism's greatest accomplishments, the integralist is necessarily anti-liberal. He would reverse what legal historian Harold Berman regarded as the signal moment of Western liberalism, in the eleventh-century investiture crisis when pope and emperor fought over who had the right to appoint bishops.[8]

Before Pope Gregory VII (1073–85) the Church had been merged with the state, and both kings and emperors claimed the right to appoint bishops. However, Gregory asserted that he alone could do so, and in response Holy Roman Emperor Henry IV demanded that Gregory abdicate. Gregory then excommunicated Henry, who travelled to Canossa in 1077 to beg pardon from the pope. The tradition has it that, before he absolved Henry, Gregory made the emperor kneel for three days bare-headed in the snow. For Berman, that was the origin of separationism, when the sacred was divorced from the secular and liberalism was born.

Separationism meant the "freedom of the church" and released a burst of ecclesiastical energy and creativity. The Cluniac reforms made every Benedictine monastery subject to the rule of a single abbot and became the model for the pope's authority of the entire Church. Churchmen systematized what had been a decentralized body of ecclesiastical learning and worked out the details of the canon law. The first universities were created as religious institutions, first at Bologna (1088) and then at Oxford (1096), Salamanca (1134), and Paris (1160). This was also when the Gothic replaced the Romanesque as the period's architectural style, beginning with the choir at St. Denis in 1144.

The investiture crisis also gave birth to the modern Western state, which began to work out its separate character and identity. Ambrogio Lorenzetti's series of frescoes in Siena was an early expression of secularism's civic virtues, as were Machiavelli's histories. America's founders also discovered the need for secular virtue in Pocock's Machiavellian Moment. Monarchical government, with its pomp and placemen, was necessarily corrupt, and in the language of republican virtue the Patriots found a justification for the break from Britain.

Separationism was an immense advantage for settler societies such as America, where it became a key element in the American creed. The 1786 Statute for Religious Freedom disestablished the Episcopal Church in Virginia and was one of only three things that Thomas Jefferson instructed be put in his epitaph. Then, as the states were deliberating over ratifying the First Amendment, the newly elected George Washington defended separationism in a 1790 letter to the Jewish congregation of Newport, Rhode Island.

> The citizens of the United States of America have a right to applaud themselves for having given to mankind examples of a large and liberal policy: a policy worthy of imitation. All possess alike liberty of conscience and immunities of citizenship. It is now no more that toleration is spoken of as if it were the indulgence of one class of people that another enjoyed the exercise of their inherent natural rights, for, happily, the Government of the United States, which gives to bigotry no sanction, to persecution no assistance, requires only that they who live under its protection should demean themselves as good citizens in giving it on all occasions their effectual support.

Today's integralists are Catholics, but historically they more than anyone were the beneficiaries of the separation of church and state.

Since many of them are descendants of immigrants from Great Britain or Ireland, they might want to recall what integralism meant there. The Church of England was established by law as the country's official religion, and until Emancipation Catholics were subject to laws that, as Montesquieu observed, did all the hurt that could possibly be done in cold blood.[9] If they heard mass, they were subject to a year's imprisonment, and if they converted anyone to their faith, they were guilty of treason. They could not send their children to a British university, and if they sent them abroad to study, they forfeited all their goods. They were not permitted to come within ten miles of London or travel more than five miles from their house. Of such laws, the best that Sir William Blackstone could say was that they were seldom enforced to their utmost rigor.[10]

Separationism is always a fragile compromise, and today it's threatened in Communist China, the greatest example of integralism today. China spies on its citizens though its closed-circuit TV cameras. There are 600 million of them, nearly one camera for every two citizens. Their information is relayed to government databases, and with the assistance of the country's sophisticated facial recognition software, the country expects to be able to identify everyone, everywhere, within three seconds of anything happening. The degree of control over people's lives exceeds that of any country at any time, more than even George Orwell imagined in his dystopian *1984*.

That's going to ensure that the Communist Party stays on top of things. More than that, however, China's goal is society's regeneration through the country's "social credit system." The CCTV videos are reviewed, and people are ranked according to good and bad behavior, with bad behavior including minor social ills such as jaywalking, putting your trash in the wrong garbage bin, and ordinary rudeness. People with low social credit scores are shamed and deprived of the access to market goods. Their internet speeds are reduced, and they're denied good jobs and banned from air travel. Their children are kept out of prestigious schools, and their dogs can be taken from them. It's the kind of soft totalitarianism from which liberalism was meant to protect us, and on this the progressive conservative is on the same side as the libertarian.

Harold Berman thought that the Investiture Crisis marked the birth of modernity. The state would have its realm, but a separate domain would be reserved for not only the church but also the private right of conscience that Washington praised. But history has no end point, and there's a new investiture crisis in China, where the Communist government has its own list of state-sanctioned Catholic bishops. Both Church and state insist on their exclusive appointment power, and a 2018 concordat between the two doesn't seem to have resolved the issue.

Even in America, with its First Amendment protections, a secular state has begun to trench on the Church through an expansive set of civil rights that depart from Church teachings. Apart from the state, social media platforms have banned or shadow-banned religious believers who stray from socially acceptable beliefs, and some have seen in this the rise of a soft-despotism that resembles the Chinese social credit system. If integralism comes to America, it won't be in the form of Catholic ultramontanism but in a diametrically opposed woke culture.

Today's integralists should therefore recognize that they are the beneficiaries of America's separationism and that the common good also includes the individual rights of liberalism. We have the right not to be pushed around, to keep what we've earned, to get ahead as best we can, and to worship as we want. A defense of the common good that sacrifices these rights is self-defeating.

In particular, the integralist should abandon the slippery slope conceit that any departure from the liberalism of the founders leads necessarily to today's woke culture. Liberalism doesn't have to turn illiberal and self-destruct, and that was the point of Lionel Trilling's *The Middle of the Journey*, which contrasted two extremists: a repellant communist sympathizer and a paranoid conservative based on Whitaker Chambers. You have to choose between the two of us, the Chambers character tells the liberal. No I don't, says the liberal.

Like Trilling, Charles Péguy (1873–1914) also refused to choose between two extremes. Péguy defended the unjustly accused Captain Alfred Dreyfus at a time when France was bitterly divided, with left-wing anticlerical Dreyfusards on one side and right-wing

Catholic anti-Dreyfusards on the other. Péguy was in the middle. He couldn't support the Left's efforts to suppress Catholicism, and then in 1910 the former atheist had a religious awakening and published a devotional poem, *The Mystery of the Charity of Joan of Arc*. The right-wingers immediately took notice. Péguy must now be on our side, they thought. But he wasn't, and he wrote a little masterpiece, *Notre Jeunesse*, to explain.

The mystique of the Dreyfusard cause had been degraded by the politicians, but one doesn't have to go along with them. And so I'll abjure nothing, he said, neither the purity of republican liberalism nor my religion. I won't be a monarchist and a nationalist of the Right; instead, I'll be a republican nationalist faithful to the civic virtues of the French Revolution. At which both sides gave up on him. Or he gave up on them. No matter. He wrote that you might find, in his writings, some things that might be called the *Memoirs of an Ass*. Or the *Memoirs of an Imbecile*. But none that could be called the *Memoirs of a Coward*.[11] When the First World War began, the forty-one-year-old Péguy died on the field of honor on the second day of the Battle of the Marne.

In history, nothing is determined and just has to happen. The integralist who thinks otherwise, who tells us that the founders' liberalism must necessarily lead to a profoundly immoral society, is simply parroting *The Communist Manifesto*, which argued that bourgeois liberalism drowns out "the most heavenly ecstasies of religious fervour, of chivalrous enthusiasm, of philistine sentimentalism, in the icy water of egotistical calculation." If this were right, if the degradation had been required as an iron law of history, if this is how liberalism must necessarily end, are we supposed to blame drag queen story hours on George Washington? How absurd!

c. Traditional Conservatism

Libertarianism draws its roots in the English social contract theories seen in Algernon Sidney (1623–83) and John Locke (1632–1704). As a reaction to this, Russell Kirk's *The Conservative Mind* (1953) described a traditional conservatism that doesn't think that anything of real interest can be derived from thought experiments about bargains made in a hypothetical state of nature and which instead draws its strength from the Anglo-American tradition of ordered liberty. The traditional conservative believes that long-established rules are presumptively worthy of respect even when their purpose seems obscured. Many of those rules are second-best solutions to greater problems that would emerge were they abolished.

Progressive conservatism will agree with much of this. Like Burke and Michael Oakeshott, he is suspicious of rationalism in politics, of the idea that statecraft should be governed by abstract principles from an altitude of thirty thousand feet above its subjects. He doesn't think that politics is like geometry and believes that John Dickinson, our forgotten founder, had it right when he said that "experience must be our only guide."[12] But, like Burke, the progressive conservative knows that traditions sometimes stand in need of reform, and he would not wish to revisit the older laws that unjustly discriminated against racial, gender, and sexual minorities.

That's something that Kirk forgot. He believed that society was naturally divided into different classes, and while this is an anodyne sentiment, if all it means is that by our efforts we'll sort ourselves out into different economic groups, that wasn't all that he meant. In describing what he called the virtues of the old south, he wrote of "the immense problem which must exist whenever two races occupy the same territory" and "the menace of a debased, ignorant, and abysmally poor folk."[13] That was the Kirk who admired John C. Calhoun. No wonder that, in a 501-page book on conservatism, Kirk could not refer to Abraham Lincoln except dismissively. But Lincoln is the founder of American progressive conservatism, and his promise of social and economic mobility for all races is its core tenet.

Conservatives took a wrong turn when William F. Buckley defined them as "someone who stands athwart history, yelling Stop," as though all changes were for the worse. If so, there could never be anything like progress, and Buckley's magazine, *National Review*, needn't have abandoned its support for Jim Crow in 1957.[14] But in time Buckley and his magazine recognized they were wrong, which is to say that they came to believe that progress is possible and that one can be both progressive and conservative.

d. Natural Law

Conservatives who seek to bootstrap their beliefs will sometimes describe themselves as natural lawyers. They're more than right-wingers, you're to understand. They're also philosophers who see things from a moral point of view. There are several difficulties with natural law theories, however, beginning with the leap from the positive to the normative, from what *is* to what *ought* to be the case. If we have natural preferences, that doesn't tell us that they're the ones we ought to have. By nature, we can be greedy and selfish, so calling something natural doesn't tell us it's a good instinct.[15] And if all you meant by saying something is natural is that it's a good thing to do, labels like "natural" and "unnatural" are wheels that turn nothing. They're shorthand for deeper beliefs about the good, and we could dispense with them and simply cut to what we think is good or bad.

More recent thinkers, such as John Finnis, try to sidestep the is-ought problem by identifying natural law with rational egoism and the idea that our practical reason will direct us to choose those goods that are best for us.[16] This has come to be called New Natural Law, and today it's the dominant form of natural law. But NNL fails to explain why we should sacrifice ourselves for others when there is no long-term personal gain from doing so. NNL is a theory of rational self-interest, not of conventional virtue, and when you flesh out the implications of New Natural Lawyers' ideas, they're no different from those of the Randist who thinks selfishness is a virtue.[17]

Some progressive conservatives might nevertheless call themselves natural lawyers, and the two movements overlap on many social issues, especially where this finds support in the empirical literature. Beginning in the 1960s, neoconservatives in journals such as *The Public Interest* (1965–2005) brought their economic skills to bear in reporting on social pathologies such as the rise in unwed birth rates and in so doing buttressed the intuitions of the natural lawyers. The natural lawyers had been right about common-sense morality, and what the empirical scholars had given them was the evidence to back up their armchair philosophizing.

e. Neoconservatism

Neoconservatism was a school of thought first associated with foreign policy realists such as Sen. Henry ("Scoop") Jackson (D-WA) and Jean Kirkpatrick. Both thought that the post-Watergate Democratic Party had wrongly abandoned the tough stand that earlier Democrats had taken against Soviet expansionism and that in its place the party's McGovernites had adopted a soft-headed idealism. The early neoconservatives also included former liberals such as Irving Kristol and Norman Podhoretz who recognized the failures of Lyndon Johnson's Great Society welfare programs.

In time, neoconservatism became a very different animal, however, and abandoned foreign policy realism. It credited false information about the threat posed by Saddam Hussein and indulged in a fantasy that the Middle East could be remade along Western, democratic lines. With the second generation of neocons, people like Bill Kristol (son of Irving) and John Podhoretz (son of Norman), they became the war party while Trump led a peace party. They were the idealists, and Trump was the realist.

The progressive conservative will have a great deal of sympathy for the earlier generation of neoconservatives, who were on the right side of the issues of their day. But he parts company with what the neocons became forty years later. Like Trump, he'll understand the necessity of accepting the enormous differences in customs and forms of government in other countries and will reject the idealism of the second generation of neocons, that war party that thinks that the world can be remade in our image.

*　*　*

The fabric of progressive conservatism, scarcely visible beneath the folds of the other variants of conservatism, shares elements of all of them but also departs from each. It's not a fusion of the different things that conservatism has meant that purports to find a unifying thread in all its irreconcilable elements. But it does claim that it represents an authentically Republican Party, one that is electable.

And all it asks other conservatives to do is abandon that which they know repels or confuses voters and could never be enacted.

It also adds the content missing from other conservative theories. The integralist claims that he seeks the common good but has little idea how to produce a jobs economy. The traditional conservative can't say anything about tariff or antitrust policies, and there isn't a natural law response to what the right marginal tax rate might be.

The libertarian does have answers, but they're the wrong ones if he wants to shrink the state down to nothing. Nevertheless, progressive conservatives and libertarians are often on the same side. They are both willing to learn from economists about the difference between policies that work and ones that don't. Both think that entrenched hierarchies in government and business keep people immobile and don't miss them when they've been buried by capitalism's creative destruction. Both admire the brilliant innovator who rose to the top with a new product and reaps its enormous profits and less so his children with their fancy-pants MBAs. Both are on the side of social and economic mobility and the friendless new man who makes his way without an old-boy network to prop him up. He might have a bit of dirt under his fingernails, but he's not been turned into a woke executive by his desire to ingratiate himself with a left-wing establishment.

But wait, says the right-wing intellectual. You want to promote the common good. Fine, but where's your theory? Ah, you noticed that, did you, answers the progressive conservative. You're right. I don't have a theory. I think they're baloney. They offer a false security and not the nuanced and adaptable answers needed for the multitude of problems life throws at you. "It is illogical to guillotine a prince and replace him with a principle," said Ortega. "The latter, no less than the former, places life under an absolute autocracy."[18] Besides, political ideologies deepen our divisions and weaken our sense of fraternity with each other. "An intellectual hatred is the worst," said Yeats, and we've proven him right.

In place of a theory then, I propose the republican virtue of the founders, the desire to see everyone flourish, the willingness to tackle corruption and love of country. And so, supple and not circumscribed, progressive conservatism will seek the common good, and like the key that nicely fits the slot, the bolt that slides itself into place, its rightness will be recognized by all who desire a better country. It is the secret driver of American politics and when adopted will make Republicans America's natural governing party.

CHAPTER SIXTEEN

A Contract with America

In 1994 REPUBLICANS retook Congress with a Contract with America that signaled that the party had aligned itself with the Tea Party movement. Today, the party should offer a progressive conservative Contract with America that aligns itself with the Trump agenda and promise to enact it in 2024 when it captures Congress and the White House.

The contract must propose radical change if it's going to address our pressing problems. Anything less won't attract the voters Trump brought to the party. Do not confuse progressive conservatives with the timid, weak sisters in the Republican Party who are afraid to fight the good fight, who tinker with miniscule changes, and who never take on the swamp. Lincoln didn't back down, not even when all his cabinet was against him. Theodore Roosevelt could stare down boat robbers and "robber barons," and Eisenhower led a crusade against foreign fascists and domestic racists. Like them, the progressive conservative will propose bold reforms where these are needed while defending with equal vigor all that is valuable in the American experiment.

1. *Republicans will protect American families*

2. *Republicans will fix our broken K–12 schools*

3. *Republicans will reform higher ed*

4. *Republicans will reform health care to protect Americans*

5. *Republicans will fix a broken immigration system*

6. *Republicans will enact just tax laws*

7. *Republicans will eliminate wasteful regulations*

8. *Republicans will close the door to wasteful corruption*

9. *Republicans will defend democracy*

10. *Republicans will appoint courageous judges who will defend a virtuous and democratic republic*

11. *Republicans will protect free speech rights on social media*

12. *Republicans will promote pride in America*

1. Republicans Will Protect American Families

Few things are more important than the spiritual health of American families, which rescue people from soul-destroying isolation and which raise our children to be responsible adults. Married people are more likely to be emotionally stable and have productive lives and as parents are more likely to pass on these traits to their children. Children raised in a married household are 82 percent less likely to live in poverty than children in single-parent households.[1]

In recent years, however, the family has been buffeted by economic forces and a decline in cultural standards. While 72 percent of all adults ages eighteen and older were married in 1960, the figure is now below 50 percent, the lowest point in recorded history. The retreat from marriage has been marked by the rise of single parenthood and informal cohabitation. A younger generation of millennials and Zoomers often have little reason to expect they'll ever get married.

This has happened for a variety of reasons. After no-fault

divorce, women learned that they had less reason to think that their marriages would last and rationally decided to enter the work force. Even if they stayed married, the rise in tax rates created a need for two-income households. There's also an educational mismatch between the sexes since women graduate from college in greater numbers than men. In addition, the declining economic prospects of blue-collar men and college grads burdened by educational debts has made many of them unmarriable. Apart from economic factors, cultural changes such as feminism, individualism, and the collapse of a family-oriented ethos have made marriage seem easier to pass up.

Today, however, we've begun to recognize how this harms us, and conservative cultural entrepreneurs might well be on the winning side. In the nineteenth century, the Regency rakes gave way to the Victorian era, and it's foolish to think this couldn't happen again. Given the pathologies of our current society and the evidence linking them to the decline of marriage, that's not so wild a dream. In fact, it's what the evolutionary biologist would predict.

While the legislator can't enact cultural changes, there are nevertheless things that he can do to help restore traditional family structures. The chief of these is a jobs economy that helps make men better marriage prospects. Often, that's all one needs to do. Give us a job and we can take care of ourselves. We could also make it easier to get married and have children through more generous tax credits for children in married households. The tax credit at present is $3,600 per child, and progressive conservatives should give some thought to increasing this.[2] Finally, and importantly, the decline in our education system has imposed burdens on parents and children that the reforms suggested in the next two sections will redress.

2. Republicans Will Fix Our Broken K–12 Schools

The best way to empower parents is to put them in charge of their children's education. With the assistance of the Biden Education Department, teachers' unions are pushing Critical Race Theories in our high schools. Radical groups also seek to sexualize elementary school children. We own the kids, says the Left, and parents should get out of our way. In the 2021 Virginia election, parents told the Democrats they wouldn't stand for this, and their protest elected a Republican governor.

The remedy is parental choice. The federal government should serve primarily as a source of flow-through funding for low- and middle-income parents to permit them to send their kids to the public, private, or parochial schools of their choice. That's going to mean defunding most of the Department of Education top-down K–12 programs, which cost $50 billion a year and which have created a blob of education bureaucrats. With the money saved, an expanded tax credit treatment might be offered to parents for tuition at private and parochial schools.

Having done that, Republicans will take their hands off the wheel. They're not going to be able to micromanage what's taught in the nation's classrooms from Washington. That's a job for the parents, and parental choice is the answer. It's also a job for elected school boards, which parents will have to wrest from the control of politicized teachers' unions.

3. Republicans Will Reform Higher Ed

While a country benefits from a well-educated class of higher ed graduates, too many kids go to college today. In part, that's a consequence of a degraded K–12 system, where a BA is now made to take the place of what was formerly a respected high school graduation certificate. Reforming K–12 education would go a long way to curing that problem. So too would vocational schools that train students for jobs in such things as plumbing and health care that today pay more than many of the jobs available to college grads.

We also need to reform higher ed from inside the beast. Its humanities departments exist because it's assumed that that their content has intrinsic worth, but they're staffed by instructors who teach that there's no mental or spiritual benefit to be gained from their study. Were they correct, they'd have explained why their jobs shouldn't exist. But they do, and American higher ed has become a poor investment that has made millions of millennials and Zoomers unemployable debt slaves. The fault lies with federal policies that encourage colleges to run up the tuition tab and then deny student borrowers a bankruptcy discharge when they cannot pay off the loan.

Other First World countries recognized that government-subsidized student loans permit poor kids to attend college and that that was a good thing. But having done this, they then told the colleges that they'd have to cap their tuition if they wanted their students to benefit from student loans. They recognized that universities would otherwise have an incentive to jack up tuition. And that's just what happened when we didn't make the same bargain with American higher ed. The federal government made a no-strings loan guarantee to the universities, and they took it to the bank. Over the last twenty years, there's been a 154 percent increase in tuition at private universities and a 221 percent increase at public ones. Over the same period time, the consumer price index rose only 54 percent.[3] An older generation remembers tuition in the range of $2,000 to $3,000 a year. If you worked in the summer, you could easily afford that. Now it's $50,000 to $70,000 for most private colleges.

The government-backed loans increased the financial burden on students, and it also corrupted higher education. They freed universities from the discipline of private markets and led them to admit students who had no business in university. If the ill-educated students couldn't get jobs after graduation, too bad for them. That wasn't something the universities had to worry about, and that in turn resulted in the ridiculous course offerings ("Cultures of Basketball" in the English Department) at the Oberlins of America.

To remedy this, the federal government should refuse to guarantee educational loans for students who want to attend colleges that charge more than a specified amount for tuition. At our good state schools, in-state tuition seldom exceeds $25,000 a year, and schools that charge more than that should be self-financing and foreswear federal loan guarantees. If pressed, our colleges might find a way to reduce the administrative bloat that consumes a significant and increasing component of their budgets. The best schools are not starving in any event. Harvard's endowment is thirty times larger than its yearly revenue from tuition and fees, and it has been suggested that it's not so much a university as an asset fund that does some teaching on the side.

That's not enough, however. What do you do about the student who has rung up a crushing student debt burden? The numbers are astounding, a total of $1.7 trillion in student debt owed by 43 million people. The Federal Student Aid program is the country's biggest consumer lender.[4]

Nearly eleven million borrowers are delinquent or in default. A total of thirty-two million – one in ten Americans – are either not able to pay or are paying so little that it all goes to interest and they can't reduce their loan balances.[5] Loans in excess of $100,000 are not uncommon.[6] Imagine trying to dig your way out of that. You can't. You can't even begin to do so. Instead, you'll roll over the principal from year to year and watch it increase from the interest rate charges.

The problem is made worse by usurious debt servicing charges. Five million student debtors have been asked to enter into a repayment agreement with private parties such as Sallie Mae. When that happens, an amount equal to 16 percent of the principal is added to the outstanding balance. If the debtor resumes paying, the first 16 cents of every dollar are taken by the servicer, then penalties and interest are taken out, and anything that remains is applied to the principal. For millions of Americans, this turns a difficult loan into an impossible one.

That's debt slavery. It's a form of permanent servitude. What incentive do you have to go out and find a job if whatever you'd earn would go to your creditors? How could you dream of marrying, buying a home, having kids, doing all the things that an older generation took for granted? That has resulted in a generation of young people who are alienated from our economy and society. If they have been radicalized, if they've given up on our economic system, it's hard to fault them. They've been slapped in the face by free markets in the form of the student-loan racket.

There's a silver bullet that could cure all this: bankruptcy. An entrepreneurial society requires risk-takers, and you won't take risks when you're a debt slave. That's why the fresh start bankruptcy offers has long been a vital element of American dynamism. Formerly student debt could be discharged in bankruptcy, but this began to change in 1976. Back then the students were thought to be rich kids, and the debt load was a lot lower. That's not true anymore, however. We've betrayed the millennials and Zoomers and need to give them a fresh start on life through a bankruptcy discharge for student debt.[7]

Right-wingers are unsympathetic to bankruptcy relief for student debt. However, supply-siders should see some value to it. What they showed, in the Laffer Curve, is that reducing a very high marginal tax rate can actually result in greater tax revenues for the government. A rate of 100 percent wipes out the incentive to go out and produce, so there's no income and nothing to tax. Debt slavery, where all your upside is owed to Uncle Sam, is like a 100 percent tax, and 100 percent of nothing is nothing. A fresh start in bankruptcy would encourage the debtor to get out there and get on with his life.[8]

Right-wingers also worry that student debt forgiveness would burden America's taxpayers since 80 percent of the loans are backed by the US government. However, we'd reduce the financing burden if we capped tuition, as I recommend above. In addition, a fair chunk of the existing debt load has already been written off as bad debt from borrowers who are never going to repay their loans. A Brookings Institution report predicts that nearly 40 percent of the 2004 entry cohort of student borrowers may default on their loans by 2023.[9] That number must be much higher today since the average cost of tuition has more than doubled since 2004. So the burden of a discharge is smaller than one might think. Creditors don't lose anything when bad debt is discharged. They've already lost it.

The Biden administration is beginning to experiment with debt forgiveness, but the way it's going about it perpetuates the problem. It is not coupling it with a demand to reduce tuition, so the plan really amounts to a giveaway to higher ed. It's also not about to police the administrative bloat and the wasteful courses at our universities. If Republicans took carriage of the problem, however, they could kill two birds with one stone by reforming higher ed at the same time as they cure the debt slavery problem.

The universities have created the student debt problem by running up the cost and teaching worthless courses, and they should be held financially accountable when their graduates declare bankruptcy on student loans. That would relieve the burden taxpayers bear under the present system, and schools would think twice before running up the tuition tab. They might even start bringing it down. They would also start paying closer attention to whether their graduates can get jobs. Too many universities offer frivolous courses that make employers run the other way from applicants, and these students aren't good bets to repay their loans. If the university bore the financial risk, it would almost certainly change what it teaches. STEM courses would flourish, and so would the humanities courses that betoken a serious student. But watch for gender study programs to disappear quickly.

The federal government can't micromanage what's taught in our colleges, but it can let the market work and let higher ed pay for the way it has made its students unemployable and debt-ridden. And while the government can't censor what's taught, it can take on the censors who trench on the academic freedom of faculty and students. All federal funds should be withdrawn from universities that punish students and faculty for expressing a conservative or religiously orthodox opinion.

Would all this be thoroughly disruptive? Most certainly. But American higher education badly needs a dose of creative destruction.

4. Republicans Will Reform Health Care to Protect Americans

Few things cost Republicans more than the party's failure to enact health care legislation when they controlled all three branches between 2017–19. Led by right-wingers such as Speaker Paul Ryan, congressional Republicans took a powder on the issue as congressional Republicans did when Eisenhower proposed health care reform, and the party paid the same price in the 2018 congressional elections as it had in 1954.

The rest of the First World offers its citizens some form of universal medical care. Some of it is financed by the taxpayer, as in Britain and Canada. Some of it is paid for through mandatory insurance plans, which comes down to the same thing. We have a mixed system under which around 91 percent of us have some form of coverage.[10]

About half of us are covered through our jobs by employer-based plans. In 2019, the average such plan cost $7,188 a year per person, of which the employer paid 82 percent of the premium, or $5,950 a year. The plans are subsidized by the tax code, which permits employers to deduct 100 percent of the cost as a business expense and which doesn't treat this amount as a taxable benefit in the hands of the employee. Employee contributions to health plans, which on average amount to $1,240 a year, are also excluded from taxes to the extent that the premiums are paid through a flexible savings account. That's fine. Just don't tell me we have a free-market health care system.

The problem is that employer-based plans have gaps. They don't cover the retirees, the permanently unemployed, or people who've just been laid off. Most of these people are covered by means-tested programs such as Medicaid and Medicare or by VA coverage. Another thirty million Americans are covered by a direct-purchase plan, including twenty million under an Obamacare exchange.

It's a haphazard system in which some people fall through the cracks. They include people covered by Medicaid, which doesn't pay doctors as much as an employer-based plan, with the result that about a third of the country's physicians refuse to accept new Medicaid patients. Then there are the 9 percent or twenty-eight million of us who are uninsured. Some of them are middle class people who don't qualify for Medicaid because they earn more than $17,000 a year as a single person. Some of them were priced out of the Obamacare exchanges, which were flawed because enrollees had to cross-subsidize people with catastrophic and very expensive illnesses. Some were healthy young people who didn't think they needed health insurance until they came down with catastrophic illnesses. And as good as they are, the employment-based plans make people fearful of losing their jobs and complicate switching from one job to another if you have a preexisting condition.

Something more is needed in the form of a national catastrophic health insurance plan. Middle class people who don't qualify for

Medicaid or Medicare don't worry about getting the flu. What they do fear is the disease that will bankrupt them or whose treatment they cannot afford. A majority of us report that we are very or somewhat worried about medical costs in the event of a serious illness or accident.[11]

How to fix this? We don't need to adopt a full coverage system on the model of Canadian Medicare. Instead, catastrophic coverage insurance might be mandated along with a deterrent fee that varies with a person's income. For example, the deductible payment might be zero for the poor, $2,500 for the median household, and as much as $100,000 for the very wealthy.[12] No one would find the deductible unaffordable, and the government's burden would come from all taxpayers and not off the backs of the narrower risk pool of members of an Obamacare exchange.

5. Republicans Will Fix a Broken Immigration System

Illegal immigration makes the illegal immigrant better off, but the gain comes off the backs of American citizens, especially poorer ones. In 2019 Pew Research put the total number of unauthorized immigrants at 10.5 million, about a quarter of our total foreign-born population.[13] Given Biden's open borders, that number has to be much higher today.

We need to close our borders, but the greater problem is our legal immigration system, not illegal immigration. The 1965 Immigration Act gives priority to entrants under family reunification categories, which disproportionately admit lower-skilled immigrants whose relatives arrived here recently, and it's a partisan issue for Democrats. "Republicans just don't seem to get it," observes Democratic speechwriter Dylan Lowe. "With every year that passes, Hispanic population numbers increase," and "these demographic changes will create millions of new Democratic voters over time."[14] The pre-1965 regime has been condemned as racist, but the racial aspects of the 1965 Act are precisely why Democrats support it.

If we wanted better skilled immigrants, there's no great mystery about how to do it. It's called the points system, and it was pioneered in Canada. You can find it on the web, and it's geared toward identifying people who'll make Canadians better off. You get points for speaking the language, skilled work experience, education attainments, proof of funds, and being young. You'll also be asked if you want to settle in a province where there's a match between your skills and the skills it needs.

Canada admits about 310,000 immigrants a year (nearly 1 percent of the country's total population), and 190,000 or three-fifths of them are admitted under economic categories on the basis that they'll benefit Canadian citizens. By contrast, America admits about 1,000,000 legal immigrants a year (0.3 percent of the total population), and of these 70 percent come in because of their family ties to Americans. Only about 140,000 are admitted under employment-based preferences.[15] With about 10 percent of the population of the US, Canada actually admits 50,000 more people a year on the basis that they'll make their ordinary citizens better off.

The points system has given Canada immigrants who are more skilled than their American counterparts and who assimilate more quickly into the national economy.[16] It has also given Canada smart teenagers who boost the country's PISA scores. In addition, it has been argued that if we mimicked Canada and required better skills or job credentials from immigrants, we'd significantly lower the tax burden for the native-born.[17]

In sum, the Canadian system has made the country both wealthier and more egalitarian. That's why Canadians seem generally happy with it and why it's not a hot political issue there. We need a similar system here, and Trump has recognized this. In 2016 I wrote a book on what Republicans needed to do to win the election, and Trump tweeted his support for the chapter that recommended we adopt the Canadian system. That has to be a major component of a progressive conservative Contract with America.

6. Republicans Will Enact Just Tax Laws

Americans for Tax Reform asks Republican politicians to sign a Taxpayer Protection Pledge under which they'll vote against all tax increases. But progressive conservatives don't begin by assuming that every tax increase is beyond the pale, and they'll not sign it.

What they might sign is a pledge not to raise taxes on the middle classes because right now they're cross-subsidizing the wealthiest Americans.

Our marginal income tax rates are progressive. For the middle class, they're 24 percent for income greater than $85,000, and at higher income levels they rise to 32 and 35 percent. For the very wealthy, they're 37 percent for income over $518,000. That doesn't sound unreasonable, but when account is taken of other regressive taxes, such as payroll (Social Security and Medicare), sales, corporate, and estate taxes, middle-class earners reportedly pay a higher rate than the top 1 percent. As calculated by Emmanuel Saez and Gabriel Zucman, who do take all this into account, the tax rate imposed on the median household is 37.5 percent on an income of $47,980, while that imposed on a household at the 99 percent level is 29.7 percent on an income of $566,920.[18] For the very top earners, the marginal rate is lower still.

That argues for middle class tax relief, which might come in the form of a reduction in marginal rates for the bottom three income quintiles plus an increased dependent child tax credit. It also suggests the need to look at increasing the tax base for the wealthiest Americans. Trump's Tax Cut and Jobs Act of 2017 made a start by capping mortgage interest and state and local tax deductions, which disproportionately benefited high earners, a reform the Democrats want to repeal in order to benefit the urban elites who support them.

More can be done. America's billionaires are permitted to shelter their income behind obscure loopholes, such as the "stepped-up basis" that reduces capital gains liability when a person passes on his wealth to his heirs.[19] Let's say a parent bought Amazon stock for $10,000 back when it was dirt cheap. At his death it was worth $10 million, and that will be taken to be its stepped-up value for tax purposes. The child who inherited the stock will therefore pay no capital gains tax if he sells it for $10 million. That's great if what you want is an aristocracy.

At present, the super wealthy get an enormous tax break because of the way in which companies are permitted to hide their earnings. Amazon paid no taxes in 2017 or 2018, having sheltered its earnings through research and development investments, stock-based employee compensation, and carry-forward losses from years before when the company wasn't profitable. In 2019, Amazon did pay $162 million in taxes on pretax income of $13.9 billion, but that was a tax rate of just 1.2 percent.[20] As for Mark Zuckerberg's Facebook and Larry Page and Sergey Brin's Google, they've saved many billions of dollars by shifting their profit centers to the low-tax Cayman Islands and Ireland, respectively.

7. Republicans Will Eliminate Wasteful Regulations

During the 2016 campaign, Trump promised to "drain the swamp." As we've found out, however, that's easier said than done. Laws are difficult to repeal, but it might be easier to undo the morass of excessive regulations. During the 2016 campaign, Donald Trump said that "70 percent of regulations can go," and a lot of people agree with him.[21] It's generally believed that the Code of Federal Regulations has developed a severe case of elephantiasis and that this is a leading cause of the decline in American economic growth. One study concluded that, had regulations had been held constant at 1980 levels, the US economy would have been about 25 percent larger in 2012 and that each American would have been $13,000 richer.[22]

Our regulatory state is more than a stumbling block for the economy. It's also a threat to democratic government. If you thought you were governed by laws passed by Congress and signed by the president, guess again. The rules that matter, the ones you're most likely to bump against, are much more likely to have been adopted by regulators who aren't really accountable to anyone except themselves. The regulations are found in the thousands of pages in the Code of Federal Regulations or in the interpretative advice found in agency opinion letters and policy statements.

Conservatives have proposed several solutions to the problem, but they've always come up short. First, they'd like courts to step in and second-guess the regulators, and that came up in the confirmation hearings for Justice Neil Gorsuch. In 1984 the Supreme Court held in the *Chevron* decision that courts should defer to reasonable agency interpretations of ambiguous statutes,[23] and Gorsuch argued against *Chevron* deference by the courts. But that's not going to do much of anything. Courts defer to the regulators, here and in other countries, precisely because they have the kind of technical expertise that courts lack. I'm trained in law and freely admit I don't know beans about climate change.

Second, conservatives want Congress to step in and review the agencies more closely. But then it's Congress that has created the problem by permitting the agencies to go their merry ways. If it has done so, it's because it has not felt any great political pressure to do otherwise. You don't have to tell a businessman how to make money, and you don't have to tell a politician how to count votes.

The minutiae of governing must necessarily be delegated to people who won't always be faithful to their democratic masters. What's the answer then? Let's go back to Justinian. Shortly after he became emperor of the Byzantine Empire in 527, Justinian created a law-reform commission led by Trebonius to restate all the laws. Up to then, the sources of law were found in two thousand books written over hundreds of years. Rather than tinker with things, Justinian's commission discarded rules that were inefficient, obsolete, repetitive, and confusingly overlapping, and it produced a much shorter new digest. Laws not selected for the digest were declared invalid and were never to be cited thereafter in the courts. Justinian's Code was remarkably sophisticated, and its key elements can be found in the private law systems in civil law countries today.

Similarly, a modern regulatory-reform commission should be put to work, one composed of common-sense experts who are aware of both the good and bad things regulations can do. The regulatory state, which began with Theodore Roosevelt's embrace of administrative agencies, has made us safer and healthier, and no one would want to go back to the unregulated meat-packing industry. But the reform commission, like Trebonius, should offer relief from the welter of rules so extensive and mind-numbingly detailed that no one can keep up with them. We'd retain the regulations that keep us safe but jettison rules that specify what counts as French dressing, ketchup, and cherry pies.[24] They're meant to protect consumers, but mostly they protect big firms against competition from up-and-coming competitors.

Could the commission cut back regulations by 70 percent as Trump proposed? Yes, and more so, if it corrects the biases of the deep state's rulemaking and abandons the regulator's conceit that every little error deserves to be corrected by a rule. The commission must recognize that we can't anticipate all future risks and eliminate them with a rule. The regulator's hubris that he could do so is what added twenty thousand pages of rules to thousand-page Dodd-Frank financial reform bill without really lessening the risk of a financial meltdown.

8. Republicans Will Close the Door to Wasteful Corruption

With a government as large as ours, it's not surprising that the lobbying industry is huge as well. The concern, however, is that causation might be working in both directions and that we'd have less wasteful spending and a smaller government if we could rein in the lobbyists.

Over the last ten years, companies, labor unions, trade organizations and others have spent an average of $3 billion a year on lobbying.[25] That's a good deal more than the money spend on political campaigns and more than what the two presidential candidates and the Super PACs that supported them spent in 2016.[26] For companies it's money well spent. One study reported that firms lower their tax bill by $6 to $20 for every $1 spent on tax loopholes.[27] Lobbying firms also have a significantly lower probability of being detected for fraud.[28] It all adds up, and firms that employ lobbyists have been found to outperform the market by 11 percent a year.[29]

That's not to say that all lobbying should be banned. Some of it is the grassroots lobbying by nonprofits and citizen groups on issues such as abortion and gay rights. That's not going to line the pockets of a public official, so it doesn't amount to corruption. It's also protected speech under the First Amendment's right to petition the government for a redress of grievances.

Nor is there anything wrong with money spent on corporate

lobbyists who simply inform their clients and congressional staffers about the legislation and regulations before them. It's extraordinarily difficult to bone up on all the new legislation and regulations, and for new Congressmen the learning curve is very steep. Because of this, they'll rely on lobbyists to tell them about the unintended consequences of proposed legislation and keep them abreast of new initiatives, studies, and legislation. A trade bill might seem attractive in the abstract, but it'll be far less so when a Congressman learns it'll mean major job losses in his district.[30]

What does cross the line, however, are the football tickets, expensive dinners, and travel expenses that lobbyists formerly spent on Congressmen and staffers. For example, Jack Abramoff arranged a $70,000 golf outing at St. Andrews in Scotland for House Majority Leader Tom Delay and his entourage. After this came to light, most gift-giving practices were banned by the 2007 Honest Leadership and Open Government Act (HLOGA).[31]

That was a start, but more can be done. The Supreme Court has upheld general limits to campaign contributions, and taking this a step further, contributions from suspect donors might be entirely banned. We've already done this for some kinds of donors, and such laws have been upheld by the Supreme Court. What remains is to restrict campaign giving by lobbyists along the lines proposed by a 2011 American Bar Association committee chaired by Harvard law professor Charles Fried.[32]

Lobbyists have a First Amendment right to inform Congress about policy issues and to propose solutions. But that's not a right to couple the request for legislative action with a payoff to the Congressman, and the ABA recommended restricting fundraising activities by lobbyists for congressional clients. These would include leading a fundraising effort, organizing fundraising events, serving on a campaign fundraising committee, and soliciting contributions for a campaign. The ABA also proposed a ban on bundling, the practice in which a person persuades a group of people to write checks for a candidate and then hands over all of them to the candidate committee. Such activities, said the ABA, can create "a self-reinforcing cycle of mutual financial dependency." Courts have upheld bans on contributions by other suspect donors, and a ban on lobbyist campaign contributions would likely survive a constitutional challenge.

Republicans should also close the door between K Street and Congress. Many Congressmen take lucrative jobs as lobbyists when they retire from public life. The Center for Responsive Politics reported that, out of an estimated 1,000 former members of Congress (many of whom had aged out), at least 285 were registered as lobbyists and a further 85 provided "strategic advice" for clients.[33] For the class of 2019, nearly two-thirds of retired or defeated federal lawmakers became lobbyists.[34] They come to Washington but never seem to leave it. In the cynical view of former Congressman Jim Cooper, Congress has become a "farm league" for a better-paying K Street job.[35]

Bully for them, but that's going to warp their incentives as Congressmen. Since they'd be earning far more money as lobbyists than they ever did as Congressmen, they'll have strong reasons to favor what they regard as a future employer. In one smelly case, Rep Billy Tauzin (R-LA) left Congress in 2004 to take up a $2 million salary as head of PhRMA, Big Pharma's chief lobbying organization. As chair of the Energy and Commerce Committee, Tauzin had been the chief architect of a 2003 law that prohibited the federal Medicare program from negotiating lower drug prices.

Current revolving door laws bar former members of the House of Representatives from making lobbying contacts with their former colleagues for one year. For former senators there's a two-year ban.[36] That's entirely too short, however, and in a strange-bed-fellows alliance, Senator Ted Cruz (R-TX) and Congresswoman Alexandria Ocasio-Cortez (D-NY) have proposed a lifetime ban. That's a better idea than the term limits proposed in the 1994 Contract with America. The problem isn't how long a person stays in office. It's the way he never leaves Washington thereafter.

9. Republicans Will Defend Democracy

The defense of democracy will require a reassertion of political control over an unelected bureaucracy. When conservatives take the White House, too many members of the bureaucracy regard themselves as an opposition party and with their allies in the left-wing media openly campaign against an elected president. That's a threat to democracy, and in response a conservative administration must have the courage to staff the bureaus, agencies, and endowments with leaders who will reassign and terminate the careers of left-wing bureaucrats who are merely playing politics.

In addition, our electoral laws are sorely in need of reform. The federal government should enact laws to guarantee the integrity of our elections as it did in the 1960s when federal voting rights laws ended the practice of burdening African Americans at the polls. States are not required to hold direct presidential elections, but if they do so the rule in each state is one-citizen, one vote, and their procedures cannot amount to the disparate treatment of citizens,[37] and what's needed today is a federal law prescribing a uniform set of anti-fraud rules.

We have the most permissive electoral laws in the First World, and they invite voter fraud. The reforms that progressive conservatives have in mind would simply match those in most other countries, and what's wrong with that? The left-winger's hysterical opposition to this and his indifference to fraud comes down to saying that we alone in America understand democracy and that countries such as Canada and France are little better than dictatorships.

So here is what we need to bring us in line with the rest of the world.

- Voters must provide an official identification card bearing their photograph and address.

- Every vote must be tabulated by hand, on election day, by scrutineers from both parties.

- Absentee voting fraud has been called "the tool of choice for vote thieves"[38] and should be banned unless the voter swears that he will be out of the jurisdiction on election day.

- Ban vote harvesting. That's where third parties collect and deliver completed ballots, and they've been known to fill in ballots for Democrats and toss votes for Republicans. Election officials have no way to police this since it happens before the ballots are turned in.

Americans deserve no less if we wish to restore the confidence that is sorely lacking in our democracy.

10. Republicans Will Appoint Courageous Judges Who Will Defend a Virtuous and Democratic Republic

C.S. Lewis wrote that courage is not simply one of the moral virtues but the form of every virtue at the testing point. It is a cardinal judicial virtue and the justification for the federal bench's lifetime tenure. The greatest of judicial heroes are those who stand up to the mob, like the Eisenhower appointees who brought the civil rights revolution to the south. The most ignominious judges are those who shirk their duties and yield to the rioters' veto.

Progressive conservative appointees must be prepared to court unpopularity if justice demands it and enforce laws that reasonably promote civic virtue and that can be demonstrably justified in a free and democratic society. In particular, judges should recognize how the federal bench has contributed to the degradation of our society by its tolerance of obscenity.

11. Republicans Will Protect Free Speech Rights on Social Media

We live an important part of our lives on search engines and social media platforms, and they've become crucially important elements in our system of democracy. Through their algorithms they nudge us on how to vote, and Google, Facebook, and Twitter took the further step of banning Trump from their services after the Capitol riot. We've prided ourselves on how we defend democracy, but now foreign leaders such as former German Chancellor Angela Merkel and Mexico's Mexico President Andrés Manuel López Obrador have expressed concern about political censorship in America.

Conservatives have a legitimate beef about social media censorship. Some right-wing links disappear quickly on Google, and Amazon demonetizes (bans from receiving donations) conservative groups such as the Family Research Council. Not a few conservatives have found themselves silenced in "Facebook Jail." The new cultural hegemony, which is reinforced by a cancel culture that de-platforms, silences, and sacks employees, begins to resemble China's oppressive social credit system.

It's a novel problem where the easy answers are either too laissez-faire or too draconian. The libertarian tells us that the social media giants are private companies and therefore can do whatever they want. That's not how the common law saw things, however. Some private companies have always been impressed with public duties because of the possibility that they would abuse their market power. In the seventeenth century, Chief Justice Matthew Hale held that a ferry owner was not permitted to charge whatever it wanted when there was no one else to carry the goods across the river.[39] Similarly we regulate hotels because of their power to exploit consumers in desperate straits, and that indeed was a partial justification for the Civil Rights Act of 1964. Because of their political clout, the social media giants are no different. Unlike city newspapers and television networks, they're natural monopolies and should be regulated like public utilities.

At the other extreme, some conservatives argue that the size of the social media giants argues for breaking them up. Such theories have been discredited by the courts, however, and current antitrust thinking has it that size isn't a problem unless a dominant firm abuses its market power to extract monopoly profits. But how could that happen with the social media giants? Their services are free. That hasn't prevented them from becoming enormously rich, but their wealth comes from selling advertising and not from selling their services to consumers, and there's nothing wrong with that. It's what radio and TV do.

Besides, it's not clear whether breaking them up would make a difference. If the problem is their leftward tilt, a breakup probably wouldn't change much. There'd be a Facebook I in Menlo Park and a Facebook II down the street in Palo Alto, and they'd be run by the same kinds of people with the same slant on politics. And just how would a breakup work? Imagine sending half your Facebook friends to one company and the other half into a second. A to L here, M to

Z there. Let them try, but a year later only one company would be left. We'd all migrate to a single one of the companies to get our friends back together. The network benefits of getting all your friends on a single platform are what permitted Facebook to become dominant in the first place, and the legislator can't change the economic conditions that dictate there'll be only one firm in the industry.

Like Theodore Roosevelt, therefore, the progressive conservative will conclude that what's needed is greater regulation and not an antitrust breakup. But that's not an easy answer either. If the problem is political bias, politicians are the last people to trust. Democrats like Zoe Lofgren (D-CA) say that if there are problems here, "it's pretty obvious bias against conservative voices is not one of them." Rather, the real problem is conservative "hate speech." Turning things over to the politicians would be asking the swamp to regulate itself, and not just the swamp but the deepest of swamp dwellers, the politicians who try to silence political opponents.

The only institution that might be trusted to get it right is the judiciary. Congress should create a social media court on the model of the FISA court with members appointed by the chief justice from among the Article III bench with the power to fine a company for unreasonable suppression of legitimate political views. That would leave the social media platforms with a degree of discretion, and there's nothing wrong with that. Facebook censors pornography, and no platform should be required to carry water for Holocaust deniers and white supremacists. True calls for insurrection needn't be tolerated. On the other hand, groups that think that the 2020 election was tainted by fraud need to be part of the national conversation, and their free speech rights should be protected. It's a bit rich for companies that allowed the Russian collusion hoax to be aired on their platforms to ban accusations of voter fraud.

That's going to require an amendment to section 230 of the Communications Decency Act, which frees the social media companies from the responsibility of standing behind anything published on its platforms. The law was based upon a 1996 finding by Congress that the social media platforms "offer a forum for a true diversity of political discourse," which obviously is no longer the case. The goal is to get back to where we were before the social media platforms began to abuse their political power.[40]

12. Republicans Will Promote Pride in America

The federal government cannot force-feed pride in America on unwilling, unpatriotic citizens, nor can it command what is taught in public schools. That's the responsibility of the states and their education departments. But there is nothing wrong and possibly much to be gained if the national government seeks in noninvasive ways to instill a sense of a benign national identity.

Republicans will therefore create a National Endowment of the American Idea charged with promoting that which is admirable in our people, history, and culture. With that end in mind, the endowment will sponsor writers, producers, performers, and short videos to be shared on social media. It will complement the National Endowment of the Arts and the National Endowment of the Humanities, which should also seek to affirm America's greatness. When so much else in our media, schools, and culture denigrates America, at least one branch of our government should seek to instill pride in our country.

* * *

Beyond this, a progressive conservative administration will reinstate the successful policies of the Trump administration on matters such as trade, energy, and foreign affairs. That in itself won't suffice, however, since new problems will arise that require novel solutions. Sometimes, as in Theodore Roosevelt's time, new regulations will be required, while at other times, as during the Carter administration and today, deregulation will be called for. Sometimes we'll need to erect trade barriers, and sometimes we'll remove them because the benefits to American producers are exceeded by the added costs to consumers. Sometimes foreign policy realism will keep us out of a conflict, and sometimes our national self-interest will ask us to preserve the international order and its trade routes. It will always depend on the facts and never on abstract ideologies or soul-destroying resentments.

Pollsters tell us that many Americans, especially the young, support socialism. Progressive conservative don't believe it. They think that many, perhaps most, Americans want national catastrophic health insurance, student debt relief, campaign finance reform, and an end to tax loopholes that favor the rich. That's not socialism. Rather, those are sensible reforms, and if a progressive conservative Republican Party won't offer them, they'll be enacted by progressive Democrats. Only it will be so much worse if the issues are given away to the Democrats. That's why progressive conservatives aren't reactionaries and why they can't permit the Democrats to be the sole agents of change. It's also why they don't give in to despair about America.

After years of Democratic incompetence and national humiliation, most Americans will welcome progressive conservatism. But merely showing that you're better than the other guy is too low a bar when the other guy is today's Democrat. Instead, progressive conservative Republicans should seek to show that, in all their policies, they uniquely desire the common good and that they are still the party of Abraham Lincoln, Teddy Roosevelt, and Dwight Eisenhower. If they do so, they'll be chosen to govern the country, now and hereafter. *Esto perpetua!*

ACKNOWLEDGMENTS

I AM MOST GRATEFUL to the many people who've helped me: Mark Baulerlein, Dan Bonevac, Nick Capaldi, Alan Collinge, Don Devine, John Fonte, David Goldman, Allen Guelzo, Deal Hudson, David Keating, Rob Koons, Pierre Lemieux, Joyce Malcolm, Dan McCarthy, Mark Pulliam, Stephen Presser, Eric Rasmusen, John Samples, Brad Smith, and my old friend Bob Tyrrell. Al Regnery was an invaluable source of advice, and Chris DeMuth read the book through and saved me from several blunders. Finally, let me pay tribute to two great American patriots no longer with us: Angelo Codevilla and Jim Wooton.

Portions of the book have appeared in the *Wall Street Journal*, the *American Spectator*, and the *New York Post*. Parts of Chapter 4 appeared in the Fall 2021 issue of *National Affairs*, and parts of Chapter 9 appeared in the summer 2020 issue of *Modern Age*.

I also thank George Mason's Scalia Law School for its generous support, Deborah Keene and Peter Vay at the Scalia Law Library, Yen Kha and Katherine Hickey for secretarial help, and José Coradin for tech support.

My heartfelt thanks to everyone at Encounter Books: to the production team of Nola Tully, Amanda DeMatto, and Mary Spencer, to the marketing team of Sam Schneider and Lauren Miklos, and especially to Roger Kimball. Thanks also to Michael J. Totten for his superb editorial work.

Finally, and as always, my most heartfelt thanks go to my wife, Esther Goldberg.

December 1, 2021

BIBLIOGRAPHY

Acemoğlu, Daron. *Introduction to Modern Economic Growth*. Princeton: Princeton University Press, 2009.

Acemoğlu, Daron and James A. Robinson. *Economic Origins of Dictatorship and Democracy*. Cambridge: Cambridge University Press, 2006.

Acemoğlu, Daron and James A. Robinson. *Why Nations Fail: The Origins or Power, Prosperity, and Poverty*. New York: Crown, 2012.

Adams, Henry. *Adams*. Library of America, 1983.

Adams, John. *Revolutionary Writings 1755–1775*. New York: Library of America, 2011.

Ambrose, Stephen E. *Eisenhower*. 2 vols. New York: Simon & Schuster, 1983–84.

Arieli, Yehoshua. *Individualism and Nationalism in American Ideology*. Cambridge: Harvard University Press, 1966.

Arum, Richard and Josipa Roksa. *Academically Adrift: Limited Learning on College Campuses*. Chicago: University of Chicago Press, 2010.

Audretsch, David B., Robert E. Litan, and Robert J. Strom (eds.). *Entrepreneurship and Openness: Theory and Evidence*. Northampton: Edward Elgar, 2009.

Ball, Howard. *Murder in Mississippi: United States v. Price and the Struggle for Civil Rights*. Lawrence: University Press Kansas, 2004.

Balz, Dan. *Collision 2012: Obama vs. Romney and the Future of Elections in America*. New York: Viking, 2013.

Bailyn, Bernard. *The Ideological Origins of the American Revolution*. Cambridge: Harvard University Press, 1967

Barro, Robert J. and Xavier Sala-i-Martin. *Economic Growth*. Cambridge: MIT Press, 2d ed. 2004.

Bartlett, Donald L. and James B. Steele. *The Betrayal of the American Dream*. New York: Public Affairs, 2012.

Bartels, Larry M. *Unequal Democracy: The Political Economy of the New Gilded Age*. New York: Russell Sage, 2008.

Baumgartner, Frank R., Jeffrey M. Berry, Marie Hojnacki, David C. Kimball, and Beth L. Leech. *Lobbying and Policy Change: Who Wins, Who Loses, and Why*. Chicago: University of Chicago Press, 2009.

Beatty, Jack. *Rascal King: The Life and Times of James Michael Curley*. Boston: Da Capo Press, 1992.

Bell, Daniel. *The Cultural Contradictions of Capitalism*. New York: Basic Books, Anniversary Edition, 1996.

Bell, Graham. *Selection: The Mechanism of Evolution*. Oxford University Press, second edition. 2008.

Betts, Julian R and Y. Emily Tang. *A Meta-Analysis of the Literature on the Effect of Charter Schools on Student Achievement*. Seattle: Center for Reinventing Public Education, 2014.

Bishop, Bill. *The Big Sort: Why the Clustering of Like-Minded America is Tearing Us Apart*. Boston: Mariner, 2009.

Black, Conrad. *Franklin Delano Roosevelt: Champion of Freedom*. New York: PublicAffairs, 2003.

Black, Conrad. *Richard M. Nixon: A Life in Full*. New York: PublicAffairs, 2007.

Blackstone, William. *Commentaries on the Laws of England*. Avalon.law.yale.edu.

Blau, Francis D. and Christopher Mackie (eds.). *The Economic and Fiscal Consequences of Immigration*, Washington, DC: National Academy Press, 2016.

Boatright, Robert G. *Interest Groups and Campaign Finance Reform in the United States and Canada*. Ann Arbor: University of Michigan Press, 2011.

Boix, Carles. *Democracy and Redistribution*. Cambridge: Cambridge University Press, 2003.

Borjas, George J. *Heaven's Door: Immigration Policy and the American Economy*. Princeton: Princeton University Press, 1999.

Borjas, George J. *Immigration Economics*. Cambridge: Harvard University Press, 2014.

Borjas, George J. *We Wanted Workers: Unraveling the Immigration Narratives*. New York: Norton, 2016.

Bowles, Samuel, Herbert Gintis, and Melissa Osborne Groves, eds. *Unequal Chances: Family Background and Economic Success*. Princeton: Princeton University Press, 2005.

Bowsky, William M. *A Medieval Italian Commune: Siena under the Nine, 1287–1355*. Berkeley: U. California P., 1981.

Branch, Taylor. *Pillar of Fire: America in the King Years 1963–65*. New York: Simon & Schuster, 1999.

Brandt, Carl G. and Edward M. Shafter. *Selected American Speeches on Basic Issues, 1850–1950*. Boston: Houghton Mifflin, 1960.

Brill, Steven. *Class Warfare: Inside the Fight to Fix America's Schools*. New York: Simon & Schuster, 2011.

Brooks, Arthur C. *The Battle: How the Fight between Free Enterprise and Big Government Will Shape America's Future*. New York: Basic Books, 2010.

Brynjolfsson, Erik and Andrew McAfee. *The Second Machine Age: Work, Progress, and Prosperity in a Time of Brilliant Technologies*. New York: W. W. Norton, 2014.

Buchanan, James M. and Gordon Tullock. *The Calculus of Consent: Logical Foundations of Constitutional Government*. Ann Arbor: University of Michigan Press, 1962.

Buckley, F. H., editor. *The American Illness: Essays on the Rule of Law*. New Haven, Yale University Press, 2013.

Buckley, F. H. *The Once and Future King: The Rise of Crown Government in America.* New York: Encounter, 2014.

Buckley, F. H. *The Way Back: Restoring the Promise of America.* New York: Encounter, 2016.

Buckley, F. H. *The Republic of Virtue: How We Tried to Ban Corruption, Failed, and What We Can Do About It.* New York: Encounter, 2017.

Buckley, F. H. *The Republican Workers Party: How the Trump Victory Drove Everyone Crazy, and Why It Was Just What We Needed.* New York: Encounter, 2018.

Buckley, James L. *Saving Congress from Itself: Emancipating the States and Empowering their People.* New York: Encounter, 2014.

Burke, Edmund. *Reflections on the French Revolution.* London: J. Dodsley, third edition. 1790.

Butterfield, Herbert. *The Whig Interpretation of History.* New York: W. W. Norton, 1965.

Cacioppo, John T. and William Patrick. *Loneliness.* New York: W. W. Norton, 2008.

Cain, Bruce E. *Democracy More or Less: America's Political Reform Quandary.* Cambridge: Cambridge University Press, 2014.

Carbone, June and Naomi Cahn. *Marriage Markets.* Oxford University Press, 2014.

Card, David and Orley Ashenfelter, eds. *Handbook of Labor Economics.* Amsterdam: North Holland, 2007.

Carnevale, Anthony P., Tamara Jayasundera, and Ban Cheah. *The College Advantage: Weathering the Economic Storm.* Washington: Georgetown Public Policy Institute, n.d.

Carney, Timothy P. *The Big Ripoff: How Big Business and Big Government Steal Your Money.* Hoboken: John Wiley, 2006.

Case, Anne and Angus Deaton. *Deaths of Despair and the Future of Capitalism.* Princeton: Princeton University Press, 2020.

Chakrabarti, Rajashri and Paul E. Peterson (eds.), *School Choice International: Exploring Public-Private Partnerships.* Cambridge: MIT Press, 2009.

Cicero. *De Officiis.* Trans. Walter Miller. London: Loeb, 1913.

Cobbett, William. *Rural Rides.* London, Folio, 2001.

Cohen, G. A. *If You're an Egalitarian, How Come You're So Rich?* Cambridge: Harvard, 2000.

Cohen, Joshua, editor. *For Love of Country: Debating the Limits of Patriotism.* Boston: Beacon, 1996.

Corak, Miles, editor. *Generational Income Mobility in North America and Europe.* Cambridge: Cambridge University Press, 2004.

Creighton, Donald. *The Young Politician.* Toronto: Macmillan, 1952.

Creighton, Donald. *The Old Chieftain.* Toronto: Macmillan, 1955.

Croly, Herbert. *The Promise of American Life.* Boston: Northeastern University Press, 1989 [1909].

Dahl, Robert A. *Who Governs?* New Haven: Yale University Press, 1961.

Dart, Ron. *The North American High Tory Tradition.* American Anglican Press, 2017.

Dawkins, Richard. *The Selfish Gene*. Oxford University Press, 2006.

Disraeli, Benjamin. *Sybil, or the Two Nations*. London: Longmans, Green, 1871.

Disraeli, Benjamin. *Selected Speeches*. Edited by T. E. Kebbel. London: Longmans, Green, 1882.

Disraeli, Benjamin. *Coningsby, or the New Generation*. London: Longmans, Green, 1900.

Djilas, Milovan. *The New Class: An Analysis of the Communist System*. New York: Praeger, 1957.

Drutman, Lee. *The Business of America is Lobbying: How Corporations Became Politicized and Politics Became Corporate*. New York: Oxford University Press, 2015.

Dunkelman, Marc J. *The Vanishing Neighbor: The Transformation of American Community*. New York: W. W. Norton, 2014.

Eberstadt, Nicholas. M. *A Nation of Takers: America's Entitlement Epidemic*. West Conshohocken, Pennsylvania: Templeton Press, 2012.

Eberstadt, Nicholas. *Men Without Work: America's Invisible Crisis*. West Conshohocken: Templeton Press, 2016.

Edelman, Peter. *So Rich, So Poor: Why It's So Hard to End Poverty in America*. New York: Twenty Years, 2012.

Edwards, H. W. J. *The Radical Tory*. London: Jonathan Cape, 1937.

Eisenhower, Dwight D. *Eisenhower Papers Series*. Edited by Louis Galambos et al. Baltimore: Johns Hopkins University Press.

Eisenhower, Dwight D. *Public Papers of the Presidents of the United States: Dwight D. Eisenhower*. Washington: GPO, 1960. *Presidential Papers of Dwight David Eisenhower* (hereafter PPDDE)

Eisenhower, Dwight D. *Mandate for Change 1953–1956*. Garden City: Doubleday, 1963.

Eisenhower, Susan. *How Ike Led: The Principles behind Eisenhower's Biggest Decisions*. New York: Thomas Dunne, 2020.

Ewald, William B. *Eisenhower the President: The Crucial Days: 1951–60*. Englewood Cliffs: Prentice-Hall, 1981.

Farrand, Max, editor. *The Records of the Federal Convention of 1787*. New Haven: Yale University Press, revised edition. 1937).

Faust, Drew Gilpin, editor. *The Ideology of Slavery: Proslavery Thought in the Antebellum South, 1830–1860*. Baton Rouge: Louisiana State University Press, 1981.

Faux, Jeff. *The Servant Economy: Where America's Elite Is Sending the Middle Class*. New York: John Wiley, 2012.

Ferrell, Robert H. *The Diary of James C. Hagerty: Eisenhower in Mid-course, 1954–1955*. Bloomington: Indiana University Press, 1983.

Finn, Chester E. *Troublemaker: A Personal History of School Reform since Sputnik*. Princeton: Princeton University Press, 2008.

Finnis, John. *Natural Law and Natural Rights*, Oxford: Oxford University Press, second edition. 2011.

Fitzhugh, George. *Sociology for the South, or The Failure of the Free Society*. A. Morris: Richmond, 1854.

Fitzhugh, George. *Cannibals All! Or Slaves without Masters*. Cambridge: Harvard University Press, 1988.

Foot, Philippa. *Natural Goodness*. Oxford: Oxford University Press, 2001.

Foner, Eric. *Free Soil, Free Labor, Free Men: The Ideology of the Republican Party Before the Civil War*. New York: Oxford University Press, 1995.

Foster, R. F. *Lord Randolph Churchill: A Political Life*. Oxford: Oxford University Press, 1981.

Frank, Thomas. *What's the Matter with Kansas?* New York: Henry Holt, 2004.

Frank, Thomas. *Listen, Liberal: Whatever Happened to the Party of the People?* New York: Henry Holt, 2016.

Frank, Thomas. *The People, No: A Brief History of Anti-Populism*. New York: Metropolitan, 2020.

Frey, Bruno. *Happiness: A Revolution in Economics*. Cambridge: MIT Press, 2008.

Frey, Bruno S. and Alois Stutzer. *Happiness and Economics: How the Economy and Institutions Affect Human Well-Being*. Princeton University Press, 2002.

Friedman, Tom. *The World is Flat: A Brief History of the Twenty-First Century*. New York: Farrar, Straus and Giroux, 2005.

Fukuyama, Francis. *The End of History and the Last Man*. New York: Avon, 1992.

Fukuyama, Francis. *The Origins of Political Order: From Prehuman Times to the French Revolution*. New York: Farrar, Straus and Giroux, 2011.

Fukuyama, Francis. *Political Order and Political Decay: From the Industrial Revolution to the Globalization of Democracy*. New York: Farrar, Straus and Giroux, 2014.

Fund, John and Hans von Spakovsky. *Who's Counting: How Fraudsters and Bureaucrats Put Your Vote at Risk*. New York: Encounter Books, 2012.

Fund, John and Hans von Spakovsky. *Our Broken Elections: How the Left Changed the Way You Vote*. New York: Encounter Books, 2021.

Galbraith, James K. *Inequality and Instability: A Study of the World Economy Just Before the Great Crisis*. New York: Oxford University Press, 2012.

Gellner, Ernest. *Nations and Nationalism*. Ithaca: Cornell University Press, 1983.

Genovese, Eugene. *The World the Slaveholders Made: Two Essays in Interpretation*. New York: Pantheon, 1969.

Gigerenzer, Gerd. *Gut Feelings: The Intelligence of the Unconscious*. New York, Penguin, 2008.

Gillens, Martin. *Affluence and Influence: Economic Inequality and Political Power in America*. Princeton: Princeton University Press, 2012.

Golden, Daniel. *The Price of Admission: How America's Ruling Class Buys Its Way into Elite Colleges – and Who Gets Left Outside the Gates*. New York: Three Rivers, 2006.

Goldin, Claudia and Lawrence F. Katz. *The Race between Education and Technology*. Cambridge: Harvard University Press, 2008.

Goodin, Robert E, Philip Pettit, and Thomas W Pogge (editors). *A Companion to Contemporary Political Philosophy*. Oxford: Blackwell, 1993.

Gordon, Rebecca H. and Thomas M. Susman. *The Lobbying Manual*. Washington: ABA Book Publishing, fifth edition, 2016.

Grant, George. *Lament for a Nation*. Toronto: McClelland and Stewart, 1965.

Grant, George. *The George Grant Reader*. Edited by William Christian and Sheila Grant. Toronto: University of Toronto Press, 1998.

Greenfeld, Liah. *Nationalism: Five Roads to Modernity*. Cambridge: Harvard University Press, 1992.

Greenwood, Michael J. and John M. McDowell. *Legal US Immigration: Influences on Gender, Age, and Skill Composition*. Kalamazoo: W. E. Upjohn, 1999.

Grisez, Germain. *Contraception and the Natural Law*. Milwaukee: Bruce, 1964.

Grossman, Gene M. and Elhanan Helpman. *Special Interest Politics*. Cambridge: MIT Press, 2001.

Halper, Stefan. *The Beijing Consensus: How China's Model Will Dominate the Twenty-First Century*. New York: Basic, 2010).

Hamilton, W. D. *Narrow Roads of Gene Land*. Oxford: W. H. Freeman, 1996.

Hamburger, Philip. *Separation of Church and State*. Cambridge: Harvard University Press, 2002.

Hamburger, Philip. *Is Administrative Law Unlawful?* Chicago: University of Chicago Press, 2014.

Hamilton, Alexander. *The Papers of Alexander Hamilton*. Edited by Harold C. Syrett and Jacob E. Cooke. New York: Columbia University Press, 1962.

Hankins, James. *Virtue Politics: Soulcraft and Statecraft in Renaissance Italy*. Cambridge: Harvard University Press, 2020.

Hanushek, Eric A. and Alfred A. Lindseth. *Schoolhouses, Courthouses, and Statehouses: Solving the Funding-Achievement Puzzle in America's Public Schools*. Princeton: Princeton University Press, 2009.

Hanuskek, Eric A. Stephen Machin and Ludger Woessmann, editors. *Handbook of the Economics of Education*. San Diego: North-Holland, 2011.

Hanushek, Eric A., Paul E. Peterson, and Ludger Woessmann. *Endangering Prosperity: A Global View of the American School*. Washington: Brookings Institution, 2013.

Harman, Oren. *The Price of Altruism*. New York: W. W. Norton, 2010.

Hasen, Richard L. *Plutocrats United: Campaign Money, the Supreme Court, and the Distortion of American Elections*. New Haven: Yale University Press, 2016).

Hawley, Joshua David. *Theodore Roosevelt: Preacher of Righteousness*. New Haven: Yale University Press, 2008.

Hayek, F. A. *Law, Legislation, and Liberty*. Edited by Jeremy Shearmur. University of Chicago Press, 2022).

Hegel, G. W. F. *The Philosophy of History*. Translated by J. Sibree. New York: Dover, 1956.

Heidenheimer, Arnold J. and Michael Johnston, *Political Corruption: Concepts & Contexts*. New Brunswick: Transaction, 2002.

Herrnstein, Richard J. and Charles Murray. *The Bell Curve: Intelligence and Class Structure in American Life*. New York: Free Press, 1996.

Hitchcock, William I. *The Age of Eisenhower: America and the World in the 1950s*. New York: Simon & Schuster, 2018.

Hofstadter, Richard. *The Age of Reform*. New York: Vintage, 1955.

Hofstadter, Richard. *The Progressive Historians: Turner, Beard, Parrington*. New York: Vintage, 1970.

Hook, Sidney. *The Hero in History*. New York: Cosmo, 2008.

Howe, Daniel Walker. *What Hath God Wrought: The Transformation of America, 1815–1848*. New York: Oxford University Press, 2009.

Hoxby, Caroline M., editor. *The Economics of School Choice*. Chicago: University of Chicago Press, 2003.

Hume, David. *A Treatise of Human Nature*. Oxford: Oxford University Press, 1967.

Hume, David. *Hume: Political Essays*. Cambridge University Press, 1994.

Huntington, Samuel P. *Who We Are: The Challenges to America's National Identity*. New York: Simon & Schuster, 2004.

James, Robert Rhodes. *Lord Randolph Churchill*. London: Phoenix, 1959.

Janowski, Zbigniew. *Homo Americanus: The Rise of Totalitarian Democracy in America*. South Bend: St. Augustine's, 2021.

Jefferson, Thomas. *Writings*. Library of America, 1984.

Jones, Maldwyn. *American Immigration*. Chicago: University of Chicago Press, 1992.

Judis, John and Ruy Teixeira *The Emerging Democratic Majority*. New York: Simon & Schuster, 2002.

Judt, Tony. *Ill Fares the Land*. New York: Penguin, 2010.

Kagan, Robert A. *Adversarial Legalism: The American Way of Law*. Cambridge: Harvard University Press, 2001.

Kammen, Michael. *A Machine That Would Go of Itself: The Constitution in American Culture*. New York: St. Martin's, 1994.

Kendi, Ibram X. *How to Be an Antiracist*. New York: One World, 2019.

Klein, Michael C. and Michael Pettis. *Trade Wars Are Class Wars*. New Haven: Yale University Press, 2020.

Kluger, Richard. *Simple Justice*. New York: Knopf, 1975.

Kojève, Alexander. *Introduction to the Reading of Hegel: Lectures on the Phenomenology of Spirit*. Trans. J. H. Nichols. Ithaca: Cornell University Press, 1969

Kirk, Russell. *The Conservative Mind: From Burke to Eliot*. Seventh revised edition. Washington: Regnery, 1995.

Kohn, Hans. *American Nationalism: An Interpretive Essay*. New York: Macmillan, 1957.

Kolko, Gabriel. *The Triumph of Conservatism: A Reinterpretation of American History, 1900–1916*. New York: Free Press, 1963.

Kotkin, Joel. *The New Class Conflict*. Candor, New York: Telos, 2014.

Kramnick, Isaac. *Bolingbroke and his Circle: The Politics of Nostalgia in the Age of Walpole*. Ithaca: Cornell University Press, 1992.

Krause, Eleanor and Isabel Sawhill. *What We Know and Don't Know about Declining Labor Force Participation Rates: A Review*. Washington: Brookings Institution, 2017.

La Raja, Raymond J. *Small Change: Money, Political Parties, and Campaign Finance Reform*. Ann Arbor: University of Michigan Press, 2008.

Larson, Arthur. *A Republican Looks at his Party*. New York: Harper, 1956.

Lasch, Christopher. *The Revolt of the Elites and the Betrayal of Democracy*. New York: W. W. Norton, 1995.

Lessig, Lawrence. *Republic, Lost: How Money Corrupts Congress – and a Plan to Stop It*. New York: Twelve, 2011.

Levy, David W. *Herbert Croly of the New Republic: The Life and Thought of an American Progressive*. Princeton: Princeton University Press, 1985.

Lincoln, Abraham. *Lincoln: Speeches and Writings 1832–1858*. Library of America, 1989.

Lincoln, Abraham. *Lincoln: Speeches and Writings 1859–1865*. New York: Library of America.

Lipset, Seymour Martin. *Continental Divide: The Values and Institutions of the United States and Canada*. Toronto: C. D. Howe, 1989.

Lipset, Seymour Martin. *American Exceptionalism: A Double-Edged Sword*. New York: W. W. Norton, 1996.

Lipset, Seymour Martin and Gary Marks. *It Didn't Happen Here*. New York: W. W. Norton, 2001.

Lowe, Dylan. *Permanently Blue: How Democrats Can End the Republican Party and Rule the Next Generation*. New York: Crown, 2010.

Machiavelli, Niccolò. *Discourses on Livy*. Translated by Harvey C. Mansfield and Nathan Tarcov. Chicago: University of Chicago Press, 1996.

Madison, James. *The Papers of James Madison*. Edited by Robert A. Rutland et al. Chicago: University of Chicago Press, 1962.

Maier, Pauline. *American Scripture: Making the Declaration of Independence*. New York: Vintage, 1997.

Marx, Karl. *The Eighteenth Brumaire of Louis Napoleon*. Translated by Daniel DeLeon. Chicago: Charles H. Kerr, third edition, 1913.

Mason, Liliana. *Uncivil Agreement: How Politics Becomes Our Identity*. Chicago: University of Chicago Press, 2018.

MacIntyre, Alasdair. *After Virtue*. Notre Dame: University of Notre Dame Press, second edition, 1984.

McCraw, Thomas K. *Prophet of Innovation: Joseph Schumpeter and Creative Destruction*. Cambridge: Harvard University Press, 2007.

McDonald, Forest. *Novus Ordo Seclorum: The Intellectual Origins of the Constitution*. Lawrence: University Press of Kansas, 1985.

McDonald, Ted, Elizabeth Ruddick, Arthur Sweetman, and Christopher Worswick, editors, *Canadian Immigration: Economic Evidence for a Dynamic Policy Environment*. Kingston, Ontario: McGill-Queen's University Press, 2010.

McFarland, Andrew S. *Neopluralism: The Evolution of Political Process Theory*. Lawrence: University Press of Kansas, 2004.

McGerr, Michael. *A Fierce Discontent: The Rise and Fall of the Progressive Movement in America*. New York: Oxford University Press, 2003.

Mettler, Suzanne. *The Submerged State: How Invisible Government Policies Undermine American Democracy*. Chicago: University of Chicago Press, 2011.

Mettler, Suzanne. *Degrees of Inequality*. New York: Basic, 2014.

Mill, John Stuart. *Collected Works*. Indianapolis: Liberty Fund, 2006.

Mill, John Stuart. *Three Essays on Religion*. New York: Henry Holt, 1879.

Mitchell, Josh. *The Debt Trap: How Student Loans Became a National Catastrophe*. New York: Simon & Schuster, 2021.

Moe, Terry M. *Special Interest: Teachers Unions and America's Public Schools*. Washington: Brookings Institution, 2011.

Monypenny, William II. *The Life of Benjamin Disraeli*. New York: Macmillan, 1913.

Montesquieu, Charles-Louis de Secondat. *Oeuvres complètes de Montesquieu*. Paris: Gallimard, 1952.

Morgenthau, Hans J. *Politics Among Nations: The Struggle for Power and Peace*. Second edition. New York: Alfred A. Knopf, 1954.

Mosca, Gaetano. *The Ruling Class*. Translated by Hannah D. Kahn. New York: McGraw-Hall, 1939.

Mungiu-Pippidi, Alina. *The Quest for Good Governance: How Societies Develop Control of Corruption*. Cambridge: Cambridge University Press, 2015.

Murchison, William. *The Cost of Liberty: The Life of John Dickinson*. Wilmington: ISI, 2013.

Murray, Charles. *Losing Ground*. New York: Basic Books, 1985.

Murray, Charles. *Coming Apart: The State of White America, 1960–2010*. New York: Random House, 2012.

Nichols, David A. *A Matter of Justice: Eisenhower and the Beginning of the Civil Rights Revolution*. New York: Simon & Schuster, 2007.

Nichter, Luke A. *The Last Brahmin: Henry Cabot Lodge Jr. and the Making of the Cold War*. New Haven: Yale University Press, 2020.

Niebuhr, Reinhold. *Reinhold Niebuhr: Major Works on Religion and Politics*. Edited by Elizabeth Sifton. New York: Library of America, 2015.

Nixon, Richard. *RN: The Memoirs of Richard Nixon*. New York: Grosset & Dunlap, 1978.

Noah, Timothy. *The Great Divergence: America's Growing Inequality Crisis and What We Can Do about It*. New York: Bloomsbury, 2012.

Noonan, John T. *Bribes*. New York: Macmillan, 1984.

Norris, Pippa. *Driving Democracy: Do Power-Sharing Institutions Work?* New York: Cambridge University Press, 2008.

Oakeshott, Michael. *Rationalism in Politics and Other Essays*. London: Methuen, 1962.

Olsen, Henry. *The Working Class Republican: Ronald Reagan and the Return of Blue-Collar Conservatism*. New York: HarperCollins, 2017.

Olson, Mancur. *The Logic of Collective Action: Public Goods and the Theory of Groups*. Cambridge: Harvard University Press, 1965.

Olson, Mancur. *The Rise and Decline of Nations: Economic Growth, Stagflation, and Social Rigidities*. New Haven: Yale University Press, 1982.

Olson, Mancur. *Power and Prosperity: Outgrowing Communist and Capitalist Dictatorships*. New York: Basic Books, 2000.

Orrenius, Pia and Madeline Zavodny. *Beside the Golden Door: US Immigration Reform in a new Era of Globalization*. Washington: American Enterprise Institute, 2010.

Ortega y Gasset, José. *The Modern Theme*. New York: Torchbooks, 1961.

Orwell, George. *The Penguin Essays of George Orwell*. London: Harmondsworth, 1984.

Orwell, George. *Essays*. New York: Knopf, 2002.

Parfit, Derek. *On What Matters: Volume 3*, Oxford: Oxford University Press, 2017.

Péguy, Charles. *Notre Jeunesse*. Paris: Gallimard, 1993.

Persson, Torsten and Guido Tabellini, *The Economic Effects of Constitutions*. Cambridge: MIT Press, 2003.

Pestritto, Ronald J. *Woodrow Wilson and the Roots of Modern Liberalism*. Lanham, Maryland: Rowman and Littlefield, 2005.

Pettit, Philip. *Republicanism: A Theory of Freedom and Government*. Oxford: Oxford University Press, 1997.

Piketty, Thomas. *Capital in the Twenty-First Century*. Harvard University Press, 2014.

Pocock, J.G.A. *Virtue, Commerce, and History: Essays on Political Thought and History, Chiefly in the Eighteenth Century*. Cambridge: Cambridge University Press, 1985.

Pocock, J.G.A. *The Machiavellian Moment: Florentine Political Thought and the Atlantic Republican Tradition*. Princeton: Princeton University Press, 2003.

Popenoe, David. *Life Without Father: Compelling New Evidence that Fatherhood and Marriage Are Indispensable for the Good of Children and Society*. New York: Free Press, 1996.

Putnam, Robert. *Bowling Alone: The Collapse and Revival of American Community*. New York: Simon & Schuster, 2000.

Rajan, Rajhuram and Luigi Zingales. *Saving Capitalism from the Capitalists*. New York: Crown Books, 2003.

Rauch, Jonathan. *Demosclerosis: The Silent Killer of American Government*. New York: Random House, 1994.

Rauch, Jonathan. *Government's End: Why Washington Stopped Working*. New York: Public Affairs, 1994.

Ravitch, Diane. *Slaying Goliath: The Passionate Resistance to Privatization and the Fight to Save America's Public Schools*. New York: Knopf, 2020.

Renan, Ernest. *Qu'est-ce qu'une nation?* Paris: Presses-Pocket, 1992.

Rhee, Michelle. *Radical: Fighting to Put Students First*. New York: HarperCollins, 2013.

Richardson, Heather Cox. *To Make Men Free: A History of the Republican Party*. New York: Basic Books, 2014.

Ripley, William Z. *Main Street and Wall Street*. Boston: Little Brown, 1927.

Roosevelt, Theodore. *Works: Administration–Civil Service*. New York: Collier, 1897.

Roosevelt, Theodore, *The foes of our own household*. New York: Doran, 1917.

Roosevelt, Theodore. *American Ideals*. New York: G. P. Putnam, 1920.

Roosevelt, Theodore. *Roosevelt's Writings*. Edited by Maurice Garland Fulton. New York: Macmillan, 1920.

Roosevelt, Theodore. *The Rough Riders.* New York: Library of America, 2004.

Roosevelt, Theodore. *Letters and Speeches.* New York: Library of America, 2004.

Rothberg, Robert I. *The Corruption Cure: How Citizens and Leaders Can Combat Graft.* Princeton: Princeton University Press, 2017.

Ruskin, John. *Unto This Last.* New York: John Wiley, 1872.

Ruskin, John. *Praeterita.* New York: Bryan Taylor, 1894.

Rycroft, Robert S., editor. *The Economics of Inequality, Poverty, and Discrimination in the 21st Century.* Santa Barbara: Praeger, 2013.

Saez, Emmanuel and Gabriel Zucman. *The Triumph of Injustice: How the Rich Dodge Taxes and How to Make Them Pay.* New York: W. W. Norton, 2019.

Sawhill, Isabel V. *Generation Unbound: Drifting into Sex and Parenthood without Marriage.* Washington: Brookings Institution, 2014.

Schama, Simon. *Rough Crossings: The Slaves, the British, and the American Revolution,* London: BBC Books, 2005.

Schumpeter, Joseph A. *Capitalism, Socialism and Democracy.* London: Routledge, 1942.

Schlesinger, Arthur M. *The Vital Center: The Politics of Freedom.* New York: Houghton Mifflin, 1949.

Schlesinger, Arthur M. *The Disuniting of America: Reflections on a Multicultural Society.* New York: W. W. Norton, 1998.

Schweizer, Peter. *Extortion: How Politicians Extract Your Money, Buy Votes, and Line their Own Pockets.* Boston: Houghton, Mifflin, Harcourt, 2013.

Schweizer, Peter. *Clinton Cash: The Untold Story of How and Why Foreign Governments and Businesses Helped Make Bill and Hillary Rich.* New York: Harper, 2015.

Sesardic, Neven. *Making Sense of Heritability.* Cambridge: Cambridge University Press, 2005.

Shlaes, Amity. *The Forgotten Man: A New History of the Great Depression.* New York: Harper, 2007.

Shlaes, Amity. *Coolidge.* New York: Harper, 2013.

Shugart, Mathew S. and John M. Carey. *Presidents and Assemblies: Constitutional Design and Electoral Dynamics.* Cambridge: Cambridge University Press, 1992.

Siedentop, Larry. *Inventing the Individual: The Origins of Western Liberalism.* Cambridge: Harvard University Press, 2014.

Skowronek, Stephen, Stephen M. Engel, and Bruce Ackerman, editors. *The Progressives' Century: Political Reform, Constitutional Government, and the Modern American State.* New Haven: Yale University Press, 2016.

Skinner, Quentin. *The Foundations of Modern Political Thought: The Renaissance.* Cambridge: Cambridge University Press, 1978.

Skinner, Quentin. *Visions of Politics: Renaissance Virtues.* Cambridge: Cambridge University Press, 2002.

Smith, Bradley A. *Unfree Speech: The Folly of Campaign Finance Reform.* Princeton: Princeton University Press, 2001.

Smith, Jean Edward. *FDR*. New York: Random House, 2008.

Smith, Jean Edward. *Eisenhower in War and Peace*. New York: Random House, 2012.

Smith, Hedrick. *Who Stole the American Dream?* New York: Random House, 2012.

Smith, Richard Norton. *Thomas E. Dewey and His Times*. New York: Simon & Schuster, 1982.

Smith, Tara. *Ayn Rand's Normative Ethics: The Virtuous Egoist*, Cambridge University Press, 2006.

Sombart, Werner. *Why Is There No Socialism in the United States?* Armonk, New York: M. E. Sharpe, 1979.

Sorel, Georges. *Sorel: Reflections on Violence*. Cambridge: Cambridge University Press, 1999.

Sowell, Thomas. *Charter Schools and Their Enemies*. New York: Basic, 2020.

Starn, Randolph. *Ambrogio Lorenzetti: The Palazzo Publico, Siena*. New York, George Braziller, 1994.

Stebenne, David L. *Modern Republican: Arthur Larson and the Eisenhower Years*. Bloomington: Indiana University Press, 2006.

Stiglitz, Joseph E. *The Price of Inequality: How Today's Divided Society Endangers Our Future*. New York: W. W. Norton, 2012.

Strain, Michael R. *The American Dream Is Not Dead (But Populism Could Kill It)*. West Conshohocken: Templeton Press, 2020.

Sullivan, Teresa A., Elizabeth Warren, and Jay L. Westbrook. *The Fragile Middle Class: Americans in Debt*. New Haven: Yale University Press, 2000.

Tamir, Yael. *Liberal Nationalism*. Princeton: Princeton University Press, 1993.

Tawney, Richard H. *Equality*. New York: Harcourt, Brace, 1929.

Taylor, Alan. *American Revolutions: A Continental History*. New York: W. W. Norton, 2016.

Teachout, Zephyr. *Corruption in America: From Benjamin Franklin's Snuff Box to Citizens United*. Cambridge: Harvard University Press, 2014).

Trilling, Lionel. *The Middle of the Journey*. New York: New York Review Books, 2008.

Trilling, Lionel. *The Liberal Imagination*. New York: New York Review Books, 2008.

Turner, Frederick Jackson. *The Frontier in American History*. Mineola: Dover, 1996.

Tyack, David. *Seeking Common Ground: Public Schools in a Diverse Society*. Cambridge: Harvard University Press, 2003.i.

Wagner, Steve. *Eisenhower Republicanism: Pursuing the Middle Way*. Dekalb: Northern Illinois University Press, 2006. Walberg, Herbert J. and Joseph L. Bast, editors. *The Patriot's Toolbox*. Chicago: Heartland Institute, 2017.

Watson, George. *The Lost Literature of Socialism*. Cambridge: Lutterworth Press, second edition, 2010.

Weil, Simone. *L'Enracinement*. Paris: Gallimard, 1949.

West, Darrell M. *Billionaires: Reflections on the Upper Crust*. Washington: Brookings Institution, 2014.

Wicker, Tom. *One of Us: Richard Nixon and the American Dream*. New York: Random House. 1991.

Wilkinson, Richard and Kate Pickett. *The Spirit Level: Why Greater Equality Makes Societies Stronger.* New York: Bloomsbury, 2009.

Wilson, James. *Collected Works of James Wilson.* Edited by Kermit L. Hall and Mark David Hall. Indianapolis: Liberty Fund, 2007.

Wilson, William Julius. *The Truly Disadvantaged: The Inner City, the Underclass, and Public Policy.* University of Chicago Press, second edition. 2012.

Wood, Gordon S. *The Creation of the American Republic, 1776–1787.* University of North Carolina Press, 1998.

Wood, Gordon S. *The Radicalism of the American Revolution.* New York: Vintage, 1993.

Woessmann, Ludger et al., *School Accountability, Autonomy, and Choice Around the World.* Cheltenham, UK: Edward Elgar, 2009.

Yarbrough, Jean M. *Theodore Roosevelt and the American Political Tradition.* Lawrence: University Press of Kansas, 2012.

Zahavi, Amotz and Avishag Zahavi. *The Handicap Principle: A Missing Piece of Darwin's Puzzle.* Oxford University Press, 1997.

NOTES

CHAPTER ONE

1. Péguy, 115.
2. The British record on slavery was superior to that of America at the time, and the difference has been the subject of several books, notably by Simon Schama and Alan Taylor.
3. Victor Morton, "New York Times 1619 Project leader calls it 'honor' to inspire riots, statue attacks," *Washington Times*, June 20, 2020.
4. *Aeneid* IV.412.
5. Foot, 107.
6. Nickolas Kristof, "Can We Put Fox News on Trial with Trump?" *New York Times*, Feb. 10, 2021.
7. Margaret Sullivan, "Fox News is a hazard to our democracy. It's time to take the fight to the Murdochs. Here's how." *Washington Post*, Jan. 24, 2021.
8. Max Boot, "Sadly, Fox News can't be impeached," *Washington Post*, Feb. 11, 2021.
9. Charles M. Blow, "Yes, Even George Washington," *New York Times*, June 28, 2020.
10. Michael Ruane, "'Greatest Generation' survey on race, sex and combat during World War II runs counter to its wholesome image" *Washington Post*, Dec. 20, 2021.
11. Philip J. Kain, "Hegel, History and Evil," 33 *History of Philosophy Quarterly*, (2016): 275.
12. Georg Wilhelm Friedrich Hegel, *Philosophy of History*, 31.

CHAPTER TWO

1. US Bureau of Labor Statistics, *Monthly Labor Review*, April 2020.
2. Robert E. Scott and Zane Mokhiber, "The China toll deepens: Growth in the bilateral trade deficit between 2001 and 2017 cost 3.4 million US jobs, with losses in every state and congressional district," *Economic Policy Institute*, October 23, 2018.
3. Neil Bhutta et al., "Changes in US Family Finances from 2016 to 2019: Evidence from the Survey of Consumer Finances," Federal Reserve Bulletin, Sept. 2020.
4. Lydia Saad, "Gallup Election 2020 Coverage," *Gallup News*, Oct. 29. 2020.

5. Henry Grabar, "Of course Trump hates Brutalism," *Slate*, July 31, 2018.

6. Chris Kahn, "Despite report findings, almost half of Americans think Trump colluded with Russia," Reuters, March 26, 2019.

7. Kimberley Strassel, "Inside the Clinton dossier and the con behind the Russiagate scandal," *New York Post*, Nov. 5, 2021.

8. Jonathan Turley: "Has the media finally awoken to Hunter Biden?" *The Hill*, Dec. 12. 2020.

9. Becket Adams, "NPR says it won't cover Hunter Biden news because it's a 'waste' of time," *Washington Examiner*, Oct. 22, 2020.

10. Brad Hoylman, "Joe Biden Loves his son. We should all be so lucky." *Washington Post*, Oct. 28, 2020.

11. Adam Popescu, "There's a new artist in town. The name is Biden." *New York Times*, Feb. 28, 2020.

12. Jay Rosen, "Donald Trump is crashing the system. Journalists need to build a new one." *Washington Post*, July 13, 2016.

13. Michael D. Shear, Noah Weiland, Eric Lipton, Maggie Haberman, and David E. Sanger, "Inside Trump's Failure: The Rush to Abandon Leadership Role on the Virus," *New York Times*, July 18, 2020.

14. Thomas Franck, "Biden says Covid surge needs to be solved at state level, vows full federal support," CNBC, Dec. 27, 2021.

15. Caroline Kelly, "'I will not take his word for it': Kamala Harris says she would not trust Trump alone on a coronavirus vaccine." CNN, Sept. 5, 2020.

16. Hannah Ray Lambert, "Here's how many people had protest charges dropped in September," KOIN, Oct. 6, 2020.

17. Margaret Sullivan, *Washington Post*, Sept. 4, 2017. See also Carlos Lozada, "How antifa justifies stifling speech, clobbering supremacists," *Washington Post*, Sept. 3, 2017; Mark Bray, "What the 'alt-left' antifa activists actually believe," *Washington Post*, Aug. 20, 2017; Perry Stein, "What draws Americans to anarchy? It's more than just smashing windows," *Washington Post*, August 10, 2017.

18. Neil MacFarquhar, "Murders Spiked in 2020 in Cities Across the United States," *New York Times*, Sept. 27, 2021.

19. Robby Soave, "'Silence Is Violence': D.C. Black Lives Matter Protesters Adopt Strategy of Intimidating Random White People," *Reason*, Aug. 25, 2020.

20. Frances Mulraney, "Moment Portland city commissioner, who demanded $18 million police budget cuts and said most 911 calls are unnecessary, calls cops on her LYFT driver in argument about open windows," *Daily Mail*, Nov. 11, 2020. Aaron Feis, "Portland politician who called 911 over Lyft spat blames 'white supremacists,'" *New York Post*, Nov. 15, 2020.

21. Shane Dixon Kavanaugh, "Portland Mayor Ted Wheeler pepper sprays unmasked man who confronted him with video camera," *The Oregonian*, Jan. 26, 2021.

22. Bill Hutchinson, "Chicago Sees 18 Homicides in Deadliest Day in 60 Years," ABC News, June 9, 2020.

23. Sorel, 61.

24. Id. 67.
25. Charles M. Blow, "An Insatiable Rage," *New York Times*, June 14, 2020.
26. Caroline Vakil, "FBI finds scant evidence Jan. 6 attack was coordinated," *The Hill*, Aug. 20, 2021.
27. Martin Weil and Amy B. Wang, "Six Jan. 6 officers may face discipline," *Washington Post*, Sept. 13, 2021.
28. Robert Kagan, "Our Constitutional Crisis is Already Here," *Washington Post*, Sept. 23, 2021.
29. Barton Gellman, "Trump's next coup has already begun," *The Atlantic*, Dec. 6, 2021. GOP leaders "are attempting to destroy the foundations of American democracy." Jeffrey Goldberg, "A Party, and Nation, in Crisis," *The Atlantic*, Dec. 6, 2021.
30. Ben Smith, "How the Media Could Get the Election Story Wrong, *New York Times*, Aug. 2, 2020.
31. Avi Asher-Schapiro, "Leak prosecutions under Trump chill national security beat," Committee to Protect Journalists, March 6, 2019.
32. Sharyl Attkisson, "It looks like Obama did spy on Trump, just as he apparently did to me," *The Hill*, Sept. 20, 2017.
33. David Weigel, "Das Capitol: How a bunch of pro-union, anti-Republican protesters turned the hallways of the Wisconsin state house into a commune," *Slate*, Feb. 25, 2011.
34. Mark Moore, "GOP Lawmakers Rip Nancy Pelosi for 'Enemies of the State' Diss," *New York Post*, Aug. 25, 2020.
35. Anne Applebaum, "History Will Judge the Complicit," *The Atlantic*, July–August, 2020.
36. Maura Judkins, "The extremists next door," *Washington Post*, Jan. 18, 2021.
37. Paulina Enck, "Nikole Hannah-Jones Calls for 'Consequences,' 'Deprogramming' for Republicans," *The Federalist*, Jan. 12, 2021.

CHAPTER THREE

1. Even then, they were often too much for Roosevelt, who invented the term "muck-raker" to ridicule their "hysterical sensationalism." Theodore Roosevelt, *The Man with the Muck Rake*, (Brandt and Shafter, 1906), 278, 281.
2. Ken I. Kersch, "Constitutional Conservatives Remember the Progressive Era," in Skowronek, 147.
3. Croly's book had a strong influence on later New Dealers and also on Theodore Roosevelt, whom Croly had shamelessly buttered up. Croly was very possibly a source for Roosevelt's 1911 New Nationalism speech in Osawatomie, Kansas. Yarbrough, 205–20; Levy, 132–41.
4. So called by Richard Hofstadter in *The Progressive Historians*. Roosevelt read Turner's essay, but in his histories of the west Roosevelt never abandoned the racial "germ" theory. Yarborough, 52–83.

5. See Theodore Roosevelt, "Nationalism and Popular Rule," *The Outlook*, Jan. 21, 1911.

6. Quoted in Hofstadter, *The Progressive Historians*, 47.

7. Schumpeter, 83.

8. Burke, 29, 47–48.

9. "Principles are often more effective guides for action when they appear as no more than an unreasoned prejudice, a general feeling that certain things simply 'are not done'; while as soon as they are explicitly stated speculation begins about their correctness and their validity." Hayek, 85.

10. Cobbett, 3.

11. Disraeli, *Sybil*, 76–77.

12. Hansard, July 12, 1839; Edwards, 189.

13. *Shropshire Conservative*, Aug. 31, 1844; Monypenny, II. 231.

14. Speech at Edinburgh on Reform Bill, October 1867. Monypenny, II. 488.

15. On Tory Democracy, see Foster; R. E. Quinault, "Lord Randolph Churchill and Tory Democracy, 1880–1885," 22 *The History Journal*, (1979): 141.

16. Ruskin, *Praeterita*, 13; Watson, 45–49.

17. Ruskin, *Unto this Last*, 17. Ruskin anticipated the Marxist Antonio Gramsci, who coined the term "economism" to express his rejection of economic determinism and the idea that ideologies and social arrangements are dictated by economic relationships. Rather, it was the other way around, he thought, with the dominant ideology determining the bounds of political possibilities.

18. Gad Horowitz, "Conservatism, Liberalism and Socialism in Canada," 32 *The Canadian Journal of Economics and Political Science* (1966): 143; See also Donald Creighton's two-volume biography of Sir John A. Macdonald, *The Young Politician* and *The Old Chieftain*. The revival of interest in progressive conservatism in Canada began with the work of George Grant.

CHAPTER FOUR

1. Trilling, 184. Trilling attributed the thought to T. S. Eliot, "Tradition and the Individual Talent," in Eliot, 13. See also Eliot, 402.

2. C. Vann Woodward, "George Fitzhugh, Sui Generis," in George Fitzhugh, *Cannibals All!*, vii, xxx.

3. Fitzhugh, *Sociology for the South*, 248. On Fitzhugh's importance as a thinker, see Eugene Genovese, *The World the Slaveholders Made*, 129.

4. George Fitzhugh, "Southern Thought" and "Southern Thought Again," in Faust, 274 ff.

5. Lincoln, *Speeches and Writings 1859–1865*, 97–98

6. Id., (February 22, 1861), 213.

7. Id., (speech in Cincinnati, Ohio, September 17, 1859), 85.

8. Richardson, 111.

9. John D. Hicks and John D. Barnhart, "The Farmers' Alliance," 6 *North Carolina*

History Review (1929), 254. Thomas Frank's *The People, No* is a useful study of the rise of populism up to (but not after) the William Jennings Bryan campaign of 1896.

10. Theodore Roosevelt, "Machine Politics in New York City," in *Works: Administration – Civil Service*, 118.

11. Henry Adams, "The Education of Henry Adams," in *Adams*, 1101.

12. Kolko argued that the push for regulation came from large firms, which saw this as a barrier to entry and competition from smaller firms, which is not the free marketer's idea of conservatism.

13. Theodore Roosevelt, "Nationalism and Progress," *The Outlook*, Jan. 14, 1911.

14. Roosevelt, *Letters and Speeches*, 799.

15. Roosevelt, *The foes of our own household*, 92.

16. Smith, *FDR*, 278.

17. Black, 316.

18. Id., 251.

19. Smith, *FDR*, 289.

20. Id., 324.

21. *Saturday Evening Post*, Jan. 29, 1949. Lodge was the son of Theodore Roosevelt's political friend Henry Cabot Lodge Sr. but unlike his father was an interventionist who provided crucial support for the American adoption of the NATO treaty and subsequently for the Vietnam War.

22. While labeled "Mr. Conservative," Taft was not a right-wing absolutist. "If the free-enterprise system does not do its best to prevent hardship and poverty, even for those who can't be shown to deserve it, it will find itself superseded by a less progressive system which does." Robert A. Taft, "The Housing Problem," Congressional recording, Jan. 17, 1946. What Eisenhower had mostly objected to in Taft was the latter's isolationism.

23. Presidential Papers of Dwight David Eisenhower (hereafter *PPDDE)*, Volume. 15, Part 6, Chapter 13, 1402. See also Ferrell, *Diary of James Hagerty*, 130–31.

24. Hitchcock, 259–60.

25. Ferrell, *Diary of James Hagerty*, 129. See William S. White, "Eisenhower Warns G.O.P. Right Wing – Chides Knowland: Insists Party Must Follow a Progressive Course or Face Loss of Influence," *New York Times*, Dec. 3, 1954.

26. Letter to Clifford Roberts, Dec. 7, 1954. *PPDDE*, Volume. 15, Part 6, Chapter. 13, 1429. See also *PPDDE*, 1953:158.

27. See, e.g., *PPDDE*, 1953:426–27.

28. Eisenhower, *Mandate for Change*, 275; *PPDDE*, 1953:415.

29. Susan Eisenhower, 189–201; Eisenhower, *Mandate for Change*, 326.

30. *PPDDE*, at 1953:182.

31. Id., 1953:813–22.

32. Smith, *Eisenhower*, 710–11.

33. Eisenhower's criteria for appointing Warren were "character and ability" first, then "high ideals, a moderately progressive social philosophy." Kluger, 567–68.

34. Nichols, 250–51.

35. Id., 158–68.
36. Niebuhr, 671.
37. Larson, 19. Arthur Larson was the butt of Barry Goldwater's ridicule in *The Conscience of a Conservative*.
38. Hitchcock, 244.
39. Black, *Nixon*, 585.
40. Id., Wicker, 413, 535.
41. Black, *Nixon*, 623.
42. He was also the person who instituted wage and price controls, took American off the gold standard, and announced that he was a Keynesian. With right-wingers, he decisively parted company.
43. Wicker, 487–94.
44. The issue was "whether the White community in the South is entitled to take such measures as are necessary to prevail, politically and culturally, in areas in which it does not predominate numerically? The sobering answer is Yes – the White community is so entitled because, for the time being, it is the advanced race." "Why the South Must Prevail," *National Review*, Aug. 24, 1957.
45. Schlesinger, *Vital Center*, x.
46. F. H. Buckley, "How Trump Won in Two Dimensions," *Wall Street Journal*, Aug 9, 2017.

CHAPTER FIVE

1. Donna Barne and Divyanshi Wadhwa, "Year in Review," World Bank, Dec. 20, 2019.
2. Tami Luhby, "The American Dream is Out of Reach." *Money*, June 4, 2014.
3. Balz, Chapter 22.
4. Aaron Blake, "Donald Trump's best speech of the 2016 campaign, annotated," *Washington Post*, Aug. 19, 2016.
5. Chuck Devore, "Trump's Policy 'Magic Wand' Boosts Manufacturing Jobs 399% in First 26 Months Over Obama's Last 26," *Forbes*, March 11, 2019.
6. Marx, 21–22. Social mobility was also the answer to Werner Sombart's *Why Is There No Socialism in the United States?*
7. J. G. A. Pocock, *The Machiavellian Moment: Florentine Political Thought and the Atlantic Republican Tradition*, (Princeton University Press, 2003) 466–67, 486–87. See also Bailyn, 34–54; Wood, *The Creation of the American Republic*, (University of North Carolina Press, 1998) 14–17.
8. For the questionable business practices of the Clinton money-making machine, see generally Schweizer.
9. "Cutting Ties to the Clinton Foundation," *New York Times*, Aug. 30, 2016.
10. Isabel Vincent, "Charity Watchdog: Clinton Foundation a 'Slush Fund,'" *New York Post*, April 26, 2015.

11. Steven Nelson, "Senate committee investigating alleged Hunter Biden drive, smoking-gun email," *New York Post*, Oct. 14, 2020.

12. Catherine Kim, "Poll: 70 percent of Republicans don't think the election was free and fair," *Politico*, Nov. 9, 2020.

13. Randall Bennett Woods, "F.D.R. and the Triumph of American Nationalism," 19 *Presidential Studies Quarterly*, (1989): 587.

CHAPTER SIX

1. Wood, *The Radicalism of the American Revolution*, 71.

2. Edward N. Wolff, "Recent Trends in Household Wealth in the United States: Rising Debt and the Middle Class Squeeze – An Update to 2007," Working Paper 589, Levy Economics Institute of Bard College (2010); Edward N. Wolff, "The Asset Price Meltdown and the Wealth of the Middle Class," NBER Working Paper 18559 (2012).

3. Steven N. Kaplan and Joshua Rauh, "It's the Market: The Broad-Based Rise in the Return to Top Talent," 27 American Economic Association, (2013): 35.

4. See also Emmanuel Saez and Gabriel Zucman, "Wealth Inequality in the United States since 1913: Evidence from Capitalized Income Tax Data," 131 *The Quarterly Journal of Economics*, (2016): 519; Lawrence Katz and David Autor, "Changes in the Wage Structure and Earnings Inequality," Ashenfelter and Card, IIIA.1463. There has been essentially no income growth for the bottom 50 percent since the end of the 1970s even after taking welfare payments, taxes, and inflation into account. Klein and Pettis, 177.

5. Piketty and Saez 2003, Table B-5.

6. Emmanuel Saez, Striking it Richer: The Evolution of Top Incomes in the United States (updated with 2018 estimates) at https://eml.berkeley.edu/~saez/saez-US topincomes-2018.pdf, February 2020. The figures are based on pretax and pre-welfare benefits. Realized capital gains were included and nontaxable fringe bene-fits excluded. Incomes were deflated using the Consumer Price Index.

    The middle class has also shrunk in size. The Pew Research Center counted the number of adults in each income quintile and reported that the size of the middle class had shrunk from 61 to 52 percent from 1971 to 2016. Never Trumpers who ask us to ignore American inequality tell us that that's because some households moved into the upper class. But almost as many descended into the lower class. Rakesh Kochhar, "The American Middle Class is Stable in Size, but Losing Ground to Upper-income Families," Pew Research Center (Sept. 6, 2018).

7. "Inequality of incomes before and after taxes and transfers," 2014, *Our World in Data*. The Gini coefficient is a number between zero and one, with higher numbers representing more inequality. If everyone earned the same income (perfect equal-ity), the Gini ratio would be 0; if all the income went to the highest paid person (perfect inequality), the Gini ratio would be 1.0. No country is at either 0 or 1.0, and the range is between 0.24 and 0.63.

8. The middle-class households in quintiles three and four (20 to 60), who earned more than $37,800 and less than $87,800, paid their way. Congressional Budget Office, "The Distribution of Household Income," 2015, Supplemental Data, Table 2 (one person household), Data Underlying Figures, Summary Figure 1. See also Thomas Piketty, Emmanuel Saez, and Gabriel Zucman, "Distributional National Accounts: Methods and Estimates for the United States," 133 *Quarterly Journal of Economics*, Table I (2018): 553, 575. One should note that programs that aren't means-tested and in which rich and poor both share aren't really welfare. Instead, they're mandatory savings plans paid for through FICA deductions from our paychecks. The Congressional Budget Office therefore excludes Social Security payouts and Medicare benefits from what it considers welfare. To measure the safety net, therefore, the proper comparison is between (a) pretax income, including government wealth transfers like Social Security that aren't means-tested, and (b) income after taxes are deducted and means-tested transfers are included.

9. See data.oecd.org/inequality/income-inequality.htm.

10. Emmanuel Saez, "Income and Wealth Inequality: Evidence and Policy Implications," 35 *Contemporary Economics Policy*, (2017): 7.

11. "Changes in US Family Finances from 2016 to 2019: Evidence from the Survey of Consumer Finances," 106 Federal Reserve Bulletin, (September 2020).

12. The figure's straight line represents an Ordinary Least Squares regression. The measure of happiness is taken from social surveys. See Frey, Chapter 2.

13. Putnam, 140.

14. Miller McPherson, Lynn Smith-Lovin, and Matthew E. Brashears, "Social Isolation in America: Changes in Core Discussion Networks over Two Decades," 71 *American Sociology Review*, (2006) 353.

15. See also Cacioppo and Patrick, 260.

16. Holly Hedegaard et al., "Increase in Suicide Mortality in the United States, 1999–2018," Washington, DC: National Center for Health Statistics, April 2020.

17. Tara Parker-Pope, "Suicide Rates Rise Sharply in US," *New York Times*, May 2, 2013.

18. Dan Levin, "A Racial Slur, a Viral Video, and a Reckoning," *New York Times*, Dec. 26, 2020.

19. See Andrew Berg, Jonathan D. Ostry, Jeromin Zettelmeyer, http://www.imf.org/external/pubs/ft/wp/2008/wp0859.pdf, 98 *Journal of Development Economics*, (2012): 149; Tortsen Persson and Guido Tabellini, "Is Inequality Harmful for Growth?" 84 *American Economics Review*, (1994): 600; Alberto Alesina and Dani Rodrik, "Distributive Politics and Economic Growth," 109 *Quarterly Journal of Economics*, (1994): 465.

20. See Alberto Alesina and Roberto Perotti, "Income Distribution, Political Instability, and Investment," http://www.sciencedirect.com/science/journal/00142921 40 (1996): 1203; Terry Lynn Karl, "Economic Inequality and Democratic Instability," 11 *Journal of Democracy*, (2000) 149; Philip Keefer and Stephen Knack, "Polariza-

tion, Politics and Property Rights: Links between Inequality and Growth," 111 *Public Choice*, (2002): 127.

21. See generally Stiglitz.

CHAPTER SEVEN

1. Raj Chetty et al., "The Fading American Dream: Trends in Absolute Income Mobility Since 1940," 356 *Science* (2017): 398; Daniel Aaronson and Bhashkar Mazumder, "Intergenerational Economic Mobility in the United States, 1940 to 2000," 43 *Journal of Human Resources*, (2008) 139.

2. Daniel Aaronson and Bhashkar Mazumder, "The Decline in Intergenerational Mobility After 1980," Federal Reserve Bank of Chicago, WP 2017–05 (revised Feb.21, 2020). See also Katharine Bradbury, "Trends in US Family Income Mobility," 1969–2006, Federal Reserve Bank of Boston, Working Paper 11-10 (Oct. 20, 2011); Jason Long and Joseph Ferrie, "Intergenerational Occupational Mobility in Great Britain and the United States Since 1850," 103 *American Economics Review,* (2013): 1109.

3. "Pursuing the American Dream: Economic Mobility Across Generations," Pew Charitable Trust Economic Mobility Project, July 2012.

4. Tom Hertz, "Rags, Riches, and Race: The Intergenerational Economic Mobility of Black and White Families in the United States," in Bowles, 165.

5. Raj Chetty et al., "Is the United States Still a Land of Opportunity? Recent Trends in Intergenerational Mobility," NBER Working Paper 19844, January 2014; S. E. Black and P. J. Devereux, "Recent developments in intergeneration al mobility," in Card and Ashenfelter; Espen Bratberg et al., "A Comparison of Intergenerational Mobility Curves in Germany, Norway, Sweden, and the US," 119 *Scandinavian Journal of Economics*, (2017): 72. See Scott Winship, "Economic Mobility in America: The United States in Comparative Perspective," Archbridge Institute, December 2018.

6. On the calculation of intergenerational elasticity, see Gary Solon, "Intergenerational Income Mobility in the United States," 82 *American Economic Review*, (1992): 393; Corak, 1.

7. Bhashkar Mazumder, "The Apple Falls Even Closer to the Tree than We Thought: New and Revised Estimates of the Intergenerational Inheritance of Earnings," in Bowles, 80. Even that might understate income immobility for the very rich since the 0.6 figure is a measure for all parents and Mazumder reports that there is relatively less mobility in top income brackets. Bhatyshkar Mazumder, "Fortunate Sons: New Estimate of Intergenerational Mobility in the United States Using Social Security Earnings Data," 87 *Revue of Economics and Statistics*, (2005): 235.

8. "Economic Mobility in the United States," Pew Charitable Trusts, July 2015.

9. OECD Data, "National Accounts at a Glance 2014," Canada 537.4, US 600.8.

10. OECD, "GDP per capita and hours worked," Canada 107.9, US 104.7 in 2018.

11. The Heritage Foundation ranks Canada number 9 in the world, with a score of 77.9 in 2021. The US is number 20, at 74.8. Top-ranked Singapore comes in at 89.7. Heritage Foundation, "2021 Index of Economic Freedom."

12. See, e.g., David H. Autor, Lawrence F. Katz, and Melisa S. Kearney, "Trends in US Wage Inequality: Revising the Revisionists," 90 *Revue of Economics and Statistics*, (2008): 300; Daron Acemoğlu, "Technical Change, Inequality, and the Labor Market," 40 *Journal of Economic Literature*, (2003): 7; Lawrence F. Katz and Kevin M. Murphy, "Changes in Relative Wages, 1963–1987: Supply and Demand Factors," 107 *Quarterly Journal of Economics*, (1992): 35.

13. Herrnstein and Murray.

14. http://www.trademap.org, retrieved June 11, 2020.

15. Daron Acemoğlu and James A. Robinson, "The Rise and Fall of General Laws of Capitalism," 29 *Journal of Economic Perspectives*, (2015): 3.

16. Thomas Piketty, "About *Capital in the Twenty-First Century*," 105 *American Economic Review: Papers and Proceedings*, (2015): 1.

17. Non-taxable capital income (excluding pension funds) is less than a fifth of all national income. Thomas Piketty et al., "Distributional Diversity in the National Accounts," 109 *AEA Papers and Proceedings* at Panel B, (2019): 289.

18. For college admissions, merit is importantly identified through the student's Scholastic Aptitude Test (SAT) score, which is strongly correlated with parental income. Todd Balf, "The Story Behind the SAT Overhaul," *New York Times Magazine*, March 6, 2014. Cultural differences are magnified when like marries like and lawyers and doctors inbreed among themselves, a phenomenon labeled "assortative mating." There's more of that today than in the 1960s, when secretaries married their bosses in Doris Day comedies. Jeremy Greenwood et al., "Marry Your Like: Assortative Mating and Income Inequality," 104 *American Economic Review: Papers and Proceedings*, (2014): 1.

19. Raj Chetty et al., "Race and Economic Opportunity in the United States: An Intergenerational Perspective," 135 *Quarterly Journal of Economics*, (2020): 711.

20. One in four native Canadians is reported to live in poverty. Poverty in Canada, Canadian Poverty Institute, at povertyinstitute.ca, accessed on June 9, 2020

21. Britt McKinnon et al., "Comparison of black-white disparities in preterm birth between Canada and the United States," 118 *Canadian Medical Association Journal*, E19, E21 at Table 1 (2016).

22. Chetty, Hendren, Kline, Saez, and Turner, "Is the United States Still a Land of Opportunity?" *supra*. See also Sawhill, at 151, Figure 4.

23. Popenoe.

24. Raj Chetty et al., "Where Is the Land of Opportunity? The Geography of Intergenerational Mobility in the United States," 129 *Quarterly Journal of Economics*, (2014): 1553; Raj Chetty and Nathaniel Hendren, "The Effects of Neighborhoods on Intergenerational Mobility I: Childhood Exposure Effects, 133 *Quarterly Journal of Economics*, (2018): 1107.

25. Patricia Cohen, "'Culture of Poverty' Makes a Comeback," *New York Times*, Oct 17, 2010.

26. Chetty, "Race and Economic Opportunity," supra.

27. David Hume, "Idea of a Perfect Commonwealth," 222

CHAPTER EIGHT

1. OECD Skills Outlook 2013: "First Results from the Survey of Adult Skills," Tables A2.4, A2.1, A2.8, A2.5, (2013).

2. Claudia Goldin, "The Human Capital Century and American Leadership: Virtues of the Past," 61 *Journal of Economic History*, (2001): 263.

3. Claudia and Katz; see also Daron Acemoğlu and David Autor, "What Does Human Capital Do? A Review of Goldin and Katz's The Race between Education and Technology," 50 *Journal of Economic Literature*, (2012): 426.

4. Michael T. Nietzel, "Low Literacy Levels Among US Adults Could Be Costing the Economy $2.2 Trillion A Year," *Forbes*, Sept. 9, 2020.

5. Peter Belfiore, "Oregon Gov Kate Brown scraps need for high school students to prove proficiency in math, reading and writing before graduation because it's an 'unfair test for children who don't test well,'" *Daily Mail*, Aug. 10, 2021.

6. Andreas Schleicher, PISA 2018: Insights and Interpretations, OECD, Figure 9, 23.

7. "Education Expenditures by Country, National Center for Educational Statistics," (Washington: Dept. of Education, May 2020), Figure 1.

8. See Eric A. Hanushek et al., *Endangering Prosperity*, 96–98 (2011 results); Hanushek and Lindseth. There doesn't appear to be a relation between per-pupil spending and PISA scores in Canadian provinces either. Jim Marshall et al., "Canada's Public Schools: Are we paying more but getting less?," Johnson Shoyama Graduate School of Public Policy, April 2019.

9. Jason Richwine, "The Myth of Racial Disparities in Public School Funding," Washington: Heritage Foundation, 2011.

10. Eric A. Hanushek et al., *Endangering Prosperity*, (2011 results), 40–42.

11. Woessmann. See also Ludger Woessmann, "Public-private partnerships and student achievement: A cross-country analysis," in Chakrabarti, 13; Ludger Woessmann, "The Importance of School Systems: Evidence from International Differences in Student Achievement, Ifo Institute, University of Munich and IZA, Discussion Paper No. 10001, June 2016.

12. EdChoice (2020), "The 123s of School Choice: What the Research Says about Private School Choice Programs in America," 2020 edition.

13. "Caroline M. Hoxby, "School Choice and School Productivity. Could School Choice Be a Tide that Lifts All Boats?" in Hoxby, 287; Mark J. Holley et al., "Competition with Charters Motivates Districts," 28 *Education Next*, (2013): 13.

14. Americans worry that sectarian schools are divisive, but in Canada they were a condition for the country's unification and a necessary compromise without which

Canada would never have existed. *Adler v. Ontario*, [1996] 3 S.C.R. 609 at §29. State-supported sectarian schools don't amount to school choice when parents refuse to register their children in schools of a different religion. But when religious barriers weaken, parents pick schools for educational and not religious reasons. Today a fifth of the students now enrolled in America's Catholic schools are of another religion. Catholic School Data: Enrollment, National Catholic Educational Association, accessed June 24, 2020.

15. Digest of Education Statistics, National Center for Educational Statistics, Dept. of Education, 2–18 Tables and Figures; Public Charter School Enrollment, National Center for Educational Statistics, Dept. of Education, May 2020.

16. Betts and Tang.

17. Corey A. DeAngelis et al., "Charter School Funding: Inequity Surges in the Cities," University of Arkansas, 2020. See Karl Zinmeister, "Will Biden's Education Nominee Stand for Students or for Unions?" *Wall Street Journal*, Dec. 23, 2020.

18. Sarah Mervosh, "Viral Video Shows Boys in 'Make America Great Again' Hats Surrounding Native Elder," *New York Times*, Jan. 19, 2019.

19. Chris Weller, "Homeschooling May Be the Smartest Way to Teach Kids in the 21st Century," *Business Insider*, Jan. 21, 2018.

20. Elizabeth Bartholet, "Homeschooling: Parent Rights Absolutism vs. Child Rights to Education and Protection," 62 *Arizona Law Review* 1, (2020): 11.

21. Aria Bendix, "Do Private-School Vouchers Promote Segregation?" *The Atlantic*, May 22, 2017.

22. Rebecca Mead, "Betsy DeVos and the Plan to Break Public Schools," *The New Yorker*, Dec. 14, 2016.

23. Brill; Moe. See also Finn; Rhee; Moskowitz.

24. Open Secrets, Teachers Unions, accessed June 24, 2020.

25. *Zelman v. Simmons-Harris*, 536 US 639 (2002).

26. See, e.g., John J. Miller, "Why School Choice Lost," *Wall Street Journal*, Nov. 3, 1993. See also James E. Ryan, "Brown, School Choice, and the Suburban Veto," 90 *Virginia Law Review*, (2004): 1635.

27. Eric A. Hanuskek and Ludger Woessmann, "The Economics of International Differences in Educational Achievement," in Hanushek, Machin, and Woessmann, 89, 168–69.

28. Arum and Roksa.

29. "The Condition of College and Career Readiness," National, ACT, 2018

30. Goldin and Katz; see also Daron Acemoğlu and David Autor, "What Does Human Capital Do? A Review of Goldin and Katz's The Race between Education and Technology," 50 *Journal of Economic Literature*, (2012): 426. The Federal Reserve Bank of Chicago also reports a mismatch between what recent students had learned and the skills employers were looking for. R. Jason Faberman and Bhashkar Mazumder, "Is there a Skills Mismatch in the Labor Market?," Federal Reserve Bank of Chicago Letter, June 2012.

31. George J. Borjas, "Making it in America: Social Mobility in the Immigrant Population," National Bureau of Economic Research, March 2006. The children of immigrants enjoy greater income mobility than the children of native Americans but without making up the difference since their parents start at a lower income level. See Ram Abramitzky et al., "Intergenerational Mobility of Immigrants in the United States over two Centuries," 111 *American Economic Review*, (2021): 580.

32. Which is not to say that, on arrival, Canadian immigrants earn as much as native-born Canadians, particularly when they arrive from poor countries. Foreign skills and education credentials don't translate into dollars as much as the skills and education natives acquire in Canada. However, immigrant earnings increase sharply after arrival. David A. Green and Christopher Worswick, "Entry Earnings of Immigrant Men in Canada: The Roles of Labour Market Entry Effects and Returns to Foreign Experience," in McDonald, Ruddick, Sweetman, and Worswick, 77.

33. Abdurrhaman Aydemir, Wen-Hao Chen, and Miles Corak, "Intergenerational Earnings Mobility among the Children of Canadian Immigrants," *IZA Discussion Papers*, 2085 (2006).

34. Borjas, *Immigration Economics*, 152–53.

35. Borjas, *We Wanted Workers*, 158. George J. Borjas, "Lessons from Immigration Economics," 22 *Independent Review*, (2018) 329.

36. Blau and Mackie.

37. Finding a 2 percent drop in low-skilled wages on a 10 percent increase in immigration levels. Borjas, *Immigration Economics*, 94. See also Patricia Cortes, "The Effect of Low-Skilled Immigration on US Prices: Evidence from CPI Data," 116 *Journal of Political Economy*, (2008): 381. For a dissenting view, see David Card, "Is the New Immigration Really So Bad?," 115 *Economic Journal*, (2005): 300. Card looked at changes in the labor market in high immigration cities and reported that he did not find that immigration harmed the low-skilled native-born. In response, Borjas argues that Card fails to take adequate account of native out-migration to other US cities when faced with competition from immigrants.

38. George J. Borjas et al., "Immigration and the Economic Status of African-American Men," 77 *Economica*, (2010): 255.

39. Lisa M. Krieger, "Can a Pay Raise Fix Agriculture Industry's Labor Crisis in California? Yes and No." *Washington Post*, July 30, 2017.

40. Robert Putnam, "E Pluribus Unum: Diversity and Community in the Twenty-First Century," 30 *Scandinavian Political Studies*, (2007): 137.

41. Paul Emrath, "Government Regulation in the Price of a New Home," National Association of Home Builders, HousingEconomics.com, May 2, 2016.

42. Martin Gilens and Benjamin I. Page, "Testing Theories of American Politics: Elites, Interest Groups, and Average Citizens," 12 *Perspectives on Politics*, (2014) 564. See Gilens, Richard Hasen, "Citizens United and the Orphaned Anti-Distortion Rationale," 27 *Georgia State University Law Review*, 989 (2010–11).

43. *Where Is the Wealth of Nations? Measuring Capital for the 21st Century,*

(Washington, D.C.: World Bank, 2006). On the positive relation between economic growth and the rule of law, see Barro and Sala-i-Martin, at 526–29; Acemoglu, *Introduction to Modern Economic Growth*, 23–40.

44. Daniel Kaufmann, "Rethinking Governance: Empirical Lessons Challenge Orthodoxy," 17 (World Bank, 2003).

45. Buckley, *American Illness*, Chapter 1.

46. Anthony Kronman, "Contract Law and the State of Nature," 1 *Journal of Law, Economics, and Organization*, (1985): 5.

CHAPTER NINE

1. Whether the rule really made a difference in America has been doubted since a father could avoid it through an explicit device in a will to his younger children. Stanley N. Katz, "Republicanism and the Law of Inheritance in the American Revolutionary Era," 76 *Michigan Law Review*, (1977): 1. But see Holly Brewer, "Entailing Aristocracy in Colonial Virginia: 'Ancient Feudal Restraints' and Revolutionary Reform," 54 *William and Mary Quarterly*, Third Series, (1997): 307.

2. Jefferson, "Autobiography," in *Writings*, 1, 44.

3. Hamilton's breakthrough articles on inclusive fitness may be found in Chapter 2 of Volume 1 of his collected essays *Narrow Roads of Gene Land*. For a more extensive version of Hamilton's Rule in the statistical form proposed by George Price, see W. D. Hamilton, "Selfish and Spiteful Behavior in an Evolutionary Model," 228 *Nature*, (1970), 1218, in *Narrow Roads of Greenland*, 177–82; Harman, 367–68.

4. Dawkins. See also Bell, 367–69.

5. Note that the coefficient of relatedness $r_y - r_x$, is a negative number. The cost $-B$ is also negative, so multiplying it by the coefficient of relatedness $r_y - r_x$ gives us a positive number.

6. Gary S. Becker, "China's Next Leap Forward," *Wall Street Journal*, Sept 29, 2010.

7. Fukuyama, *The Origins of Political Order*; Fukuyama, *Political Order and Political Decay*.

8. "State of the Poor," World Bank, April 17, 2013; "A Measured Approach to Ending Poverty and Boosting Shared Prosperity," World Bank Group.

9. Liu Yi et al., "100 years of fortitude," *China Daily*, July 7, 2021.

10. Mosca, 61.

CHAPTER TEN

1. Farrand I.50 (May 31). Besides Madison, other delegates subscribed to the idea of filtration as a method of countering corruption. Farrand I.133 (Wilson, June 6); Farrand I.136 (Dickinson, June 6); Farrand I.152 (Gerry, June 7); Farrand II.54 (G. Morris, July 19).

2. Farrand I.50 (May 31).

3. Rutland, *Papers of James Madison*, IX.348.

4. Farrand I.242 n.

5. In a letter written on the same day that the delegates voted to adopt Article II on the executive branch, Madison told Jefferson that "the plan … will neither effectually *answer* its *national object*, nor prevent the local *mischiefs* which everywhere *excite disgust* agst. the *State Governments*." Farrand III.77 (Sept. 6, italics in original).

6. Farrand II.29 (July 17).

7. Farrand II.404.

8. Farrand II.399 (roll call 359).

9. Farrand II.501, II.500 (Sept. 4). James Wilson offered a similar explanation of the Constitution's method of choosing a president as an anti-corruption device at the Pennsylvania Ratifying Convention in 1787. Wilson, I.267. Hamilton, too, observed in Federalist 68 that the framers had sought to exclude the possibility of "cabal, intrigue, and corruption" in the election of presidents.

10. Ari Hoogenboom, "The Pendleton Act and the Civil Service," 64 *American History Review*, (1959) 301.

11. *US v. Blagojevich*, 794 F.3d 729 (7th Cir., 2015).

12. *McDonnell v. US*, 579 US __ (2016), reversing 792 F.3d 478 (2015).

13. Under the federal bribery statute, public officials may not "corruptly" demand, seek, or receive anything of value "in return for … being influenced in the performance of any official act," with "official act" defined as "any decision or action on any question, matter, cause, suit, proceeding or controversy, which may at any time be pending, or which may by law be brought before any public official, in such official's official capacity, or in such official's place of trust or profit." 18 USC. §§ 201(b)(2), 201(a)(3). Several other federal criminal offenses piggyback on the bribery prohibition. In the recent "Bridgegate" case, *Kelly v. US*, __ US ___ (2020), the court held that the federal fraud statutes at issue didn't criminalize political payback unless the goal was to get money or property.

14. *Citizens United v. FEC*, 558 US 310, 360 (2010).

15. *McCutcheon v. F.E.C.*, 134 S. Ct. 1434 (2014).

16. Transparency International Corruption Perceptions Index 2010 Long Methodological Brief.

17. See John G. Peters and Susan Welch, "Gradients of Corruption in Perceptions of American Public Life," in Heidenheimer, 155. See Alina Mungiu-Pippidi, 2–10, 27–33, 40–48; Rothberg, 54–58.

18. Andrei Shleifer and Robert W. Vishny, "Corruption," 108 *Quarterly Journal of Economics*, (1993): 599; Stephen Knack and Philip Keefer, "Institutions and Economic Performance: Cross-Country Tests Using Alternative Institutional Measures," 7 *Economic and Politics*, (1995): 207; Rafael La Porta, Florencio López-de-Silanes, Cristian Pop-Eleches, and Andrei Shleifer, "Judicial Checks and Balances," 112 *Journal of Political Economy*, (2004): 445; Mushfiq Swaleheen, "Economic Growth with Endogenous Corruption: An Empirical Study," 146 *Public Choice*, (2011): 23; Sutirtha Bagchi and Jan Svejnar, "Does Wealth Inequality Matter for Growth? The

Effect of Billionaire Wealth, Income Distribution, and Poverty," Institute for the Study of Labor Discussion Paper 7733, November 2013. For a review of the evidence, see Pranab Bardhan, "Corruption and Development: A Review of Issues," 35 *Journal of Economic Literature*, (1997): 1320.

19. Noel D. Johnson, Courtney L. LaFountain, and Steven Yamarik, "Corruption is Bad for Growth (Even in the United States)," 147 *Public Choice*, (2011): 377.

20. Craig A. Depken & Courtney L. Lafontain, "Fiscal Consequences of Public Corruption: Empirical Evidence from State Bond Ratings," 126 *Public Choice*, (2006) 75.

CHAPTER ELEVEN

1. Francis Fukuyama, *Political Order and Political Decay*, 25.

2. Edward Glaezer, David Laibson, José A. Scheinkman, and Christine L. Soutter, "Measuring Trust," 115 *Q. J. Econ.*, (2000) 811. Alberto Alesina and Eliana La Ferrara, "Who Trusts Others," 85 *Journal of Political Economy*, (2002): 207.

3. Alberto Alesina and Eliana La Ferrara, "Ethnic Diversity and Economic Performance," 43 *Journal of Economic Literature*, (2005): 762.

4. Buckley, *American Secession*, 69, Figure 6.1.

5. Malcolm S. Salter, "Crony Capitalism American Style: What Are We Talking About Here?" Harvard Business School Working Paper 15-025 (October 22, 2014); Carney.

6. Montesquieu, *The Spirit of the Laws*, VIII.16, 362.

7. Stiglitz, "There was a large transfer of wealth from the elderly to the government, and from the government to the bankers," 244.

8. Barry Weingast, "The Economic Role of Political Institutions: Market-Preserving Federalism and Economic Development," 11 *The Journal of Law, Economics, and Organization*, (1995): 1.

9. Ball, 84.

10. Douglas O. Linder, "Bending Toward Justice: John Doar and the Mississippi Burning Trial," at SSRN-1109-93 (2008).

11. *US v. Price*, 383 US 787 (1966).

12. The check that the separation of powers places on presidential power might be thought to give the nod to presidential government, for example. Persson and Tabellini, 23–24.

13. Buckley, *The Once and Future King*, 317, Table C-2.

14. On how stronger political parties reduce minoritarian misbehavior costs, see Philip Keefer and Stuti Khemani, "When Do Legislators Pass on Pork? The Role of Political Parties in Determining Legislator Effort," 103 *American Political Science Review*, (2009): 99.

15. 24 US 1 (1976).

16. Hasen, *Plutocrats United*, 44–45.

17. Like many other countries, we limit the amount of money people can contribute to a political campaign, but then we permit unlimited amounts to be contributed to

Political Action Committees that don't coordinate with a political party. That's led to the explosive growth of Super PAC money in politics. That's been roundly condemned by Democrats even though they outspend Republicans. But that doesn't mean more corruption since Super PACs spend ideological dollars rather than pay-for-play dollars.

18. Seth Apfel, "Prosecutorial Misconduct: Comparing American and Foreign Approaches to a Pervasive Problem and Devising Possible Solutions," 31 *Arizona Journal of International and Comparative Law,* (2014) 835. See *US v. Olsen*, 737 F.3d 625 (9th Cir., 2013) (Kozinski, C. J., dissenting); Jeffrey Toobin, "Casualties of Justice," *The New Yorker*, Jan. 3, 2011; Powell.

CHAPTER TWELVE

1. Hegel § 347, 343–44.
2. Orwell, "Notes on Nationalism," *Essays*, 865–66.
3. Orwell, "England, Your England, *id.,* 291.
4. Orwell, "What Has Kept England on its Feet?," *The Penguin Essays*.
5. Ed Pilkington, "Obama Angers Midwest Voters with Guns and Religion Remark," *The Guardian*, April 14, 2008.
6. https://www.nytimes.com/by/shane-goldmacher, Ella Koeze, Rachel Shorey, and Lazaro Gamio, "The Two Americas Financing the Trump and Biden Campaigns," *New York Times*, Oct. 25, 2020.
7. Statista, Nov. 9, 2020.
8. "True Americanism," in *Roosevelt's Writings*, 159.
9. Daniel Villarreal, "Joe Biden, Kamala Harris Tweets Backing Jussie Smollett Remain Up After Guilty Verdict," *Newsweek*, Dec. 9, 2021.

CHAPTER THIRTEEN

1. Speech at Chicago, Illinois, July 10, 1858, in *Lincoln: Speeches and Writings 1832–1858*, 456.
2. Gellner, 74.

CHAPTER FOURTEEN

1. "World military spending rises to almost $2 trillion in 2020," Stockholm International Peace Research Institute, April 26, 2021.
2. Tami Luhby, "Democrats want to offer health care to undocumented immigrants. Here's what that means." CNN, Sept. 11, 2019.

CHAPTER FIFTEEN

1. Skinner, *Renaissance Virtues*, Chapters 3–4.

2. Machiavelli II.2, 129–30. Machiavelli's *virtù* differed from Christian virtue and that of other Renaissance humanists. For Machiavelli, it was *vir virtutis*, the kind of spirited manliness that won honor and glory. His Prince was even encouraged to govern cruelly when this was necessary to remain in power. See Pocock, 166, 177; Hankins, 463–75; Skinner, *The Renaissance*, 128–38.

3. Cicero, I.vii.22, 22. See Skinner, 46–47.

4. Samuel Wales, "The Dangers of our National Prosperity," in Sandoz, *Political Sermons*, I.837, 849. The message that republican virtue was possible only in genuinely popular non-monarchical republics was repeated by Montesquieu, whose *Spirit of the Laws* was cited by the framers more than any other book. See Book III, Chapters 5–7.

5. To David Stuart, July 1, 1787, Farrand III.51.

6. Olson, *Power and Prosperity*, 19–23.

7. Stephen Spender, *The Truly Great.*

8. Berman, 85–199,. See also Cantor.

9. *Spirit of the Laws*, xix.27

10. Blackstone, IV.4.57.

11. Péguy, 145.

12. Farrand, at II.278 (August 13, 1787).

13. Kirk, 416.

14. "Why the South Must Prevail," *National Review*, Aug. 24, 1957.

15. The is-ought problem was first identified by David Hume three hundred years ago. Some moralists, wrote Hume, claim that some thing or other "is" the case and that therefore we "ought" to do it. They try to slip that in, but one thing doesn't follow from the other. Hume, *Treatise*, III.ii.V.

16. Finnis, 36. See also Grisez, 62.

17. See, e.g., Tara Smith.

18. Ortega, 35.

CHAPTER SIXTEEN

1. Robert Rector, "Marriage: America's Greatest Weapon against Child Poverty," Heritage Foundation, Sept. 5, 2012.

2. A child allowance system, in which monthly checks are sent to parents, is popular with some conservatives but does not enjoy broad support with the public. See Robert VerBruggen, "Who Wants a Child Allowance?" Institute for Family Studies, March 3, 2020.

3. Briana Boyington and Emma Kerr, "20 Years of Tuition Growth at National Universities," *US News*, Sept. 19, 2019.

4. Mitchell, 3.

5. Prepared Remarks by Secretary DeVos at Federal Student Aid's Training Conference, Dec. 3, 2019, US Dept. of Education, Washington, D.C.

6. Zack Friedman, "Student Loan Debt Statistics in 2019: A $1.5 Trillion Crisis," *Forbes*, Feb. 25, 2019.

7. Student debt can be discharged if the debtor can prove undue hardship, but this is very hard to show, and few people avail themselves of it. See, e.g., *Brunner v. New York State Higher Education Services Corp.*, 831 F.2d 395 (2d Cir. 1987).

8. Emmanuel Saez et al., "The Elasticity of Taxable Income with Respect to Marginal Tax Rates: A Critical Review," 50 *Journal of Economic Literature*, 3 (2012). In addition, the true cost to the taxpayer is not the $1.5 trillion of indebtedness but only that portion that represents the principal amount. The interest charges have been estimated to amount to a third of the total indebtedness.

9. Judith Scott-Clayton, "The looming student debt default crisis is worse than we thought," Brookings Institution: Evidence Speaks, Jan. 11, 2018.

10. "Income, Poverty and Health Insurance Coverage in the United States: 2020," US Census Bureau, Sept. 14, 2021.

11. https://news.gallup.com/poll/4708/healthcare-system.aspx.

12. Ed Dolan, "Could We Afford Universal Catastrophic Health Coverage?" Niskanen Center, June 5, 2018.

13. Jeffrey S. Passel, "Measuring Illegal Immigration: How Pew Research Center Counts Unauthorized Immigrants in the US," Pew Research Center, July 12, 2019.

14. Lowe, 136. Similarly, John Judis and Ruy Teixeira argued in 2002 that Democrats would come to dominate American politics thanks in part to growing support from immigrant communities. This assumes that Hispanics will remain loyal Democrats, but they're less likely to do so when they've been in America for generations. Trump received 30 percent of the Hispanic vote, plausibly because of defections from second- and third-generation Hispanics. See Merrill Matthews, "Could Blacks and Hispanics Hand Trump a November Victory?" *The Hill*, Oct. 30, 2020.

15. Legal Immigration and Adjustment of Status Report Fiscal Year 2019, Quarter 4, Department of Homeland Security, Table 1B; "How Many Immigrants Come to Canada Each Year," Immigration.ca, accessed July 4, 2020.

16. David A. Green and Christopher Worswick, "Entry Earnings of Immigrant Men in Canada: The Roles of Labour Market Entry Effects and Returns to Foreign Experience," in McDonald, 77.

17. Alan J. Auerbach and Philip Oreopoulos, "The Fiscal Effect of US Immigration: A Generational-Accounting Perspective," 14 *Tax Policy and the Economy*, (2000) 123; Greenwood and McDowell.

18. Saez and Zucman.

19. Robin Kaiser-Schatzlein, "This Is How America's Richest Families Stay That Way," *New York Times*, Sept. 24, 2021.

20. Tom Huddleston, "Amazon had to pay federal income taxes for the first time since 2016 – here's how much," *CNBC*, Feb. 4, 2020.

21. Many of the most wasteful regulations are at the state and local level. In 2018,

more than forty-three million people in the United States held a professional certi-
fication or license, including hairdressers and masseuses. In many cases that's simply a barrier to entry that protects established businesses.

22. Bentley Coffey, Patrick A. McLaughlin, and Pietro Peretto, "The Cumulative Cost
of Regulations," Mercatus Working Paper, April 2016.

23. *Chevron USA. Inc. v. Natural Resources Defense Council, Inc.*, 467 US 837 (1984).

24. Editorial, "Liberation Day for French Dressing," *Wall Street Journal*, Dec. 27, 2020.

25. Center for Responsive Politics, Open Secrets, Lobbying Data Summary, accessed
July 20, 2020. Lobbying firms are required to provide estimates of moneys
received from clients. Firms and organizations that lobby are also required to
reveal what they spent on in-house lobbyists.

26. Id. at Open Secrets, 2016 Presidential Race.

27. Kelleher et al., "Lobbying and Taxes," 53 *American Journal of Political Science*,
(2009) 893.

28. Frank Yu and Xiaoyun Yu, "Corporate Lobbying and Fraud Detection," 46 *Journal
of Financial and Quantitative Analysis*, (2012) 1865.

29. "Money and politics," *The Economist*, Oct. 1, 2011. See also Hui Chen, David Pars-
ley, and Ya-Wen Yang, "Corporate Lobbying and Firm Performance," 42 *Journal of
Business, Finance, and Accounting*, (2015) 444; Jin-Hyuk Kim, "Corporate Lobbying Revisited," 10 *Business and Politics*, (Sept. 28, 2008).

30. See Nicholas W. Allard, "Lobbying Is an Honorable Profession: The Right to Petition and the Competition to Be Right," 19 *Stanford Law and Policy Review*, (2008):
23, 42–49.

31. Pub. L. 110-81, 121 Stat. 735. 2 USC. § 1613.

32. "Lobbying Law in the Spotlight: Challenges and Proposed Improvements," Report
of the Task Force on Federal Lobbying Laws, American Bar Association, Section of
Administrative Law and Regulatory Practice, Jan. 3, 2011.

33. Thomas B. Edsall, "The Trouble with that Revolving Door," *New York Times*, Dec.
18, 2011.

34. Alan Zibel, "Revolving Congress: The Revolving Door Class of 2019 Flocks to K
Street," *Public Citizen*, May 30, 2019.

35. Lessig, 123.

36. 8 USC. § 207, enacted as part of HLOGA.

37. See *Harper v. Virginia Bd. of Electors*, 383 US 663 (1966); *Bush v. Gore*, 531 US 98
(2000).

38. Fund and von Spakovsky, *Our Broken Elections*, 65.

39. De Portibus Maris, I Harg. Law Tracts 78.

40. What we'll want to avoid, however, is a return to the fairness doctrine under which
the FCC required broadcasters to provide honest and balanced political view-
points. That's what kept the Rush Limbaughs off the air until the rule was repealed
in 1987.

INDEX

Abramoff, Jack, 200
absentee voting fraud, 202
absolute preferences, 110
Acemoğlu, Daron, 84
Acosta, Alex, 21
Acosta, Jim, 14
Adams, Henry, 41
Adams, John Quincy, 152
Affordable Care Act, 27, 70
Allegory of Good and Bad Government, The, 163
Allen, Woody, 97
American Dream; eclipse of, 58–59; government's duty to, 7; offshoring of, 56, 68, 86, 88; restoring of, 65; Trump's defense of, 7, 25, 55, 89
American Federation of Teachers (AFT), 97
America, 1–6, as the unknown country, 62–63
American Hustle, 124
American Revolution, 159; pride in, 2–3; refighting of, 3–5; republican virtue and, 60; as work of enslavers, 147
Americans with Disabilities Act, 51
American Spectator, 58
Americans for Tax Reform, 195
Anarchy, State, and Utopia (Nozick), 173
Antifa rioters, 17, 23
anti-nationalism, 143–150; anti-American, 149–150; catnip to elites, 145; Davos Man, 146; globalist, 145–146; identitarian, 147–149; libertarian,

143–145; patriotism, 144; politics, 147; sophisticate, 146–147; Trump's nationalism, 147
aristocracies, permanence of, 109–118; absolute preferences, 110; bequest motive, 110, 111–113; choosing future worlds, 114; "coefficient of relatedness," 112; cyclical theory of history, 115–117; entrepreneurial labor, 110; genopolitics, 117–118; Hamilton's Law, 112, 113, 115; "inclusive fitness," 112; laws of primogeniture, 109; relative preferences, 110, 113–114; rule of law, 117; selfish gene, 111; social mobility, 109; traditional aristocracies, 109
Articles of Confederation, 165
Arum, Richard, 99
Aslan, Reza, 96
Atlantic, The, 96
Atlee, Clement, 110
Atwater, Lee, 49
Avenatti, Michael, 18

Baldwin, James, 153
Band of Brothers, 6
Barr, Bill, 22
Bartholet, Elizabeth, 96
Beijing Consensus, 115
Bell, Daniel, 43
Bell Curve, The (Murray and Herrnstein), 83
Benét, Stephen Vincent, 29, 141
Bentham, Jeremy, 4